T0366565

The Chile Pepper in China

ARTS AND TRADITIONS OF THE TABLE
PERSPECTIVES ON CULINARY HISTORY

ARTS AND TRADITIONS OF THE TABLE
PERSPECTIVES ON CULINARY HISTORY

Albert Sonnenfeld, Series Editor

For a complete list of titles, see page 277.

THE CHILE PEPPER
IN CHINA

A Cultural Biography

BRIAN R. DOTT

Columbia University Press

New York

Columbia University Press
Publishers Since 1893
New York   Chichester, West Sussex
cup.columbia.edu

Library of Congress Cataloging-in-Publication Data

Names: Dott, Brian Russell, author.
Title: The chile pepper in China : a cultural biography / Brian R. Dott.
Description: New York : Columbia University Press, [2020] | Series: Arts and traditions of
the table : perspectives on culinary history | Includes bibliographical references and index.
Identifiers: LCCN 2019038653 (print) | LCCN 2019038654 (ebook) |
ISBN 9780231195324 (cloth) | ISBN 9780231551304 (ebook) |
Subjects: LCSH: Hot peppers—China—History. | Cooking (Hot peppers)—China—
History. | Cooking, Chinese—History. | Food habits—China—History.
Classification: LCC SB307.P4 D68 2020 (print) | LCC SB307.P4 (ebook) |
DDC 633.8/40951—dc23
LC record available at https://lccn.loc.gov/2019038653
LC ebook record available at https://lccn.loc.gov/2019038654

Cover design: Milenda Nan Ok Lee

Cover image: Hitoshi Kamizumi/a.collectionRF/© Getty Images

In memory of my parents,
who taught me to be curious about the natural world.

Nancy Robertson Dott
naturalist
(1929–2018)

Robert H. Dott, Jr.
geologist
(1929–2018)

CONTENTS

ACKNOWLEDGMENTS

Many people have provided me with support and assistance throughout this book project. Sarah Scheewind, Yi-Li Wu, and Evelyn Rawski all gave me valuable advice and feedback on my first stab at writing a narrative for the history of the chile. Members of the History Department at Whitman College provided feedback at various stages of the project. Audiences at presentations at the Qing History Institute at Renmin University in Beijing and at the Needham Institute in Cambridge asked probing questions that pushed me further in my understanding and analysis. Shu-chu Wei-Peng, Qiulei Hu, and Donghui He all helped me decipher cryptic passages in classical Chinese. Wencui Zhao gave me assistance with nuances of modern Chinese and helped me navigate obtaining permissions in China. Dong Jianzhong, at the Qing History Institute at Renmin University, hosted me on several occasions in Beijing, aiding in numerous ways, both scholarly and personally. Xu Wangsheng at the China Agriculture Museum in Beijing assisted by tracking down important scholarly works on chiles in Chinese. Wang Maohua brought the illustrated text by Huang Fengchi to my attention. Annelise Heinz provided research assistance at the beginning stages of the project.

Chef Wang Taohong in Beijing demonstrated a variety of cooking methods, engaged me in a stimulating culinary conversation, and taught me to look for chiles in the cuisines of traditionally nonspicy regions. Traditional Chinese Medicine practitioner Alex Tan clarified a number of medical concepts. Li Yongxian from Sichuan University expanded my understanding of the place and role of chiles in Sichuan culture. He took the time to tour me around Pixian, where I deepened my appreciation of *douban jiang*. Librarians at Harvard-Yenching, the University of Washington, Beijing University's rare book collection, and the National Library of China all provided invaluable assistance tracking down materials. At Whitman College, Jen Pope did an extraordinary job obtaining numerous books through interlibrary loan. Jennifer Crewe, at Columbia University Press, helped me turn a manuscript with potential into a much more readable book.

Whitman College and the History Department both provided travel expenses for multiple research trips to China, as well as the University of Washington Library and the Harvard-Yenching Library. Sally Bormann has aided me in this project in many ways, as an amazing editor, providing feedback, and especially as someone who pushed me to think deeper and write better.

All translations in the book are my own unless noted otherwise.

CHINESE DYNASTIES AND REGIMES

Shennong, inventor of agriculture and medicine	(legendary ruler)
Shang dynasty	c. 1766–1045 BCE (before Common Era, equivalent to BC)
Zhou dynasty	c. 1045–256 BCE
Qin dynasty	221–207 BCE
Han dynasty	207 BCE–220 CE (Common Era, equivalent to AD)
Period of disunity	221–589
Sui dynasty	589–618
Tang dynasty	618–907
Five Dynasties period	907–960
Song dynasty	960–1279
Yuan dynasty (Mongols)	1279–1368
Ming dynasty (Han Chinese)	1368–1644
Qing dynasty (Manchus)	1644–1911
Republic of China	1911–1949 (to present on Taiwan)
People's Republic of China	1949–present (mainland China)

The Chile Pepper in China

INTRODUCTION

Red chile,
Pointed chile,
Spicy chile,
So tasty!

—CHINESE FOLK RHYME

Chinese cuisine without chile peppers? Unimaginable! Yet, there were no chiles anywhere in China prior to the 1570s. All varieties of chile pepper, from sweet to extremely spicy, from long and pointed to round, belong to species native to Central America and northern South America and therefore had to be introduced to China. This book was sparked by an epiphany when I was enjoying a spicy meal at a Sichuanese restaurant in Beijing and asked myself, "How did the Chinese begin to eat something new with such an intense flavor as chile peppers?" I started seeing chiles everywhere—real dried ones hanging from the eaves of traditional homes, decorative glass ones hanging from rear-view mirrors keeping images of Chairman Mao company, in contemporary music videos, and in an eighteenth-century novel. Today chiles are so common in China that many Chinese assume they are native. Indeed, in the mid-twentieth century Mao Zedong even asserted that revolution would be impossible without chiles![1]

In the twenty-first century I presented on some preliminary findings to an audience of Chinese historians in Beijing, and many of them were astounded that chiles are not indigenous. "Surely," several asked, "some of the varieties we enjoy are native!?" While the Chinese have certainly bred varieties to suit their tastes and needs over the past few hundred years, initial introduction came from abroad. In this book I trace the intricacies and complexities of answers to two deceptively simple questions: How did chile peppers in China evolve from an obscure foreign plant to a ubiquitous and even "authentic" spice, vegetable, medicine, and symbol? And how did Chinese uses of chiles change Chinese culture?

Drawing on a wide range of sources from many genres, I place evolving uses of and views about chiles into changing cultural contexts. Many of the ways chiles were integrated into Chinese culture transcend just one field, such as food or medicine. The introduction of chiles into China contrasts with other American crops where calories or profit were prime motivations for their spread under the public patronage of local elites and officials. In fact, elite writers tended to ignore chiles more than they wrote about them. However, chiles appear in a wide variety of genres, demonstrating that they affected Chinese culture well beyond the realm of cuisine. An important theme throughout the book is the versatility that Chinese recognized in the chile as they adapted it to fit particular national, regional, and personal conditions and needs. As a plant found in many kitchen gardens it came to be naturalized as, literally, home grown. Eventually the chile even surpassed an indigenous flavor, the Sichuan pepper, in popularity. The influence of chiles as flavorings even changed Chinese language, shifting the meaning of the term "spicy" (la 辣), so that chiles and "spicy" became enmeshed and inseparable.

Integration of the chile into medical classificatory systems was essential to its spread and adoption—not just medicinally, but also for use in cooking. The chile pepper offers an excellent avenue for viewing the interconnections between elite medical literature theory and popular healing techniques developed through practice. In addition to being used in pharmaceutical cures against a wide range of maladies, chiles also became an important daily, dietary supplement for the overall maintenance of good health. In the earliest Chinese source to include chiles, from 1591, the author emphasized their aesthetic appeal. A number of later texts also underscored how people liked to grow chile plants in pots as decorations for their homes. In modern times this beauty of chiles has been carried over into souvenirs from a sacred site and decorations for the New Year. In literature and even in revolutionary songs, chiles have been used as metaphors for personality traits or revolutionary spirit.

While many aspects of the history of chiles in China apply to most of the country, there are some regions, particularly Sichuan and Hunan, where chiles have become an essential component of regional identity—embraced by insiders and assigned by outsiders. Regional identity, like national identity, is constructed, and food is one of the things around which such identities are centered. Chile consumption has become a key identity marker in these two regions, and the chile has indelibly affected their cultures. While chile use was often multifaceted, for organizational purposes each chapter focuses on a particular type of adoption or influence, with interconnections across the chapters brought together in the conclusion.

Studying the history of food gives insight into far more than cuisine. Cultural anthropologist Igor Kopytoff, in an important study for the academic analysis of items, argues that culturally specific biographies of things treat objects "as a culturally constructed entity, endowed with culturally specific meanings, and classified and reclassified into culturally constituted categories."[2] Cultural construction refers to the concept that many things are not essentially, concretely defined by their mere presence but are fashioned into sets of meanings by the surrounding context, roles, expectations, and stories of which they are a part. My analysis of chiles in Chinese culture engages with Kopytoff's proposal for a cultural biography of a thing. In this vein, I examine how the Chinese incorporated and adopted the chile into already existing cultural constructs until it became both an "authentic" and a "revolutionary" component of Chinese culture, emblematic of specific regions as well as Mao's communist revolution.

The chile is the focal point and connecting thread through this book, an introduced crop that grants a unique lens through which to analyze changing components of Chinese culture, such as gender and revolutionary symbolism. Examination of food allows scholars to engage in deep analytical readings of a variety of cultural practices: the role of food in everyday life, the intricate interconnections between cuisine and medicine, changing gender expectations, political manipulations of popular symbols, the importance of differences between regional identities, and connections with religious rituals.

Just as gender roles and national myths are culturally constructed, so too are components of a culture that are seen as contributing to "authentic" identity, be it national, regional, or ethnic. Food and culture scholar and critic Fabio Parasecoli argues that "certain ingredients, dishes, or traditions enjoy a special position in the definition of individual and communal identities. . . . Continuous negotiations define and redefine these 'identity foods' both within and outside the communities that produce them."[3] For chiles to be so thoroughly integrated into Chinese society that most Chinese today consider them indigenous means that after introduction chiles were adopted, adapted, and redefined to the extent that they came to be considered as an "authentic" or essential component of the culture. This history of the constructed authenticity for chiles in China, however, extends beyond the realm of cuisine; the chile in China is not just an "identity food," for it was also used in medicine and literature as well. Thus the chile in this cultural biography is an "identity object."

The time is ripe for a detailed, book-length study of the cultural impact of the chile in China. There are no other studies in English. In Chinese, there are two strong history articles and a short book using an anthropological lens.[4] While the articles include important insights into the history of chiles in China, the shorter format precludes in-depth analysis of cultural impacts of chile introduction. In his recent book, *The History of Spice in Chinese Food: Four Hundred Years of Chiles in China*, Cao Yu includes interesting ethnographic information about contemporary chile use based on fieldwork that is largely outside the scope of this book. In the history sections of his book, Cao's interpretations differ significantly from mine in two key areas. Cao asserts that the main agents for transmitting chiles within China were merchants. I, instead, argue that

Figure 0.1 A number of varieties of chiles at a market in Kunming, Yunnan, 2017.

farmers played a major role. Second, Cao gives a much later date for the first use of chiles as a flavoring and emphasizes Guizhou as the most important location for that use. By contrast, in this book, I explore sources that demonstrate Chinese used chiles as flavoring well before when Cao asserts it began. Furthermore, early Chinese use of chiles as a flavoring was more broadly dispersed. In works about Chinese food and the introduction of foreign crops, the chile pepper usually receives only a few passing lines or, at most, a few pages.[5] The chile pepper's importance in Chinese culture, however, is much more significant than is reflected in scholarly discourse.

Although no chiles were grown in China until about the 1570s, their popularity took off rapidly. By 1621 there were already references to them being grown widely.[6] By the eighteenth century the editors of a local history even declared that chiles had become "as indispensable in daily cuisine as onion and garlic."[7] As a trip to any market in China reveals (see figure 0.1), the chile is now a vibrant and ubiquitous component of Chinese culture. The impact of chile pepper use extends well beyond culinary practices. Mao associated the revolutionary vigor of Hunanese, including himself, with chile pepper consumption. The renowned contemporary pop singer Song Zuying, in the song "Spicy Girls," declares that "with a handful of chiles, [women] speak their minds."[8] The fiery gender anarchy of a key female character from the eighteenth-century novel *The Dream of the Red Chamber* is linked with the chile pepper. Chiles are on the table in flavorful dishes, their heat helps people's bodies adjust to high levels of humidity, their images decorate posters and doorways, and, metaphorically, they symbolize revolutionary men and passionate women. The chile is now a lively and even authentic component of Chinese culture.

1

NAMES AND PLACES

How the Chile Found Its Way "Home" to China

Foreign pepper: It comes from central Shu [Sichuan].
Now it is found everywhere.

—*SHIWU BENCAO*, MEDICAL TEXT, 1621

Although chiles originated outside China, Chinese played integral roles in their introduction and spread. Chinese merchants, pirates, smugglers, or sailors probably initially brought chiles from Southeast Asia to the central coast of China. In the Northeast, Chinese farmers likely learned about growing chiles from their neighbors in northern Korea. Once chiles were already introduced, they spread locally in ways distinct from other American crops. Instead of thriving because of elite patronage as a solution to famine, or as a way to make money, chiles gained popularity at the local level first—from the bottom up—growing in kitchen gardens.

The story of how chiles came "home" to China begins with the tale of how they traveled from the Americas to Southeast Asia. Ships with multiethnic crews played an integral role in transporting this spice, vegetable, and medicine. Their introduction from Southeast Asia was more indirect and involved less fanfare than that of other American crops. Chiles became virtually free, home-grown garden plants that subverted and substituted for moneyed-economy spices, unlike introduced cash crops such as tobacco or spice trade tropicals like black pepper. Uncovering their likely entry points into China involves a close look at naming protocols and geography.

Global Warming: The Worldwide Spread of Chiles

Chile peppers are native to Central America and northern South America. Like a number of other American crops, such as the white potato, tomato, and tobacco, chiles are in the Solanaceae family. This family also includes deadly nightshade or belladonna (native to North America and Eurasia) and the eggplant (native to South or Southeast Asia). The eggplant has been widely used in Chinese cuisine since its introduction around the fourth century CE.[1] A number of Chinese recognized the close relationship between chiles and eggplants. One early name for chiles was *laqie* 辣茄, or spicy eggplant.[2] Chiles are in the genus *Capsicum*. While chile varieties worldwide come from several recognized species of chiles, it appears the ones introduced into late imperial China (c. 1500–1920 for social and cultural practices) were probably all *Capsicum annuum*.[3] This species is an annual, and in most parts of China it must be replanted every year. In subtropical or tropical climates, some annuals can grow as perennials. Thus in some parts of southern China, *Capsicum annuum* may have behaved like a perennial (including woody stems), causing some researchers to believe that several of the early varieties introduced were from the species *Capsicum frutescens*. Wu Zhengyi and Peter Raven of the Missouri Botanical Garden, however, make a convincing case in the *Flora of China* that all early introductions were *Capsicum annuum*.[4] There are numerous varieties of *Capsicum annuum* that vary widely in shape and spiciness. Chiles in this species tolerate a wide range of climatic conditions and grow readily throughout much of Inner China (essentially the area in map 1.2).[5] They grow well in both dry and moist climates. As with the introduction of other members of this sometimes poisonous family, like the tomato and white potato initially in Europe, some early East Asian authors believed that chiles were too dangerous to eat (albeit at the same time they were documenting their cultivation).

European exploration, expansion, and trade were the initial causes of the spread of American crops to other regions of the world. Christopher Columbus mentioned chiles in his diary during his first voyage, 1492–1493: "There is also much *axi* [chile], which is their pepper, of a kind more valuable than [black] pepper, and none of the people eat without it, for they find it very healthful. Fifty caravels can be loaded with it each year in Hispaniola" (see map 1.1).[6] *Axi* or *ají* are Spanish transliterations of the Arawak (an indigenous Caribbean language) name for chiles. The term *chile* comes from the Aztec or Nahuatl name.[7] It is unclear if Columbus brought any *axi* back with him to Spain on that first journey.[8] Even if he did not bring chiles back with him on his first voyage, it is extremely likely that they were sent back to Spain during his second voyage,

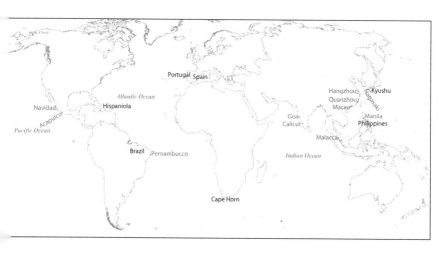

Map 1.1 The world in the sixteenth century. Created by author using ESRI ArcMap, v. 10.0.

1493–1496. In February 1494 Columbus sent twelve ships from Hispaniola back to Spain, where they arrived in April 1494. Among the items taken back was an ethnographic letter about Hispaniola, including a description of chiles, by the fleet physician, Dr. Diego Alvarez Chanca.[9] Given the carrying capacity of twelve ships and the interest of both Columbus and Chanca in chiles, 1494 is a reasonable deduction for the introduction of chiles to Spain. Despite Columbus's enthusiasm that chiles were "more valuable than black pepper," they were initially unpopular as a spice in Spain and were never transported across the Atlantic as a trade commodity. In fact, early use of peppers in Spain was as decorative plants, and many were grown in monastery gardens for their aesthetic appeal.[10] Initial use of chiles by Chinese elites similarly emphasized their aesthetic beauty rather than culinary or medical uses.

Chile plants are quite tolerant of being grown in temperate zones, and thus once a few had been established in Spain they were self-reproducing, making any need for further importation superfluous. This makes chiles quite different from other spice-trade products like black pepper or nutmeg, which require tropical climates and therefore had to be continually imported to places like Europe and China. Instead, since chiles can be grown in a variety of climates they were a disappointment for those seeking riches through the spice trade.[11]

It is impossible to be precise about the date chiles arrived anywhere in Asia. Just as was the case for Europe, there is no evidence that either the Spanish or Portuguese ever transported chiles as a trade commodity to Asia. Instead, they were probably carried in ship galleys as a flavoring for meals for crews or servants. Indeed, botanist Henry Ridley, writing in the 1930s, implied such a dispersal method within South and Southeast Asia in his *The Dispersal of Plants Throughout the World*.[12] Jean Andrews, an expert on the global spread of the chile, almost certainly building on Ridley's comments, also acknowledges inadvertent spreading via "seed in food scraps" as a possible scenario for dispersal within parts of Asia.[13] Only a few seeds would have been needed to establish chiles at various ports of call.

While chiles first arrived in Europe in Spain, it was almost certainly Portuguese ships that began moving them to Asia. The Portuguese had explored along the west coast of Africa in the 1470s, and Bartolomeu Dias rounded Cape Horn in 1488. Andrews suggests that the Portuguese introduced chiles along the east coast of Africa sometime between 1494 and Vasco da Gama's voyage into the Indian Ocean basin in 1497–1498.[14] In 1498 Portuguese ships, under da Gama, arrived for the first time in India, at Calicut. The year 1498, then, is the earliest possible date for the introduction of chiles into Asia. In 1500 Portuguese landed for the first time in Brazil. So from then on they had direct access to chiles and other crops in Brazil, as well as the indirect access via Spain. It is also possible that the Portuguese began including crew members from Brazil on their ships, who may well have brought chiles on board for flavoring their meals.

The Portuguese rapidly embraced trade in the Indian Ocean region. In 1510 they captured the key trade entrepôt at Goa, located centrally on the west coast of India. The chile was probably introduced shortly after this, perhaps in the 1520s, for "by 1542, three separate varieties of chilli were growing in India, mainly on the west coast and especially in Goa. Chillis first became well known in Bombay under the name *Gowai mirchi* (Goan pepper). According to Clusius in his *Exoticorum* (1605), the chilli pepper was also cultivated in India under the name Pernambuco [a Brazilian port city] pepper."[15] This introduction too was probably serendipitous and not through trading chiles as a commodity. From India the pepper spread, via land or sea, to Burma. The Portuguese expanded their presence to Southeast Asia when they conquered Malacca, near the tip of the Malay Peninsula, in 1511. Malacca was already a flourishing center of trade that brought together, among others, Arab, Bengali, Chinese, Filipino, Gujarati, Javanese, Malay, Persian, Ryū-kyū islander, Tamil, and Thai merchants.[16] Chiles reached this part of Southeast Asia by 1540.[17]

Portuguese merchants first arrived in southern China from Malacca in 1514. In 1522, after many aggressive actions on the part of the Portuguese, such as building a fort without permission and enslaving Chinese, the Ming government banned them from trading in China. Despite the ban, Portuguese merchant ships continued to conduct trade, albeit illegally, at ports along the southeast and central coast of China, including Zhangzhou, Quanzhou, and Ningbo.[18] In 1554 Sino-Portuguese trade officially recommenced, and in 1557 the Ming government allowed the Portuguese to set up a base of operations in Macao.[19]

The Spanish first arrived in East Asia in 1521 in the Philippine Islands. Ferdinand Magellan, en route to circumnavigate the globe, claimed the islands for the Spanish throne, but without making any settlements. The Spanish made a couple of failed attempts at establishing a settlement in the Philippines in order to compete with the Portuguese in the spice trade in the mid-sixteenth century.[20] However, it was not until the Spanish decided to link their American colonies of "New Spain" directly across the Pacific to the Philippines that they finally succeeded in establishing permanent settlements in the Philippines. The ships that made these trans-Pacific voyages are usually referred to as the Manila Galleons. The first fleet of ships to make this journey left from the port of Navidad on modern Mexico's southern Pacific coast (just north of Acapulco) in November 1564 and arrived in the Philippines in February 1565. In 1571 the seat of Spanish authority in the islands was relocated to Manila, which from then on became the main trade center for the Spanish in East Asia.[21] The Manila Galleons continued to traverse the Pacific until 1815, with some fleets continuing to use Navidad while most used Acapulco. Carlos Quirino, a historian of the Philippines, asserts that probably half of the crew of the first fleet was made up of creoles, mestizos, and Meso-American indigenes.[22] It is probable that some of these people were accustomed to eating chiles regularly and thus stocked the kitchens on the galleons with chiles for their food preparation. In addition, on later voyages wealthy passengers brought chocolate with them.[23] This would have been prepared in the style prevalent in Mesoamerica, which included chile peppers. Thus multiple people on the galleons had reasons for bringing chiles across the Pacific for personal consumption, but none sought to trade them as Columbus had once imagined.

After 1514 the Portuguese had the opportunity to introduce American crops into China; the Spanish could have done so beginning in 1565. In addition, merchants from a variety of places and ethnicities also had the same opportunity. Indeed, even though it is convenient to refer to Portuguese, Fujianese, or Dutch merchants or ships, most ships conducting trade in Asia during the sixteenth century had multiethnic crews. The British navigator William Adams actually arrived in Japan on a Dutch ship.[24] The British ship *Clove* arrived in Hirado, Japan, in 1613 "carrying seventy-four Englishmen, a Spaniard, a Japanese, and five Indians."[25] Thus even if a Portuguese or Spanish vessel brought chiles to Malacca or Manila, it may actually have been a crew member from somewhere else who transported the chiles or seeds. Roderich Ptak, a historian specializing in the history of maritime trade in East and Southeast Asia, notes that by the end of the sixteenth century the Chinese far outnumbered all other outsiders in Southeast Asia, including in the Philippines.[26] Eric Tagliacozzo, another historian specializing in maritime trade in East and Southeast Asia, shows that Chinese conducted a great deal of trade in ocean produce between Indonesia, Malaya, the Philippines, and the southeast coast of China.[27] Thus it is quite likely that Chinese crew members or merchants introduced many of the American crops, including the chile, to the coastal areas of central and southeastern China from some part of Southeast Asia.

Chinese merchants, especially those from Fujian, have a long history of ocean trade with Southeast Asia and the Indian Ocean basin. Many Fujianese had migrated to a variety of trade ports in Southeast Asia, especially during Zheng He's voyages in the early fifteenth century. Zheng He was a renowned Chinese admiral who led massive diplomatic fleets between 1405 and 1433 from China into the Indian Ocean, stopping at ports in Indonesia, India, East Africa, and the Persian Gulf. Quite a few Fujianese who participated in these large, extravagant missions chose to settle in other parts of Asia. Chinese demand for many South and Southeast Asian products made sea trade routes profitable. Black pepper, for example, was an important trade item that Chinese traders transported from ports such as Malacca to the southeast coast of China.[28] The Ming government had banned Chinese merchants from traveling abroad in 1372, but the restriction just led to large-scale illicit trade and piracy.[29] Indeed, the problems with smuggling and piracy finally led the Ming government to revoke the ban in 1567. According to Ptak, after the ban was lifted Fujianese merchants "immediately took advantage of these favorable circumstances and greatly expanded their trade to Southeast Asia and Japan." He further argues that Fujianese merchants acted as important connective links among overseas Chinese in Southeast Asia, Macao, Kyūshū, and the northern Philippines.[30] Thus Fujianese merchants, illicit or authorized, and their multiethnic crews were likely transferers of the American crops that entered China in the sixteenth century.

Local histories or gazetteers (*difangzhi* 地方志) are an essential source for historical studies of local phenomena and practices in late imperial China, including introductions of new plants.[31] They proliferated during the late imperial period publishing boom. While there are a fair number extant from the late Ming, the genre really took off during the Qing. The majority of gazetteers were written for the political jurisdictions of the district, department, prefecture, and province. They were usually revised every fifty to one hundred years. Wealthier areas tended to have shorter periods between revisions. Revisions often directly copied large sections from the previous edition, and those for larger or higher-level jurisdictions normally consolidated material from the gazetteers of smaller or lower-level jurisdictions. Typically, each revision was edited by a team drawn from the local elite, and the printing was often underwritten by the corresponding government office.

The main gazetteer chapters used for this book are "local-products" (*wuchan* 物產) sections. The local-products section in most gazetteers was itself divided into many categories, which generally included grains, vegetables, fruits, trees, flowers, bamboos, manufactured goods, minerals, medicines, and a variety of animal types. Some entries might include just a two- or three-character name, while others might include up to a page or two of description and commentary. For the gazetteers that listed chiles, the majority just gave a name or possibly also an additional alternative name. The longest entry for chiles is one page long. While the quantity of information in these local histories is not vast, it has nonetheless proved essential for my research.

The local-products sections of gazetteers often describe local, nonelite use. Both the Ming and Qing bureaucracies used laws of avoidance (no official could serve in his home province) as a counter to corruption. Thus gazetteers contained essential information about local customs, practices, beliefs, crops, and products, all of which aided officials in understanding the places where they had been posted. Indeed, the compilers of one gazetteer from 1550 observed that "when worthy scholar gentry obtain the gazetteer, they will be forever able to observe and investigate the ordinary people."[32] When the texts referred to "local" practices, there was usually an implied class to the subjects being described—generally "local" meant "nonelite locals." The recipes and descriptions of chile use from gazetteers therefore can often be read as the elite editors' perceptions of lower-class use.

The records on chiles from gazetteers demonstrate that they were being grown in a particular place at a given time. Longer entries might name varieties, describe culinary use, give medical cures, or reveal class differences for consumption. Gazetteers from all the provinces of Inner China included chiles. For many provinces, the earliest known source is a gazetteer. For some provinces the only sources are local histories.

Generally, a crop would have to have been grown in ample quantities to be sold in markets prior to gazetteer inclusion. Ming- and Qing-period historian Ho Ping-ti asserted that "it took considerable time for a new crop to be grown on a scale sufficiently significant to be recorded in a local history."[33] Thus the presence of a new crop like peanuts or chiles in a local gazetteer probably means that people had been growing it in that area for personal use for some time. Once the plant was available in markets, elites who wrote local gazetteers may only have visited larger, district-seat markets, ignoring local ones. Finally, even with mounds of peanuts or chiles in the main market, there was no guarantee an author or authors of the products section would include them. Therefore while the products sections of local gazetteers are extremely valuable sources for the study of new crops, the lack of an item does not mean the crop was not yet widely available.

Arrival of American Crops in China

Other crops from the Americas (North, Central, and South) offer some possible clues about the routes for chiles into China. The introduction of chiles, however, was almost certainly later than for the main edible American crops. The earliest known, datable record for peanuts in China is from the 1539 local gazetteer for Changshu district in Jiangsu, which was just north of Suzhou and just south of the Yangzi River.[34] Ho believed that either the Portuguese introduced the peanut directly or Fujianese merchants brought it from Southeast Asia, where it had been introduced earlier by the Portuguese.[35] Likely, crops from the Americas arrived in China a number of years prior to showing up in any written record. The 1520s is a reasonable estimate for the introduction of peanuts.

Ho demonstrated that the sweet potato entered China from two directions, decades prior to 1594, the date suggested in earlier scholarship. In 1594 sweet potatoes were brought to the attention of the governor of Fujian. However, based on other sources it is clear that cultivation had been ongoing prior to the governor's notice.[36] One route for the introduction was probably via sea into Fujian; the other was probably overland from Burma into Yunnan province. A Yunnan local history from 1563 is the earliest known record for sweet potatoes in China.[37] Again, sweet potatoes were likely grown for at least a decade before appearing in the gazetteer, so introduction by the 1550s would be reasonable.

Ho identified a district gazetteer of 1555 from Henan as the earliest reference for maize in China. As he noted, "Since this locality is far from the southeast coast and the Yunnan-Burma border, the two regions whereby a New World crop was likely to be brought into China, and since it took considerable time for a new crop to be grown on a scale sufficiently significant to be recorded in a local history, it seems reasonable to suggest that maize was introduced into China at least two or three decades prior to its first written account."[38] This would put introduction in the 1520s–1530s.

The earliest record of tobacco cultivation in China is from Fujian and dates to 1611.[39] The author of this source, Yao Lü (1573–1620), claimed that it had been introduced from Luzon (in the Philippines) and that production was then high enough that it was actually being exported back to Luzon.[40] Carol Benedict argues that tobacco, like the other crops discussed above, would have been available and also grown in China prior to reaching such a level of production, as early as the 1550s.[41] Thus these four American crops were probably introduced into China between the 1520s and the 1560s. Some came overland first, via Burma into Yunnan; others, along the central or southeast coast. Portuguese or Fujian merchant ships were the most likely initial couriers for the coastal introductions.

Chiles Into China

In their important article on chile peppers, Jiang Mudong and Wang Siming argue that chiles entered China at three main points: from Southeast Asia to the central coast, from Korea into Northeast China, and via the Dutch into Taiwan.[42] My own research, including analysis of the earliest sources for each province, dominant naming regiment by region, and likely routes for the spread of chiles, corroborates this conclusion that chiles entered China at these three points (see map 1.2, showing the date of the earliest source to mention chiles for each province of Inner China).[43] Each of the three regions that are the most likely entry points for chiles into China had their own initial names for the new crop. Different

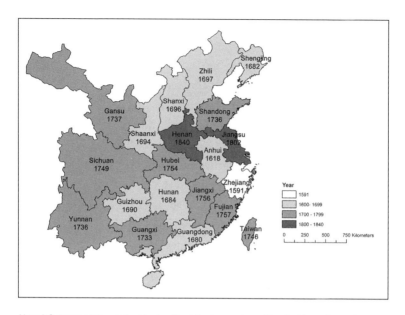

Map 1.2 Dates of the earliest texts with chiles by province. Created by author using China Historical GIS, v. 4.0 (1820 boundaries), and ESRI ArcMap, v. 10.0.

initial names are an important piece of evidence supporting multiple entry points and also reflect how locals embraced this foreign plant, making it their own. The three main initial descriptors focus on the foreign origin, the main substitution uses in local cuisine, or a more domestic, regional association, all key aspects of the multiple, varied ways this spice from the Americas began its transformation from second-class immigrant, to regional homegrown, "authentic" native.

Exactly when each of these introductions occurred is difficult to pinpoint. As mentioned above, gazetteers are generally an excellent source for tracing the introduction of other new crops. However, as is evidenced in the large lag in the record between the earliest source to mention the chile (1591) and the first appearance in a gazetteer (1671), gazetteers are not a particularly reliable source for precisely isolating the introduction dates of the chile. In addition, it is quite possible that chiles would have had to have been introduced more than once in some places. Ho argued, quite persuasively, that new crops were probably "introduced" multiple times, in multiple places: "It is foolish to believe that a certain plant can be introduced into a new area only once, and then only by a certain route. A new plant may score an immediate success in one region and remain neglected in another for a considerable time. Sometimes only through repeated trial and error can a new plant strike root."[44] Based on the earliest sources for each region, international trading conditions, and introduction dates for other parts of Asia, I give estimates below for the time when chiles probably first arrived in each of these three areas. Map 1.3 shows the three entry points.

Chiles reached the Malacca area of Southeast Asia by 1540. Given trade patterns at that time, it is extremely likely that introduction of chiles into China occurred after that. The earliest known

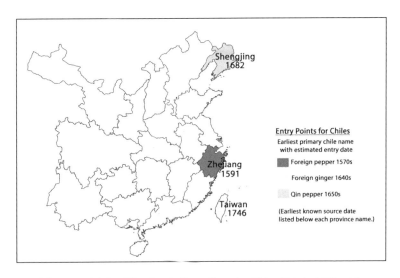

Map 1.3 Entry points for chiles. Created by author using China Historical GIS, v. 4.0 (1820 boundaries), and ESRI ArcMap, v. 10.0.

record for chiles in a Chinese source is from Hangzhou, Zhejiang, in 1591.[45] In addition, the earliest known reference to chiles in a gazetteer, 1671, is from a prefecture adjacent to Hangzhou, also in Zhejiang.[46] Thus introduction from somewhere in Southeast Asia to the central coast was clearly one route, and almost certainly the earliest. Given the likely delay between introduction and recording in a written source, chiles probably first appeared along the central coast in the 1570s–1580s, overlapping with the likely time for the introduction of tobacco. This means chiles could have come from the Malacca area, or, since the first Spanish galleons crossing the Pacific arrived in 1565, from the Philippines, or possibly both. Chinese botanist Shiu-ying Hu states that chiles were "introduced to the Philippines by the Spaniards and then into China by overseas Chinese residing there in the seventeenth century."[47] While such a route is certainly possible, Hu does not cite any sources to substantiate this claim. In addition, with Gao's 1591 description of chiles, the initial introduction definitely dates to earlier than the seventeenth century. With the Ming trade ban lifted in 1567, Chinese merchant ships were likely transmitters. As there is no evidence for an intentional import of chiles as a trade commodity, the most likely vector for introduction was via chiles brought for flavoring food for ship crew members.

Gao Lian (fl. 1573–1591), a late Ming collector and connoisseur, was the earliest Chinese author to mention chiles. He lived in Hangzhou on the central coast, so his source was also the earliest for that entry point. Gao Lian's father made a vast fortune as a grain merchant. He sought to augment his economic clout with cultural and political standing by acquiring a library and an art collection, in addition to educating his son for the civil service examinations. Gao Lian, however, like so many of his peers, was unsuccessful in the grueling, career-determining exams. Instead of the coveted prestige and social advancement of a career as an official, he gave himself over to a life devoted to the arts and good living. He pursued a myriad of elite pastimes, including art collecting, writing poetry and plays, patronage of writers, and authoring his encyclopedic work on living well. Gao lived on the shores of West Lake in Hangzhou, Zhejiang. There is no evidence that he traveled, and it is therefore likely that he encountered chiles in or near Hangzhou. His references to the aesthetic appeal of chiles are found in his extensive work on living, *Zunsheng bajian* (Eight discourses on nurturing life).[48] He did not, however, include the chile in the sections of this work on food or medicine. This is not surprising since in the opening lines of his discourse on food and drink he declared: "As for those who flavor living creatures (*shengling*) with Sichuan pepper, fragrances or rare delicacies, these are for high officials' sumptuous dinners or for offerings to celestial beings (*tianren*). They are not for a mountain hermit (*shanren*) like me; I make no record of them at all."[49] While his luxurious house with library, art collection, and study in Hangzhou seems a bit ostentatious for a "mountain hermit," this quote does convey his style, interests, and pursuit of Daoist perfection.

Gao Lian used the name *fanjiao* 番椒, or foreign pepper, for the chile.[50] This name emphasized the foreign origin of the plant (*fan*) and combined it with the name of an indigenous, intense flavoring (*jiao*), borrowing the well-known pungency of the native plant Sichuan pepper to describe the intense flavor of the new arrival. It is likely that early use in this region included substituting the chile for this native spice.

A survey of Taiwanese flora and fauna from 1746 is the earliest source from that island to include chiles. It presents the Dutch as the source for chiles on the island: "Foreign ginger (*fanjiang*) is a type of vine from Holland. . . . Foreigners (*fanren*) brought these pods [to Taiwan] to eat them."[51] This quote overtly suggests that one association of the designator *fan* was not only the source of the spice but the peripatetic foreigners who brought it specifically for personal use in their exotic cuisine. The Dutch were in Taiwan from 1624 to 1662. So introduction during the middle of that period, in about the 1640s, would be reasonable. Unfortunately, I have found no sources providing more details about this Dutch introduction. The Dutch might have become accustomed to eating chiles in their Indonesian colonies, or they may have grown them to mix in their hot chocolate. While the compilers of the work on Taiwanese flora and fauna were aware of chiles on the mainland, noting that "on the mainland (*neidi*) they are named foreign pepper," the primary use of the name "foreign ginger" supports the idea that the inhabitants on the island had invented their own name for a newly introduced crop.[52] The primary name for chiles in all the Taiwanese gazetteers consulted from between 1746 and 1894 is "foreign ginger." The only known sources from prior to the twentieth century that use this term as the primary name are all from Taiwan. Indeed, "foreign ginger" is still the most common term for chile peppers in the Taiwanese dialect (*Minnanhua*).[53]

Before examining the entrance of the chile from Korea into northeastern China, then called Shengjing (modern Liaoning), we must first take a step back to briefly look at its prior introduction into Japan. As with China, introduction into Japan almost certainly occurred after the chile arrived in Southeast Asia. In 1543 some Portuguese traders arrived aboard a Chinese ship on a small island off the southern tip of Kyūshū in Japan. Francis Xavier, along with two other Jesuits, arrived in southern Kyūshū in 1549, also aboard a Chinese vessel.[54] The Portuguese began trading in Japan shortly afterward and eventually established an important trade post at Nagasaki in 1571. Chiles likely entered Japan shortly after this, again probably brought by multiethnic crew members on a European- or Chinese-owned ship as flavoring for their own meals. From there chiles moved onto the Korean peninsula.

The earliest known record of chiles in Korea is found in the 1614 encyclopedia by Yi Su-gwang (1563–1628), who noted that "Now it is grown everywhere [in Korea]," so introduction must have occurred earlier. Yi was a military official and diplomat in the Korean Joseon dynasty (Chosŏn, 1392–1910). His *Jibong yuseol* (Topical discourses of Jibong [his penname]) was the first encyclopedia published in Korea. Yi labeled chiles as "Southern Barbarian" peppers, using a common Japanese term for Europeans. He further stated that chiles were introduced to Korea from Japan, so introduction into Korea during the Japanese unifier Toyotomi Hideyoshi's invasions of Korea (1592–1598) is reasonable.[55]

The earliest record of chiles in Shengjing dates from 1682.[56] The location for this earliest record, Gaiping district, is about 175 kilometers from northern Korea, so initial introduction into Shengjing probably occurred earlier. Another gazetteer from the area, compiled just two years later, notes that many varieties were grown.[57] Based on this data, introduction two to three decades prior to there being many varieties away from the border area would extend the likely time for introduction back to the 1650s. Indeed, transference to northeastern China from Korea, where chiles were "grown everywhere" in 1614, would be reasonable by the 1650s. The only name used for chiles in Shengjing sources prior to the twentieth century was *Qinjiao* 秦椒 or Qin pepper, thus supporting the Northeast as a separate entry point from the central coast.[58] Qin is an ancient name for the region that is now essentially Shaanxi province, in north-central China. This choice of a regional name deemphasizes the overseas origin of chiles, perhaps owing to its gradual introduction, probably farmer by farmer from northern Korea into northeastern China, possibly over a period of a couple of decades.

Examination of map 1.2 reveals another possible introduction point on China's southeast coast in Guangdong. Since many merchant ships plied the waters between various Southeast Asian ports and those along the Guangdong and Fujian coasts, chiles may also have been introduced along the southeast coast, though there is no written evidence to support this region as an entry point. Jiang and Wang argue that chiles entered this region from the central coast rather than from overseas.[59] Finding a unique name for chiles in the earliest source provides strong evidence that a particular place was a point of introduction. Yet the earliest name for chiles in both Guangdong (1680) and Fujian (1757) was *fanjiao*,[60] instead making it likely that chiles entered this region from the Chinese central coast, the earliest location where that name was used. While lack of a unique name does not preclude introduction into the southeast coast as a fourth entry point, without additional evidence it remains purely speculative.

While other crops, particularly the sweet potato, probably entered China via land from Burma into Yunnan as well as by sea, there is no evidence for chiles arriving via such a route. The earliest date for chiles in Yunnan, 1736, is later than those for the two neighboring provinces to the east (Guizhou 1690 and Guangxi 1733).[61] So introduction from the east is logical. The earliest source for Yunnan is the 1736 edition of the provincial gazetteer. Unfortunately, this source does not identify where in the province chiles were growing at that time. However, the next earliest source from Yunnan, from 1739, is from a prefecture adjacent to Guangxi and quite close to Guizhou.[62] The primary name for chiles in both of these sources was *Qinjiao*, the same name used first in the Northeast in Shengjing. Since there was not a distinct initial name for chiles in Yunnan, there is no textual support for a separate introduction from Burma. In their article on chiles, Jiang and Wang do not give any consideration to Yunnan as a possible entry point.[63]

Over the centuries many crops have entered inner China along the so-called silk roads trading routes across Central Asia into Gansu and then Shaanxi provinces. Jiang Xianming proposed this as one route for the introduction of chiles into China.[64] While it is possible that chiles followed this route, as with the southeast coast and Yunnan routes, there is no actual evidence to support such a hypothesis. In fact, other Chinese scholars are skeptical to outright dismissive of this route for chiles.[65] Furthermore, there is evidence that contradicts such a hypothesis. While the data from gazetteers certainly cannot be taken as definitive for when chiles first arrived in any particular place, it is often the only data for examining their spread. If chiles were introduced via this route, then one would expect the earliest reference for chiles in Gansu (1737) to be earlier than that for Shaanxi (1694).[66] While this contrary fact does not preclude introduction of chiles along the silk roads, it certainly does not lend any support to that possibility. In addition, if chiles had entered via the silk roads, it would be reasonable to find a different initial name for chiles in Gansu and Shaanxi, as we have seen for the other three entry points. However, the earliest name for chiles in Gansu is *Qinjiao*, implying introduction from the east, across northern China. Furthermore, James Millward notes that chiles were quite possibly introduced into Xinjiang (west of Gansu) from both India and Inner China.[67]

Once chiles were in China, they probably spread internally within market areas. Ho surmised that new crops were probably "introduced" by a variety of actors: "such as traders, travelers, emissaries, and government officials."[68] To his list of possible channels for the spread of new crops, I add another extremely important group: networks of rural farmers, for example, northeastern Shengjing farmers, for whom exchanges with nearby Korean farmers may have been more common than any interactions with sailors, traders, government officials, or elite authors.

The eighty-year gap between the earliest record of chiles and the first reference in a gazetteer makes tracing times and places for the spread of chiles difficult. Gazetteers are among the earliest sources for some of the other American crops, such as the peanut, sweet potato, and maize.[69] However, gazetteer entries for both tobacco and chiles lagged considerably behind the earliest known sources. A probable explanation for this lies in the natures of the crops themselves. Peanuts, sweet potatoes, and maize all became important crops that could be grown on previously unfarmed land, where wheat, sorghum, millet, or rice could not be grown. All three produce high-caloric edible parts, which store well. For these reasons, growing and consuming these crops spread fairly quickly. Most important for recording in gazetteers, these crops caught the attention of local elites, officials, and at least one emperor, who, out of paternalistic concerns, actively promoted the growing and consuming of these crops by the lower strata of society as famine relief.[70] In contrast, late imperial sources about chile peppers are thin, and no one explicitly advocated growing them. Chiles and tobacco did not have an impact in terms of caloric value. Tobacco, however, captured elite attention much more than chiles and developed quickly into a cash crop. Sources about tobacco are much more detailed and numerous than those about chiles, with many elite authors writing treatises about the crop.[71] In contrast, explicit references to chiles being sold in markets are rare until the twentieth century. Also, chiles sometimes served as a homegrown, free substitute for salt. Chiles competed directly with the cash-generating, government-controlled salt, a likely disincentive for the authors of gazetteers to encourage their use as a salt substitute. Chiles, additionally, were perhaps initially grown as decorative plants by the elite, such as Gao Lian, and this would have made them unlikely to appear in the products sections of local gazetteers. Also, as chiles came to be used as a spice and vegetable, they were probably grown by individual families for personal use in small plots such as kitchen gardens. No one planted them to survive or rushed to grow as many as possible in order to sell them. Under such conditions, chiles likely spread from neighbor to neighbor in areas with common markets. However, it probably took a fair amount of time until there were sufficient numbers being grown for them to appear in markets. Once there, they still would have needed to have been noticed by gazetteer compilers before appearing in the products section of a local gazetteer.

The anonymous author of the medical text *Shiwu bencao* (1621) sends a confusing message down to us about this foreign *yet local* crop. First, the author identified the chile plant as "foreign pepper," a name that should connote its overseas origin. Yet the author continues: "It comes from central Shu [Sichuan]. Now it is found everywhere."[72] It is extremely unlikely that chiles had yet reached Sichuan by 1621, and certainly they did not originate there. So why did the author believe chiles originated there? First, Sichuan had long been associated with strong flavorings. Second, the phrase "Now it is found everywhere" implies that the author found this crop to be so ubiquitous as to be indigenous and did not pause when using the name "foreign" when assigning its point of origin to Sichuan.

By the late nineteenth century the chile pepper was so well integrated as a widespread, well-known, "local" crop that it was even used to help others identify an indigenous plant. "Golden lantern [*Physalis alkekengi*]: it is also called heavenly lantern. [The plant] resembles the spicy eggplant [chile], but its leaves are larger."[73] Local names and local usages help us piece together the path of a once obscure foreign plant as it became widely used, and in some regions indispensable.

2

SPICING UP THE PALATE

The seasonal taste, who doesn't want it?
—FROM "CHILE PEPPER PASTE POEM," BY WU XINGQIN, 1783

The intense, spicy flavor of chiles was the most essential character-istic for their acceptance in China. Cuisine, however, is often a fairly conservative component of culture. Indeed, the tomato took a long time to appeal to Italians, partially owing to difficulties in integrating it into the culinary tradition.[1] In contrast, the adoption of chiles as a spice for Chinese cuisine evolved relatively quickly into a homegrown, locally spread substitute for commodified, taxed, and imported products. Indeed, they became so popular that the editors of a local gazetteer from the inland province of Shaanxi in 1755 asserted that they had become "as indispensable in daily cuisine as onion and garlic."[2] Ultimately, chiles became treated as an authentic and necessary component of Chinese cui-sine. In addition, their use also affected other cultural systems, including language.

While chiles were adopted into Chinese cuisine in a variety of ways, at first these meshed with traditional cooking and preserva-tion methods long in use. Some early sources demonstrate that chiles initially gained inroads as substitutes for other flavorings.

However, chiles soon eclipsed many of these spices and in some places even became more "authentic" than longer-used, indigenous flavorings. The fact that chiles grow well throughout Inner China also meant they were more economical than many alternatives. Thus those more detached from the moneyed economy, such as farmers and minorities living in remote areas, seem to have adopted chiles much more quickly than elites. Over time, Chinese also realized that the strong flavor of chiles helped make the highly starchy meals of the majority of the population more palatable. In addition to adding their own flavor to dishes, chiles, like other spices, enhance the other flavors in a dish. They were also used in food preservation. They could be kept for long periods through drying and pickling, and as a main ingredient in sauces. Aesthetically they added color to meals, particularly during seasons when fresh vegetables were unavailable. Furthermore, modern psychological research has shown that once a tolerance for the capsaicin in chiles has been developed, eating chiles can cause endorphin secretion, generating feelings of pleasure, and since capsaicin can trigger danger signals, thrill-seeking tendencies can be satisfied through consumption.[3]

Prior to examining the specifics of Chinese culinary adoption of chiles, it is important to briefly debunk a modern bias that privileges technology for food safety. A much trotted-out legend asserts that spices were used in the past (especially in medieval Europe) to cover up the taste of spoiled food, particularly meat. This legend derives from modern Westerners (probably in the nineteenth century) feeling superior about their cuisines and cultures compared to the perceived backwardness of the past and also of cultures outside of Western Europe.[4] During the research for this book, several people have suggested this masking ability to me as one of the reasons the chile became so popular in China.[5] This is a myth, however, both for the expensive spices used by elites in medieval

Europe and for Chinese using chiles in the early modern period. Paul Newman debunks this quite succinctly and colorfully in his book *Daily Life in the Middle Ages*: "Spices and other flavorings for food were certainly highly prized in the Middle Ages but the idea that any of them were routinely used to disguise the smell and taste of rotten meat is just silly. Once meat has spoiled, it is toxic and no amount of spices can make it safe to eat."[6] While they would not have been used for masking flavors, chiles were quite useful for helping to preserve meat, to prevent it from spoiling in the first place.

The strong flavor of chiles was read culturally as pungent (*xin* 辛), drying, hot, and connected with the health of the lungs. The integration of chiles into culinary flavoring regimens is evidenced in the ways that they were initially substituted for other well-established pungent spices, including Sichuan pepper, black pepper, and ginger. In addition, some Chinese even replaced salt with chiles. Economics, and therefore class, played a role in chile adoption. Once introduced, chiles could be grown by families in their vegetable or kitchen gardens. In contrast with other flavorings, chiles, although they required labor input, did not need to be traded for cash or some other commodity. Imported black pepper was fairly expensive. Salt too was not cheap, as its production and marketing were government controlled and taxed. For many, chiles would have been cheaper than buying Sichuan pepper at the local market. As integration increased, a sort of competition between spices developed, eventually leading to outsider chiles largely displacing the native Sichuan pepper as a daily flavoring and even shifting the very meaning of spicy (*la* 辣).

While Gao Lian, the earliest Chinese author to discuss chiles, mentioned in 1591 that chiles are spicy, the earliest source that offers a specific and concrete example of chiles as a flavoring in food is the anonymous 1621 edition of *Shiwu bencao* (The Pharmacopoeia of edible items): "The ground [fruit] is put into food, it is extremely pungent and spicy [*xin la*]."[7] As the title demonstrates, it is often difficult to separate food and medicine in Chinese cultural practices. Generally, the Chinese observed and theorized that whatever was taken into the body affects health, whether it is eaten for sustenance, for enjoyment, or as medicine. Thus as Chinese used chiles in their food they also observed medicinal affects. Although it can be hard to delineate between culinary and medicinal uses of chiles in Chinese culture, for the purposes of analyzing their integration and acceptance, it is useful to separate out different categories of chile pepper use. While I touch on several aspects of medicinal use of chiles in this chapter on food, my main analysis of the integration of chiles into the Chinese pharmacopeia will be in the next chapter.

Indigenous names for chiles were essential for allowing Chinese to access this foreign spice for local use. Some names implicitly or explicitly compared chiles to other flavorings, likely reflecting initial uses. The sheer number of Chinese names for chiles reflects regional adaptation, and it was not until the mid- to late nineteenth century that the name now widely used across much of China, *lajiao* 辣椒 or "spicy pepper," came into use in most places. Examination of the spread and adoption of chile use adds to our knowledge of regional differences within Inner China. Chiles illuminate cultural, climatic, and geographic regional distinctiveness, from mountainous interiors to the island of Taiwan. Chiles filled different niches in different locales, fitting into regionally constructed identities through culinary specialization; competing with black pepper, salt, or ginger; or fulfilling particular geographic needs, such as providing essential vitamins in mountainous areas or replacing harder-to-find flavorings. Beginning in the twentieth century, identity in some regions came to be associated with spicy chile consumption. Chiles thus became a marker for the constructed authenticity of the cuisines and the people for regions like Sichuan and Hunan.

All the sources examined in this chapter were written by members of the elite. However, some of the materials probably reflect lower-class practices. Thus it is possible to provide some limited assessment of differing rates of acceptance and integration between elites and lower classes. In addition to assessing mechanisms for indigenizing chiles for Chinese culinary use, I also delineate class cultural differences, some of which favored lower-class adoption, while others encouraged elite avoidance. Gazetteers and occasional records in other genres prove use. Yet the spottiness of the mention of chiles across all genres demonstrates overall elite reluctance to advocate cooking with this intense spice until the end of the eighteenth century.

Chinese Flavoring and Naming Regimens

For assimilation into the Chinese flavoring system, chiles had to be assessed within the framework of the so-called five flavors (*wuwei* 五味). The five-flavors categorization system is equally important for cuisine and medicine. It developed from a broader classification structure known as the Five Phases (*wuxing* 五行; often mistranslated as the five agents or five elements); the earliest recorded accounts date back to the fifth to fourth centuries BCE. Under this system, each phase (wood *mu* 木, fire *huo* 火, earth *tu* 土, metal *jin* 金, water *shui* 水) can change to create the following one, or diminish or destroy one of the others. In addition, the phases became associated or linked with myriad other categories, including times of the year, colors, directions, musical notes, senses, flavors, types of *qi*, and internal organs (for more on this system, particularly in relation to medicine, see the next chapter, including table 3.1). The five flavors and their corresponding internal organ were outlined in the *Inner Canon of the Yellow Emperor*, a third- to first-century BCE medical collection: sour (*suan* 酸) with the liver, bitter (*ku* 苦) with the heart, sweet (*gan* 甘) with the spleen, pungent (*xin* 辛) with the lungs, and salty (*xian* 鹹) with the kidneys.[8] The five flavors in this correspondence or associative system continue to influence Chinese cuisine and medicine to the present.

Many of the sources I used for this book are divided into sections based on the category of the material. For example, the local-products sections of gazetteers usually included headings such as vegetable, flavoring, medicine, mineral, and various categories of animals. Medical texts often used similar categories. A couple of early texts that include chiles classified them as a "flavoring" (*wei* 味), including the 1621 edition of the *Shiwu bencao* and the earliest gazetteer from Shaanxi,[9] thus emphasizing the importance of chiles as an enhancer within food.

Early sources on chile peppers describe their flavor as pungent or spicy. Spicy is subsumed under the broader pungent category; indeed, the left part of the character for *la* 辣 is the character for *xin* (辛). The modern food historian H. T. Huang observes that "pungent is not a well-defined single flavour but rather a group of associated flavours, piquant, pungent, acrid, peppery, spicy, hot etc. They all elicit unpleasant sensations in our bodies, burning throat, watery eyes and a runny nose. Yet in the right amount they impart a zest and excitement to food that can make them almost irresistible."[10] Hong Sen, in a work on spicy flavorings and health in Chinese cuisine, lists general attributes of pungent seasonings: "among the basic flavors, pungent is the one that is irritating and the strongest. Everything [that is pungent] stimulates the stomach, promotes digestion,. . . and is used to augment delectableness. In addition, [pungent flavorings] have the effects of fighting damp, and controlling [internal] cold wind."[11] In ancient times the pungent category encompassed the onion family (including garlic), ginger, cassia cinnamon, and Sichuan pepper.[12] Sichuan pepper or flower pepper, sometimes also known in English as fagara, was a very important indigenous pungent spice as well as a medicine in ancient China. Indeed, two types of Sichuan pepper were discovered among food dishes in the well-known second-century BCE Han period tombs at Mawangdui.[13] Huang argues that, among the five flavors, pungent is the one that has had the largest change over time:

> The onion group, cassia and ginger are still popular, fagara (Szechuan peppercorn) less so. New spices such as sesame, anise, fennel, clove and black pepper have entered and stayed on the scene. But it is the introduction of the chilli or *Capsicum* pepper from the New World that has had the greatest impact on Chinese cuisine. It is probably eaten in larger amounts and by more people than any other spice in China, or for that matter, all over the world. The popular Szechuan and Hunan cuisines that we know of today would be mere provincial curiosities without the intervention of the chilli pepper.[14]

Chiles greatly affected the pungent category within the five flavors, becoming a key spice and even displacing the indigenous Sichuan pepper. Like other pungent flavors, while the spiciness of chiles was sometimes initially seen as irritating or even painful, many people came to appreciate their bite and ability to enhance the flavors of other ingredients in a dish. Quite a few seem to have been attracted to the rush caused by capsaicin activating pleasure-inducing endorphins and causing thrill-seeking stimulation.

The loss in popularity of Sichuan pepper through the usurpation of some of its roles by chiles, combined with the borrowing of its name for other spicy flavors, makes a brief exploration of it important for this book on chiles. The plants that provide this spice, *Zanthoxylum bungeanum*, are small trees in the Rutaceae family native to several regions in China. It is a relative of the North American prickly ash. The dried seed pod (the pericarp) of the Sichuan pepper has a strong, distinctive and pungent flavor. The spherical seed pod or shell is dull red or brown in color when ripe and typically splits in half when dried (see figure 2.1). The pods are occasionally picked green as well, for a slightly different flavor. In addition to their flavor, the shells also have a numbing or anesthetic property. In Chinese this numbing characteristic is referred to as *ma* 麻. The small, round, black seeds are classified as slightly toxic in the traditional pharmacopeia (several are shown in the lower right of figure 2.1). The seeds often fall out of the shells but sometimes are actively removed when the shells are used for flavoring food. Both the seeds and shells are used in medicine. There

Figure 2.1 Sichuan pepper, 2019.

are a number of names in Chinese for this spice, some of which denote varietal differences. The most basic name is *jiao* 椒, which is usually translated into English as pepper. The fact that the name consists of a single character reinforces that this spice dates back to ancient times. Most ancient texts referred to key staple crops using single-character names that were originally pictographs of the plant, including *tao* 稻 (rice), *ji* 稷 (foxtail millet), *shu* 黍 (broom-corn millet), *shu* 菽 (soybean), and *mai* 麥 (wheat and barley).[15] Later, as varieties developed and new species were introduced, many plants were named using two, and sometimes more, characters in order to clarify differentiation, for example, *xiao mai* (small *mai*) for wheat and *da mai* (large *mai*) for barley. In the late imperial sources examined for this research, Sichuan pepper or fagara was still sometimes referred to just using the single character *jiao*. More commonly, however, the names contained two characters, *jiao* plus an additional, modifying character. *Huajiao* 花椒, meaning "flower pepper," describes the shape of the open seed pod with attached stem. The *Shu* 蜀 in *Shujiao* is an ancient name for the region now essentially Sichuan; this name emphasizes Sichuan as the place of origin. The "chuan" in *Chuanjiao* 川椒 also refers to Sichuan. *Qinjiao* 秦椒 means pepper from the Qin region.[16] This name emphasizes origination in the territory of the ancient state of Qin (roughly modern Shaanxi province), although the name was used quite broadly. Qin pepper is also a name that was used for chiles. In a modern compilation of 3,249 recipes dating from the Zhou until the end of the Qing, representing all regions, numerous recipes contain Sichuan peppers, demonstrating the importance of this spice in earlier times.[17] Despite the centuries-long, widespread use of the native Sichuan pepper as a pungent spice, the chile pepper eventually surpassed it as a popular flavoring, demonstrating, like the tomato for Italian cuisine, that constructed authenticity does not necessarily correlate with indigeneity.[18]

The earliest name for chiles highlighted their foreign origin, but over time other naming practices became dominant. Plants introduced into China were often given names that both emphasized their foreignness while also identifying a key use. For example, what Westerners call black pepper (*Piper nigrum*) originated in the tropical zones of the Indian subcontinent. Pepper vines require a tropical climate to produce their fruit, and until quite recently black pepper needed to be imported into China on an annual basis. The first record of its introduction into China dates its arrival to the Later Han dynasty (25–220 CE).[19] In the West, traditionally the whole ripe pepper corns, including the black outer peel, are ground, resulting in the black-and-white speckled powder. In China, however, there was, and still is, a preference for grinding the peeled immature seeds, resulting in a white powder. This form of ground "black pepper" is also now available in the United States and Europe as "white pepper." While "white pepper" would be a more accurate description of *Piper nigrum* in China, I will use the name black pepper since it is the common English-language name (and the Latin name) for this spice and the plant it comes from. Black pepper is known in Chinese as *hujiao* 胡椒. During the Han period *hu* referred to non-Han peoples from—as well as the lands in—the so-called Western Regions (*xiyu* 西域), including India.[20] *Jiao* meant Sichuan pepper. Thus Chinese identified black pepper as being foreign/Western/Indian pepper. The renowned late Ming botanical and medical scholar Li Shizhen (1518–1593) noted that black pepper (*hujiao*) "has *jiao* in its name because its spicy pungency is like *jiao*, but it is not a true *jiao*."[21] Black pepper, like the native Sichuan pepper, was classified as pungent for both flavoring and medicine. By the Later Han, then, the character *jiao* was used for intensely flavorful spices. The foreign or imported spice was named by borrowing from an indigenous one. A similar structure can be seen in many of the Chinese names for chiles.

Many of the numerous names for chiles were quite localized. Of the fifty-seven different Chinese names for the chile in historical sources I have identified, fifty-three can be linked to specific places. Of those fifty-three names, thirty-three occurred in only one province. Thus at least 58 percent of the total of fifty-seven Chinese names for chiles were local. In addition, a further eight names were found only in two or three neighboring provinces, bringing the total for regionally marked names to at least 72 percent.[22] Such localization of names underscores how idiosyncratic this nonetheless rapid and widespread culinary and medicinal use was.

Some chile names probably reflect a major initial use in certain areas. For example, chiles were sometimes used as a replacement for other flavorings, and the names of substituted items could be reflected in names for chiles. The earliest recorded name for chiles, *fanjiao* 番椒,[23] reveals two key aspects of early Chinese understandings of the plant. In this context *fan* can more narrowly be related to minorities or foreigners; more broadly it means people outside the majority Han ethnic group.[24] Thus Gao Lian, the author of the earliest text to mention chiles, was conscious that chiles were not native. As was the case for black pepper, *jiao* was borrowed from the pungent native spice, Sichuan pepper. In the classic drama *The Peony Pavilion* (1598), the only other known sixteenth-century text to mention chiles, Tang Xianzu (1550–1616) identifies chiles as *lajiao* 辣椒, or "spicy pepper," also borrowing the native spice's name.[25] In his medical text from 1758, Wang Fu (1692–1759), echoing Li Shijian's commentary about black pepper, emphasized the choice of *jiao* in names for chiles as linked to flavor: "Foreign Pepper [*fanjiao*]: . . . Another name is spicy pepper [*lajiao*]. It is not actually [in the Sichuan] pepper [family]. [The use of *jiao*] in the name is due to its flavor."[26] The intense flavor of chiles clearly struck a palatal note of similarity with Sichuan pepper for early eaters of this introduced spice, helping it along its path to acceptance and indigenization. Gao was almost certainly not using chiles in his food or medicine (see chapter 5). Still, since *jiao* had been appropriated into the name of this newly arrived plant, it is likely that it was initially used by others in ways similar to Sichuan pepper as a pungent (*xin*) flavoring.

The overlap in naming between chiles and Sichuan pepper became intertwined in the northerner Wang Xiangjin's botanical work *Qun fang pu* (Assembly of perfumes) (1621). Wang noted that "foreign pepper" was "also called Qin pepper [秦椒]." The inclusion of a second name in the entry for "foreign pepper" was augmented by a separate statement found a few pages earlier under the entry for Sichuan pepper: "Another name is Qin pepper. It is a product of the Qin territory, hence its name. The Qin pepper now [grown] in the north is a different species [than the one from Qin]."[27] So Qin pepper could designate a variety of Sichuan pepper that originated in Qin or chile peppers grown in the North. The "North" (*beifang* 北方) is a vague term, but often meant the provinces through which the Yellow River flowed and those to their north. Based on data from local gazetteers, Qin pepper was the earliest name used for chiles for three northern provinces: Shengjing, Zhili, and Shandong.[28] Wang Xiangjin's entry for chiles gives foreign pepper as the primary name and Qin pepper as secondary. Likely he chose foreign pepper as the primary name to align with Gao. The inclusion of Qin pepper in two separate places reflects the naming regimen in place in the North, including his home province of Shandong. Thus Wang's descriptions provide evidence supporting different entry points for chiles into China. "Foreign pepper," in the lower Yangzi area, shows conscious knowledge that chiles came from overseas, while Qin pepper as a name for chiles seems to emerge first in Shengjing and supports the theory that they entered northwestern China from the Korean peninsula.

Why would people in Shengjing use the name Qin pepper for chiles when that name already referred to another spice? The use of the same name for different plants or places and multiple names for the same plant or place are common phenomena in Chinese sources. There are even standard Chinese phrases for describing this: *tongming yiwu* 同名異物 means the "same name for different things (or plants)," and *tongwu yiming* 同物異名 means the "same thing (or plant) with different names."[29] Indeed, clarifying such uses for plant names was one of the motivations Li Shizhen gave for writing his work on medical ingredients, the *Bencao gangmu* or *Systematic Materia Medica* or *Compendium Pharmacopeia*.[30] There would have been a natural affinity to use a name that was already associated with a pungent flavoring. For written works there was a strong impetus to use names found in earlier sources. In addition, Qin pepper was probably not used widely in Shengjing for Sichuan pepper. Indeed, *huajiao* or flower pepper seems to have been more common.[31] Finally, a product that was likely introduced gradually from farmer to farmer from northern Korea into southern Shengjing would not readily have been viewed as "foreign," as in from "overseas," and thus *fanjiao* or "foreign pepper" probably would not have struck a chord. As can be seen from map 1.2 and table 2.1, chiles seem to have spread from Shengjing to Shandong and Zhili. Regional names like *Qinjiao* were important for the spread of chile use, informing new regional adopters of the general category of the new crop, pungent like Sichuan pepper, and thus how it might be integrated into local culinary practices.

While early names including *jiao* imply that chiles were used in food in ways similar to Sichuan pepper, several gazetteers actually make this connection explicitly. Even though Sichuan pepper was native to China and there were no government price controls, it still had to be purchased in markets. The plants that produce

TABLE 2.1
"Qin Pepper" as a Name for Chiles in the North

Province	Date of earliest source	How "Qin pepper" was used as a name in gazetteers
Shengjing (modern Liaoning)	1682	Used exclusively until 1909
Shandong	1729	Used exclusively until 1841
Zhili (modern Hebei)	1732	Used as only primary name until 1874

Sichuan pepper are small trees that typically would have used up too much space in most kitchen or vegetable gardens. Instead, they were mostly grown in mountainous areas. The seed shells were harvested and sold in markets. Considerably cheaper than black pepper or salt, Sichuan pepper would still have been more expensive than chile peppers, which a family could grow in its own garden. Chen Jiru, in his agricultural manual from around 1639, noted that chiles "can be used in place of [*chong* 充] Sichuan pepper [*huajiao*]."[32] The earliest known gazetteer to include chiles, from 1671 from Zhejiang, also mentions that they "can be substituted [*dai* 代] for Sichuan pepper [*jiao*]."[33] The relatively early dates for these two sources, combined with some of the choices for early names, demonstrate that the practice of substituting chiles as a flavoring for Sichuan pepper developed quickly. The association of chiles with the pungency of Sichuan pepper extended across Inner China; the earliest name for chiles included the character *jiao* 椒 in eighteen of the twenty provinces of Inner China (including Shengjing and counting Taiwan separately from Fujian).

Categorization of chiles within the five flavors was extremely important for its acceptance. As noted above, *la*, or spicy, is subsumed under the broader category of *xin*, or pungent. The earliest texts to include chiles across several genres all emphasize the flavor as spicy or pungent. In 1591 Gao Lian, the author of the earliest of any text including chiles and the earliest botanical text to mention chiles, described the flavor as spicy.[34] The earliest medical text, from 1621, employed both terms, calling the flavor "pungently spicy" (*xin la*).[35] The earliest gazetteer to include chiles, from 1671, did not describe the flavor directly but included spicy in the name, *laqie* or spicy eggplant.[36] In a late seventeenth-century gardening text, Gao Shiqi compares chiles to two other important pungent flavorings: "Their flavor is intensely pungent, exceeding that of ginger and cassia-cinnamon."[37] What is significant in this context is not just that the author might have thought chiles could be used in place of ginger or cassia-cinnamon, but also that he used other common pungent flavorings as a point of reference for readers who might not be familiar with chiles. Thus categorization and naming were key steps in helping Chinese to understand how to use chiles in their cooking. Adoption took place relatively quickly, with an anonymous author even declaring as early as 1621 that "now it is found everywhere."[38] The rapid spread of chiles would not have occurred without basic classification via nomenclature and comparison.

Deeper Culinary Integration

Chiles as a flavoring within dishes, rather than as the main ingredient, dominated their culinary use in late imperial Inner China. Chinese cooking methods employed a fair amount of preprepared sauces, including a variety of fermented soy sauces, flavored oils, various vinegars, preserved vegetables, and thicker pastes.[39] The use of chiles in infused oils, vinegars, and pastes shows that Chinese inserted chiles into these existing cooking methods.

The earliest known recipe book containing chiles, *The Harmonious Cauldron*, dates to around 1790 and is attributed to Tong

CHILES AS FLAVORING IN COMPOUNDED INGREDIENTS
(Tong Yuejian, c. 1790)

Chile Pepper Paste

Mash chile peppers.
Add sweet sauce, a cube of lard, diced bamboo shoots,
a little oil.
Fry.

Chile Pepper Oil

Start with sesame oil.
Place whole chile peppers in the sesame oil and fry completely.
Remove the chiles, preserving the oil in a can for future use.

Chile Pepper Meat

Choice of meat: 1 jin (½ Kg)
Vinegar: 1 cup
Salt: 4 qian (20 g)
Boil [off liquid].
Just before it is done, add a little chile pepper oil.

Yuejian. This text includes a short discussion of key ingredients prior to listing specific recipes. In this overview Tong emphasized chiles as additives for flavoring, including ground chiles, chile-infused sesame oil, and chile paste. In the few specific recipes where he calls for dishes to include chiles, he calls for chile paste twice and chile oil once. In one further instance he calls for whole fried chiles, but as an alternative for vinegar sauce.[40] In the box we can see Tong's recipes for the key compounded flavorings of chile pepper paste and chile pepper oil, as well as a recipe that called for the oil. Thus, Tong fit chiles into typical Chinese culinary practices of using sauces, flavored oils, and pastes to enhance dishes.

Key sauces or pastes, such as chile pepper paste, have numerous variations, often related to regional or even personal taste. The variety of chile used can vary, and some recipes (like Tong's) call for bamboo shoots, while others add garlic.[41] Overall, however, the basic form includes mashed chiles, some oil, and sometimes a thickener (lard for Tong, and flour in the poem cited in the chapter epigraph and analyzed in chapter 5). Another recipe, from a Zhejiang gazetteer, used a different characteristic of chiles: "locals grind the fruit and mix it with meat and beans; this is called spicy eggplant [chile] paste."[42] Here the preserving characteristics of chiles were called into use, allowing for long-term storage of meat in the sauce to add further flavoring (the chile's antimicrobial properties are covered in more detail in the next chapter on medicine).

In addition to being incorporated into dishes as an additive in some type of flavoring composite such as a paste or oil, fresh or dried chiles could be added directly to a dish. While the distinctions between fresh and dried chiles are not clearly delineated in pre-twentieth-century Chinese sources, general characteristics are recognized across culinary traditions. Fresh chiles add flavor, color, and texture to dishes. In a dish, the heat from fresh chiles tends to appear on the palate quickly (see figure 2.2). Prior to refrigeration and widespread use of greenhouses, fresh chiles would have been available for a short period of time after harvest in late summer to early autumn. This period would have been longer in warmer climates. Therefore drying was (and still is) a common way of preserving chiles. Dry chiles retain much of the flavor and spice of the fresh and will keep well for months (see figure 2.3). The drying process does alter some of the flavors, for example, concentrating sugars, as in raisins. Drying in bunches in the sun was most typical, but drying indoors adjacent to fires was used as well. Dry chiles were used whole, chopped (including flakes), or ground.

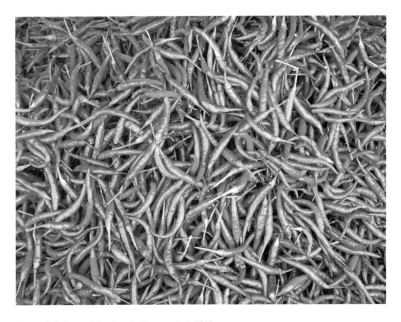

Figure 2.2 Fresh chiles in a Beijing market, 2015.

Heating dried chiles brings out their flavor and spiciness. The spiciness from dried chiles tends to build up more slowly but may last longer than from a comparable fresh chile. Compared to whole dried chiles, chopped or powdered ones will infuse their flavor more throughout the entire dish, especially if they are added early in the cooking process.[43] One nineteenth-century Chinese source noted that "when ground they are extremely spicy."[44] Placing chiles directly into dishes, rather than as part of a sauce or oil, also meshed with earlier uses of pungent ingredients. Sichuan pepper could be used fresh but was usually used dried—either whole or ground. Black pepper, as it was imported, was always used dried and was usually ground. Members of the *Allium* family, such as garlic and onions, were typically used fresh, although they could be kept for long periods of time.

Figure 2.3 Dried and ground chile peppers in a market in Dunhuang, 2016.

This variety of uses for chiles, as one ingredient in composite sauces, as a substitute for another flavor, or as a flavoring in its own right, can be seen in a number of seventeenth- and eighteenth-century gazetteers. While examination of recipes in Tong's work offers some insight into the specifics of chiles as flavoring, they are not as useful for tracing early culinary use of chiles as are gazetteers. A number of gazetteers include a general characterization of the flavor of chiles, and several provide more specific uses. Table 2.2 lists excerpts about the flavor of chiles from a number of late

TABLE 2.2
Chiles as Flavoring in Selected Seventeenth- and Eighteenth-Century Gazetteers

Year	Province (location)	Source	Text about chiles
1690	Guizhou (South, interior)	*Qian shu* by Tian Wen	"Used as a substitute for salt" (2.3a).
1694	Shaanxi (North, interior)	*Shanyang xianzhi*	"The flavor is extremely spicy" (3.50a).
1736	Shandong (North, coastal)	*Shandong tongzhi*	"The fruits are much more pungent than *huajiao* [Sichuan pepper]" (24.2b).
1737	Gansu (Northwest, interior)	*Chongxiu Suzhou xinzhi*	"It can be used to make dishes pungent" (*ce* 6.11a).
1746	Taiwan (South, coastal)	*Taihai caifeng tukao*	"It is pungent and spicy" (2.8a).
1757	Fujian (South, coastal)	*Anxi xianzhi*	"The flavor is spicy" (4.10a).
1759	Jiangxi (South, interior)	*Jianchang fuzhi*	"The flavor is spicy" (9.3a).
1764	Guangxi (South, interior)	*Liuzhou xianzhi*	"The flavor is pungent and spicy" (2.27).
1765	Hunan (South, interior)	*Chenzhou fuzhi*	"The pod is sliced and used to flavor food in sauces, vinegar, savory oils, and preserved vegetables" (15.12a).
1766	Guangdong (South, coastal)	*Enping xianzhi*	"The flavor is spicy. . . . After each picking locals put them in sauces" (9.10b–11a).
1776	Zhejiang (Central, coastal)	*Haining zhouzhi*	"During the winter months a little is put in soup. It is also used in food" (2.55a).
1779	Shengjing (North, coastal)	*Shengjing tongzhi*	"The flavor is very pungent" (106.9a).

seventeenth- and eighteenth-century gazetteers, demonstrating widespread use of chiles—contrasting with the lack of chiles in recipe collections from the same time period. The gazetteer entries sometimes reflect elite authors' views about others—be they lower-class locals, minorities, or people from other regions. In addition, gazetteer entries could also be a place to introduce plants or products to readers who were unfamiliar with them.

The emphasis on spiciness covered a broad range geographically: coastal and inland, as well as northern, central, and southern. Some of the more specific uses listed in the table were similar to Tong's later recipes. Chiles were used to add spice to other flavorings, such as sauces, vinegars, and oils. In addition, they were used more directly in spicing up standard dishes, such as preserved or pickled vegetables and soups. A couple of the earlier sources seem to be introducing this new spice to the readers: "The flavor is extremely spicy," and "The fruits are much more pungent than Sichuan pepper." The editors of these two gazetteers may have been warning their readers that "just a pinch" will do! It is also possible to read the Shandong gazetteer from 1736 as a competition between spices: since chiles were described as "much more pungent," they could have been an economical replacement for Sichuan pepper. The emphasis across these gazetteer entries on pungency and spiciness shows an important path for the indigenization of this American crop.

By the mid-nineteenth century, chiles largely replaced Sichuan pepper in many regional cuisines. Lan Yong has concretely tracked the trend of the decline in the use of Sichuan pepper by examining the recipes in the collection edited by Liu Daqi (mentioned earlier). Lan categorized the 3,249 recipes in Liu's collection by dynastic period and whether or not they included Sichuan pepper. While Liu's collection is certainly not a scientific sampling, Lan's data does show a downward trend in Sichuan pepper use from the Ming to the Qing, which correlates with the introduction of chiles around the 1570s:

Ming period recipes (1368–1644)   29.7 percent contained Sichuan
                                                        pepper
Qing period recipes (1644–1911)   18.9 percent contained Sichuan
                                                        pepper[45]

In their article on spiciness in Sichuan cuisine, Zheng Zhu and Zang Xiaoman also argue that consumption of Sichuan pepper across China declined dramatically during the Qing.[46] Sichuan pepper is still quite popular in Sichuan and Yunnan, where it is often used in combination with chiles in dishes creating the so-called *ma-la* or numbing-spicy flavor. Even in places where the Sichuan pepper is still commonly used, however, the chile pepper plays a dominant role in flavoring.

A good example of chiles replacing Sichuan pepper can be seen in the comparison of the lists of ingredients from two Chinese cabbage recipes shown in the box, one from the late eighteenth century[47] and the other from the twenty-first century.[48]

Fried Chinese Cabbage (c. 1790)	*Spicy Chinese Cabbage* (2005)
Chinese cabbage	Chinese cabbage
sesame oil	sesame oil
soy sauce	salt
vinegar	vinegar
sugar	sugar
Sichuan pepper	**chile pepper**
bean sprouts	
garden cress	

The eclipsing of the Sichuan pepper by the chile demonstrates that constructed authenticity does not require indigeneity and is an example of chile pepper usage actually altering a Chinese cultural practice. Chile peppers in cuisine surpassed the Sichuan pepper in the early to mid-nineteenth century.[49] This was about the same time period when the name *lajiao* 辣椒 or spicy pepper was becoming more common across much of China. Thus as chiles displaced the native *jiao* (Sichuan pepper), this immigrant crop was taking on a more universal name, *lajiao*, emphasizing its dominant flavor.

In a related phenomenon, the explicit identification of chiles as being foreign decreased over the course of the nineteenth century. In all the gazetteers I examined for this book that contained chiles (dating between 1671 and 1936), 120 listed a primary name for chiles that identified them as foreign; however, only 26 of those date to after 1899. Thus as the spice became more and more integrated into Chinese culture, its foreignness largely disappeared. This is another sign of the chile becoming an "authentic" component of Chinese culture.

Today across China the vast majority of people, when they are not referring to a particular variety, call the chile *lajiao* or spicy pepper. As we have seen, such uniformity in naming was certainly not the initial practice. While the name *lajiao* was first used quite early, in 1598, in Tang Xianzu's *Peony Pavilion*, it was not used in a gazetteer until 1733.[50] Indeed, the name was not used widely across Inner China until the mid- to late nineteenth century (see table 2.3). *Lajiao* had been used in only three provinces by the beginning of the nineteenth century, but by the end of that century it was being used in seventeen of the twenty provinces of Inner China (including Shengjing and counting Taiwan separately from Fujian). Thus by the early twentieth century naming for chiles was moving toward uniformity and a national consensus. An important exception to

TABLE 2.3
Date of the Earliest Use of *Lajiao* as a Name for Chiles
in Gazetteers, by Province

Years	Names of provinces (in chronological order)
1733–1754	Guangxi, Guangdong, Shaanxi
1802–1854	Jiangsu, Sichuan, Hubei, Hunan, Anhui, Fujian, Guizhou, Zhili
1871–1894	Jiangxi, Zhejiang, Shandong, Gansu, Taiwan, Yunnan
1903–1931	Henan, Shengjing, Shanxi

the use of *lajiao* is Sichuan, where the common name is *haijiao* or sea pepper (see below for a discussion of this name). Scholarly articles about chiles in Sichuan, however, tend to use *lajiao*.[51] Indeed, nearly all the Chinese secondary sources that I have consulted about chile peppers dating from after 1949 use *lajiao* as the primary name for chiles. Thus as nationalism emerged and developed in China, along with the development of national universities and publishing houses with nationwide penetration, the name for chiles was also nationalized.

The more universal name *lajiao* underlines the use of the chile as a spicy flavoring in its own right. The shift to this name also reveals another way that Chinese uses of chiles have changed their culture—in this case the very meaning of the character *la* 辣 or spicy. Indeed, Wang Maohua, Wang Cengyu, and Hong Seung Tae, in their article on chiles in East Asia, proclaim that "it was only after chiles had been introduced that the Chinese were able to embrace a truly, genuinely spicy [*la*] flavor."[52] While the shift in the meaning of *la* was well under way by the mid-nineteenth century, published dictionaries were more conservative in preserving long-standing definitions.

The dominant dictionary for much of the Qing period was the *Kangxi zidian* (Kangxi character dictionary). This imperially commissioned work was completed in 1716. *La*, drawing on a second-century source, was defined as "very pungent" (*xin shen*).[53] The definition of *xin* as a flavoring in the *Kangxi zidian* was "the flavor of hard metals (*jingang* 金剛)." This description connected the flavor of *xin* with its corresponding phase in the Five Phases, metal. There is also an example in the *Kangxi zidian* of a usage of *xin* that identified specific pungent plants: "For New Year's Day, the mixture of scallions, garlic, garlic chives, knotweed, and mustard is called 'Five Pungents Dish.' "[54] Here we see a list including several of the standard pungent flavorings. This list, because of the conservative nature of definitions, particularly the propensity to refer to much earlier precedents, unsurprisingly did not include the chile. Published definitions of *la* did not acknowledge this character's connections with chiles until the twentieth century. Eventually, chiles became directly linked to the meaning of *la* in a number of twentieth and twenty-first century dictionaries.[55] In the *Hanyu da zidian* (Large Chinese character dictionary), from the early 1990s, the first definition of *la* is "the sharp and stimulating flavor of ginger, garlic or chile pepper."[56] The *Xiandai Hanyu guifan cidian* (Standardized modern Chinese dictionary) (2004) emphasizes chiles in the definition for *la*, moving them to the front: "The sharp and stimulating flavor of chile pepper, garlic, or ginger."[57]

Thus chiles have become a signifier for the very meaning of *la* or spicy. Indeed, in the following modern phrases *la* is widely seen as meaning *lajiao*—chile pepper:

*Wo xiang chi **la** de.*	I want to eat spicy food.
*Wo bu chi **la** de.*	I don't eat spicy food.
*Wo pa **la**.*	I am afraid of spice (or I cannot eat spicy food).

While *la* is still used to describe the intense flavor of things like garlic and ginger, as a general classifier it is usually standing in for *lajiao*. Thus by the mid- to late twentieth century the intense spiciness of chiles shifted the way *la* is used in Chinese writing and speaking.

Even though records of the culinary use of chiles date back to 1621, the elite authors of recipe books all ignored this spice until Tong Yuejian included it in his *The Harmonious Cauldron*, written about 1790. Thus by the early nineteenth century chiles had finally broken into this genre. The brash chile was no longer excluded from writing about the kitchens of the elite, demonstrating the deeper integration. We can see a further example of the shift of elite writing about chiles from preferring the plant as decorative to acknowledging its importance as an alimentary crop in two gazetteers from the Hangzhou region, the home of Gao Lian. In the 1686 edition of the Hangzhou prefectural gazetteer, chiles were included at the end of the entry on eggplant: "There is another slender and long variety. Its color is pure cinnabar. Several can be placed in a pot for pleasure. It is called spicy eggplant. It is inedible (*bu ke shi* 不可食)."[58] The 1776 edition of the gazetteer from Haining department, within Hangzhou prefecture, begins by quoting the earlier prefectural gazetteer entry, reproducing the text verbatim up through the name, but editing out its predecessor's statement that it was inedible. The Haining gazetteer then continued: "During the winter months a little is put in soup, it also used in food. The round, slender ones are called heavenly eggplant."[59] In this gazetteer the authors not only acknowledged that it was used in food, they even give a specific example of its use in soup. It is well on its way toward this chapter's opening epigraph poem's query, "The seasonal taste, who doesn't want it?"[60] Furthermore, they also recognized that more than one variety was being grown. These two contrasting sources demonstrate how many elite authors eventually moved away from biases against this passion-inducing, shiny seed pod.

Regional Use

Regional conditions, including climate, geography, and local culinary traditions, created localized circumstances that influenced chile adoption and use. While environment certainly played a role in regional chile use, I am not arguing that it played a singular role. As with almost all historical changes, multiple factors and causes were involved. Variations in the adoption of chiles linked to place can be seen in other examples of substitution apart from Sichuan pepper. Chile peppers were also described as proxies for black pepper (*hujiao*), ginger, and salt. For each of these flavorings, however, equivalency seems to have been restricted to a particular region. While specific substitutions helped chiles gain traction in particular areas, it is important to emphasize that chiles were also used in numerous other ways in those places as well. While a particular use may have dominated in some regions, multiple uses were employed everywhere.

Because chiles and black pepper were both classified as pungent, replacement was logical. Since black pepper had to be imported to China, the chile being used as an alternative was strongly influenced by economic factors. In his 1688 gardening text, Chen Haozi notes that "people use them [chiles] in many dishes. Ground very fine, they are used in the winter months as a substitute for black pepper."[61] Chen, like Gao, was from Hangzhou and also apparently did not travel much outside of the Jiangnan region.[62] Therefore it is likely that central coastal elites sometimes used chiles in place of black pepper. Several gazetteers, all from the interior provinces of Hubei and Hunan, explicitly commented on chiles being used as a substitute for black pepper, a number of others included names for chiles that imply parallel usage, and one even stressed the superiority of chiles.

Table 2.4 lists a number of names for chile peppers, which included *hujiao* (black pepper). The inclusion of "black pepper" in these names for chiles implies a similar use as a flavoring, as well as

TABLE 2.4
Chile Pepper Names Found in Gazetteers That Reference Black Pepper

Name including black pepper	Province	Year	Used as primary or secondary name	Gazetteer	Described as substitute for black pepper
Big black pepper da hujiao 大胡椒	Hubei	1758	Primary	Qishui xianzhi, 2.37a	No
Big black pepper	Hubei	1794	Primary	Qishui xianzhi, 2.35b	No
Big black pepper	Hubei	1866	Primary	Chongyang xianzhi, 4.54b	No
Big black pepper	Hubei	1868	Primary	Tongshan xianzhi, 2.68b	No
Big black pepper	Hubei	1884	Primary	Huangzhou fuzhi, 3.63b	No
Earth black pepper di hujiao 地胡椒	Hunan	1765	Secondary	Chenzhou fuzhi, 15.12a	Yes
Earth black pepper	Shaanxi	1814	Primary	Hanzhong xuxiu fuzhi, 22.4a	No
Earth black pepper	Hunan	1818	Secondary	Longshan xianzhi, 8.12b	Yes
Earth black pepper	Anhui	1826	Secondary	Fanchang xianzhi, 6.20b	No
Earth black pepper	Shaanxi	1832	Primary	Xuxiu Ningqiang zhouzhi, 3.32a	No
Earth black pepper	Hunan	1871	Primary	Baojing xianzhi, 3.16b	No

Name	Province	Year	Primary/Secondary	Source	Superiority
Earth black pepper	Shaanxi	1924	Primary	*Hannan xuxiu junzhi*, 22.4a	No
Surpasses black pepper sai hujiao 赛胡椒	Hubei	1777	Primary	*Yunxi xianzhi*, 4.6a	No
Surpasses black pepper	Hubei	1866	Secondary	*Fang xianzhi*, 11.10b	No
Surpasses black pepper	Hubei	1921	Secondary	*Hubei tongzhi*, 22.16a	No
Spicy black pepper la hujiao 辣胡椒	Jiangxi	1860	Primary	*Yuanzhou fuzhi*, 10.2a	No
Black pepper horn Hujiao jiao 胡椒角	Jiangxi	1871	Secondary	*Fengxin xianzhi*, 1.38a	No
Nose black pepper hujiao bi 胡椒鼻[a]	Fujian	1834	Secondary	*Chongyin Yong'an xian xuzhi*, 9.3a	No
(none)	Hunan	1824	—	*Fenghuang tingzhi*, 18.11b	Yes, "by many"
(none)	Hunan	1877	—	*Qianzhou tingzhi*, 13.11a	Yes, "by many"
(none)	Hubei	1866	—	*Laifeng xianzhi*, 29.9b	Yes

[a] The meaning of this name is not clear. It could refer to the chile being longer than black pepper. However, *bi* 鼻 also has a less used, literary meaning of originate, starting, or initiating (*Hanyu dazidian*, 1983), which could place chiles in a position of superiority vis-à-vis black pepper.

a physical or flavor comparison. "Big black pepper" almost certainly refers to the fact that chile pepper pods are larger than black pepper corns. "Surpasses black pepper" and "spicy black pepper" both suggest chiles were considered spicier than black pepper. The origin of "earth black pepper" perhaps comes from the knowledge that the chile pepper plant grows more closely to the ground than black pepper vines. "Black pepper horn" describes the curved shape of the common spicy chile pod. All but one of these references came from interior provinces, where, presumably, black pepper would have been rarer and more expensive than along the coast, where merchants delivered it from South Asia. For the one source from a coastal province, Fujian, the gazetteer is from a district in the interior of the province, much closer to Jiangxi than to the coast. The use of chiles as a black pepper substitute seems to have been greatest in the central Yangzi River basin, Hubei and Hunan in particular (see map 2.1). The name "surpasses black pepper" also implies competition or even supplanting. The flavor of the locally grown chile was stronger and more intense than the imported, expensive spice. Even though chiles were not native, they were *homegrown*. Thus the fact that individuals or families could cultivate rather than import chiles added to their constructed authentication and regional importance.

The earliest name for chiles in Taiwan provides evidence for yet another regional variation in adoption. A survey of Taiwanese flora and fauna in 1746 stated that "foreign ginger (*fanjiang* 番薑) is a type of vine from Holland. . . . Foreigners (*fanren*) brought these pods [to Taiwan] to eat them." While the compilers of this work noted that "on the mainland (*neidi*) they are named foreign pepper,"[63] the primary use of the name foreign ginger in the earliest Taiwanese sources supports the theory of Taiwan as an entry point for chiles, since the inhabitants invented their own name for the plant. Foreign ginger is the primary name for chiles in all but one of the Taiwanese

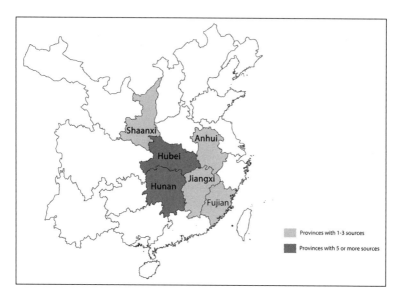

Map 2.1 Provinces where some chile names included the name for black pepper. Created by author using China Historical GIS, v. 4.0 (1820 boundaries), and ESRI ArcMap, v. 10.0.

gazetteers I examined dating between 1746 and 1895. Prior to the twentieth-century, Taiwanese sources were the only ones to use this term as the primary name for chiles. Indeed, foreign ginger is still the most common term for chiles in the Taiwanese dialect (Minnan-hua).[64] Ginger is native to southern China and grows in sub-tropical climates (like Taiwan) as well as tropical climates. Ginger is used as a flavoring in a wide-range of Taiwanese dishes, including Hakka-style stir fry, stewed pigs' feet, and fried squid.[65] The name choice demonstrates that it is likely that Taiwanese initially incorporated chiles into their cuisine within the same niche as ginger, another pungent flavor, rather than Sichuan pepper, black pepper, or salt.

Chiles are also described as a substitute for salt in a number of late imperial texts. Chiles, however, never completely replaced salt. Salt, sodium chloride, is essential for human life. Sodium in particular is necessary for a variety of physiological functions in the body, including nerve impulses, muscle contraction and relaxation, blood pressure regulation, and fluid balance. However, only a relatively small amount of sodium is needed for these purposes. Most people consume far more salt because of its flavor-enhancing abilities. It was in this use of salt as a flavoring, rather than its life sustaining properties, that the chile served as a substitute.

The production, shipping, and sale of salt were handled through late imperial government licenses, which of course added to its price. Both the Ming and Qing governments brought in substantial income through salt licenses and taxes.[66] Because of the licenses and taxes there was also widespread salt smuggling—Tao-chang Chiang estimates probably half of the salt consumed during the Qing came from smuggled rather than licensed salt. Evaporative salt production from brine water at the surface was mainly along the sea coast (amounting to 84 percent of total production in the nineteenth century), but it was also done on a much smaller scale at northwestern salt lakes. The major centers for evaporation of brine water drawn from below the surface were in Sichuan, Shanxi, and Yunnan. Salt production required maintaining equipment as well as labor input, costs that needed to be recouped through the price of the final product. In addition, salt passed through a number of hands between the producers and consumers (whether it moved legally or was smuggled), again adding to the price. The inland, mountainous provinces of Guizhou and Guangxi had the most limited access to salt. Indeed, Guangxi was the only province to have no salt production whatsoever.[67] The earliest reference for chiles being substituted for salt comes from Tian Wen's text about Guizhou from 1690, where he notes that salt was uncommon. He goes on to state that chiles were "used as a substitute for salt. The pepper's characteristic [flavor] is very pungent. It is used as a substitute for salty [flavoring] just to deceive people's tongues."[68] Tian, who was governor of Guizhou at the time,[69] was clear that he found chiles a poor replacement for salt. Instead of enhancing the flavor of food, as he implied salt does, chiles, he believed, merely deceived people. As "salty" is a separate category from "pungent" in the five flavors, it makes sense that he would question the ability of chiles to easily substitute for salt as a flavor enhancer. In addition, as the top government representative in the province, he may have also felt it was his duty to support use of a product that brought in substantial revenue to the central government. The price of salt was probably the main cause for people to substitute it with chiles. Ray Huang observed that "when the monopoly system was in disarray, retail prices could soar to three or four times the normal level, as was the case in Hukwang [Hubei and Hunan] during the 1610s. On such occasions, this daily necessity was literally beyond the means of common people."[70] In the 1620s there was another, more widespread crisis in the salt industry as many salt merchants neared bankruptcy resulting from official as well as merchant mismanagement, corruption, government demands for more revenue, and banditry, which again resulted in higher prices for salt.[71] Thus at the same time as chiles were spreading further during the 1610s–1620s, the price of salt spiked upward in some areas, probably adding to the popularity of the recently introduced spice as an economical alternative. According to Chen Wenzhao in a short article on chiles in Hunan, the difficulties of transporting salt throughout that province, combined with the ease of growing chile peppers, resulted in farmers deciding that chiles were a wonderful, economical flavoring.[72] Perhaps even more than for black pepper, particularly since salt consumption was universal, economics then seems to have been not just a factor for those who replaced salt with chiles, but one for the overall adoption of chiles.

Later authors of Guizhou gazetteers were more explicit about who they believed were substituting the chile pepper for salt:

1722 *Sizhou prefectural gazetteer*: "The local minorities use it as a substitute for salt."

1741 *Guizhou provincial gazetteer*: "Minorities use it as a substitute for salt."

1818 *Zheng'an departmental gazetteer*: "The locals use it as a substitute for salt."[73]

Non-Han populations made up the majority of Guizhou until about the mid-nineteenth century, and the province was essentially a frontier zone well into the eighteenth century.[74] Minority groups who lived up in the mountains, farthest from the cities, were the least integrated into the moneyed economy,[75] which would have included salt. The provincial gazetteer is not precise about where the minorities who substituted chiles for salt lived, but both Sizhou and Zheng'an are mountainous regions, distant from cities. In neighboring Guangxi, substituting chiles for salt was similarly associated with non-Han minorities, particularly the Yao and Miao, also in a mountainous region.[76] It is not surprising that minority groups would at times find it difficult to purchase salt through the monopoly system and therefore substituted economical chiles. Furthermore, since chiles are "high in vitamins A and C, iron, calcium, and other minerals," they caught on particularly well "in remote and mountainous regions where other high-vitamin foods could not grow well."[77] Thus minorities living in Guizhou and Guangxi, especially those in the mountainous regions, were probably drawn to chiles for their economy in comparison to salt, and then expanded their use owing to positive impacts on health.

In gazetteers the earliest use of the name "sea pepper" (*haijiao* 海椒) for chiles occurred in 1684 in Hunan. This is also the earliest known entry for Hunan. While the name implies knowledge that chiles were brought from overseas, it appears only in gazetteers from inland provinces (see map 2.2). Therefore it could be that the name referenced introduction to the interior from the coast, rather than from overseas. It might also suggest that it was initially observed as a pepper used on the sea, in ships by sailors, or particularly with seafood or fish. While it is impossible to pin down the exact meaning of the origins of the name, it definitely had limited geographic scope, and it never held salience as a name along the coast. Today the vernacular term for chiles in Sichuan, one of, if

Map 2.2 Provinces where the name "sea pepper" was used for chiles (all interior). Created by author using China Historical GIS, v. 4.0 (1820 boundaries), and ESRI ArcMap, v. 10.0.

not the most, quintessential provinces for daily consumption of chiles, is still sea pepper. Certainly the importance of chiles as the dominant characteristic of Sichuan cuisine is in no way decreased by the continued use of this name, which underscores that chiles are not indigenous to this land-locked locale.

The geography and climate of various regions in China caused some people in those areas to adopt chiles in ways that initially substituted them for other flavorings. The fact that chiles grew easily in these areas allowed their use to take off. Chiles were used in place of black pepper largely in the interior, where the imported black pepper would have been scarcer and probably more expensive. In subtropical Taiwan, chiles were associated with ginger and were probably used in ways similar to that pungent flavoring. Salt was scarcest and most expensive in Guizhou and Guangxi, where records emphasized that minorities replaced salt with chiles. One of the reasons chiles became popular in China was that they could fit into different niches. People living in some places, like mountains, probably found that chiles filled a need for a crop they could grow themselves that is high in vitamins, while others could not afford salt in every meal and chiles offered a viable flavoring alternative. Economics and geography, while never single factors, certainly affected the reasons why particular people developed a taste for this spice.

Varieties

One indirect method of judging the popularity of a particular crop is to assess how many cultivated varieties (cultivars) of the plant were being grown. An increase in the number of varieties, or at least an increase in the emphasis on varieties in sources, is a strong sign for use and also of popularity. Thus numerous references to cultivars of chiles are a strong counter to an argument that the lack of chiles in many sources meant that few Chinese were eating them. Varieties accommodated different individual tastes, regional preferences, and the matching of varieties with different dishes or even cooking styles. Chinese sources began to mention multiple varieties of chiles by the late seventeenth century.[78] Mention of varieties increased over the eighteenth century, and by the mid-nineteenth century even short entries in gazetteers often mentioned at least two varieties. While it is likely that multiple varieties of *Capsicum annuum* entered China, some of the varieties discussed in later sources, particularly by the mid-nineteenth century, were almost certainly bred in China for particular flavors, spiciness, shapes, or colors, a concrete example of how coming to China changed the chile pepper itself.

It is difficult to pinpoint how many cultivars of chiles were grown in China during the late imperial period. In her article on chile names in China, Hu Yiyin lists twenty-eight varietal names that she came across in various sources from the late imperial and Republican periods.[79] In their article, Wang, Wang, and Hong list thirty-three cultivar names for China.[80] During my research I discovered forty-two separate names for varieties. However, about half of these names seem to be regional nomenclature variants rather than botanical varieties, which means, based on written sources, there were possibly on the order of twenty varieties being grown in China by the mid- to late nineteenth century. It is worth noting, however, that the Japanese botanical scholar Itō Keisuke published a series of illustrations in the late nineteenth century of fifty varieties of chile peppers.[81] Thus it is quite possible that Chinese were growing more varieties than were being recorded.

Many of the sources were unspecific about the varieties—just mentioning that there are two varieties, such as long and round, red and green, or big and small (see figures 2.4 and 2.5). The earliest specific variety mentioned was the "Goddess pepper" (*tianxian jiao*)

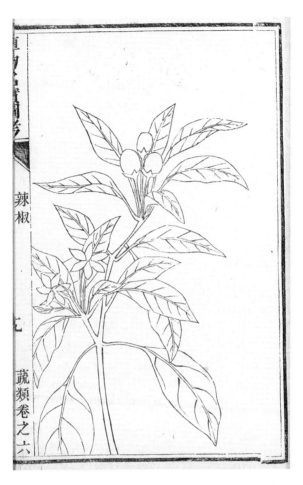

Figure 2.4 Woodblock print of an unidentified round variety of chile. Wu Qijun, *Zhiwu mingshi tukao* (Illustrated treatise on the names and natures of plants) (1848), j. 6.19a. Courtesy of C.V. Starr East Asian Library, Columbia University.

from 1689; the name was probably a commentary on the beauty of the shiny, red chile.[82] The most commonly mentioned variety was the "facing heaven pepper" (*chaotian jiao* 朝天椒). Since many authors addressed the fact that the pointed fruit in this variety grew upward, the implication was that many pointed varieties grew

Figure 2.5 Facing heaven chiles from the Chengdu region of Sichuan, 2015.

downward.[83] Many sources emphasized the fruit in this variety as being extremely spicy,[84] but some did not comment one way or the other. Today a moderately spicy, pointed variety with this name and the characteristic of growing upward is particularly popular in the Chengdu region of Sichuan (see figure 2.5).[85] While the general appearance of some Qing varieties may be similar to their modern counterparts, flavor has probably changed to some degree. Other commonly mentioned late imperial varieties include the following:

pointed ones: chicken toe pepper, goat horn pepper, cow horn pepper, Buddha's hand pepper, and seven sisters pepper
round ones: lantern pepper, chicken heart pepper, button pepper, cherry pepper, and persimmon pepper.

Beginning in the early to mid-nineteenth century, the specific cultivar name "persimmon pepper" (*shizijiao* 柿子椒) became fairly common. While this name could well have been used for different varieties across regions, it was often used for the sweet or bell pepper. Several sources described this variety as being red or yellow and not very spicy.[86] Indeed, bell peppers are now generally categorized as sweet rather than pungent, within the five flavors. Both shape and color probably played the largest role in the development of this name. Given that persimmons require a fair amount of processing before they are used in cooking, the name probably did not come from parallel use in dishes beyond adding color.[87] The emphasis on using bell peppers to add color to dishes in modern times is reflected in a more common contemporary name, *caijiao* 彩椒 or colored peppers. Another modern name, *tianjiao* 甜椒 or sweet pepper, emphasizes its nonspicy flavor.

Discussion of various cultivars can be a reflection on ways in which a particular crop was being integrated and eventually indigenized. Chiles in China were certainly bred for particular flavors, colors, and shapes to meet local needs. The names of cultivars reflect local naming regimens, often evoking well-known local shapes such as chicken toes, goat horns, chicken hearts, and cherries. The "Buddha's hand" variety almost certainly refers to the citrus fruit of that name, which has a series of finger-like segments or sections. Long chile peppers are shaped very much like the individual "fingers" of the Buddha's hand fruit. The "seven sisters" variety is described as usually having seven fruits on each branch. Throughout China the seventh day of the seventh month—double-seven— was a time to celebrate the yearly joining of the Weaving Maid and the Cowherd. In some parts of southern China, particularly in Guangzhou, double-seven is referred to as the Festival of the Seven Sisters, referring to the Weaving Maid and her six sisters.[88] Thus as varieties increased, so too did this imported plant's integration into a variety of regional cultural traditions.

Adaptation of the chile by Chinese cultivators continues to the present. These new cultivars vary widely, fulfilling a wide-range of desires. A pale-yellow cultivar of the Hangzhou chile (*Hangjiao* 杭椒), called "white pepper" (*baijiao* 白椒), is used primarily for delicate flavor rather than spice. The "facing heaven pepper" (*chaotian jiao* 朝天椒) variety popular around Chengdu, Sichuan, provides the qualities of both a vegetable and spice. The intensely red "beauty pepper" (*meiren jiao* 美人椒) provides color as well as spice (lower left in figure 0.1). The extremely hot "spicy little rice grain" (*xiaomi la* 小米辣) is also quite popular, particularly in regions known for intensely spicy cuisine (top center in figure 0.1). The "wrinkly chile" (*zhoupi lajiao* 皱皮辣椒) is an example of one bred largely for visual curiosity (see figure 2.6; also pictured on the right in figure 0.1). These and many additional varieties were and continue to be developed in order to adapt chiles to specific conditions in particular regions of China and preferences of Chinese, resulting in changes to the overall diversity of *Capsicum annuum*.

Chiles as Vegetables

For many Chinese who ate chiles regularly, they were far more than a spicy flavoring. For them, chiles were also vegetables. This was particularly true for fresh chiles but also some types of preserved chiles. Thus chiles as food, not just in food, furthered their acceptance. Chiles were used as the main ingredient in some dishes and even occasionally eaten by themselves. In the gazetteers where the editors divided products in categories, over 80 percent identified chiles as a vegetable (*shu* or *cai*). In the agricultural or botanical texts that included chiles, and provided categories, just over

Figure 2.6 Wrinkly chile (*zhoupi lajiao*), Kunming, Yunnan, 2017.

half listed chiles as vegetables. Of the three medical texts that divided ingredients by categories, chiles were identified as a vegetable in two. In his compendium on plants from 1848, Wu Qijun (1789–1847) observed that "in Jiangxi, Hunan, Guizhou, and Sichuan [chiles are] grown as a vegetable."[89] Wu Qijun, who was born in Henan, is a stark contrast to the approximately 90 percent failure rate of the civil service exam. In 1817 he not only passed but achieved the coveted number one slot, granting him special titles and a fast track up the bureaucracy. He served in a variety of positions in Fujian, Hubei, Hunan, Jiangsu, Jiangxi, Shanxi, and Yunnan, rising to the position of governor in several of them. He also held high positions in the very lucrative government salt bureau. Over the course of his career, he had opportunities to observe chile pepper usage in a wide range of places.[90] Sources describing chiles as vegetables show that fresh chiles could be chopped and included as a main ingredient in a dish, not just as a flavoring. In addition, several sources emphasize that the pods could be munched on raw (see table 2.5).

While these five works demonstrate that the practice of eating raw chiles as vegetables was broadly distributed across Inner China, they also reveal that a number of elite authors viewed this type of

TABLE 2.5
Selection of Sources Showing Chiles as Raw Vegetables

Date	Author	Province	Title	Text about chiles
1764		Guangxi	Liuzhou xianzhi	"They can be eaten raw" (2.27).
1820	Guo Lin	(Jiangsu and Zhejiang)	Chu yuan xiao xia lu	"Northerners eat stacks of raw ones from plates, dipping them in salt" (18).
1828		Hunan	Yongzhou fuzhi	"The locals often take green ones and eat them raw, skin and all" (7shang.8a).
1848	Wu Qijun	(multiple)	Zhiwu mingshi tukao	"Poor people actually eat them as raw vegetables" (6.19b).
1886		Zhili	Shuntian fuzhi	"When they are green they can be eaten raw" (50.6a).

consumption as something practiced by "others." Guo Lin, who lived in the central coastal Jiangnan area, ascribed the practice to a geographic other, namely, "northerners." While Guo's comment about northerners "dipping them in salt" does not imply poverty, two of the other sources do associate the eating of raw chiles with the lower classes. In the Yongzhou gazetteer from Hunan, the author distanced the practice from himself, projecting it onto "locals," almost certainly a veiled class demarcation. Wu Qijun was the most explicit about the class differences for raw chile consumption, asserting that only "poor people" eat them raw like vegetables. In contrast, he claimed that the elite used them only as flavoring in the form of chile paste.[91]

The treatment of chiles as vegetables may also be seen in names that made use of the character for the popular vegetable eggplant (*qie* 茄). The earliest gazetteer to include chiles, from 1671, named them *laqie* or spicy eggplant.[92] Other variations employing *qie* for chiles included *jiaoqie* or peppery eggplant and *qiejiao* or eggplant pepper.[93] The eggplant and chile are both in the Solanaceae family. The plants have similar leaf, flower, and seed shapes. The eggplant was introduced into China from South or Southeast Asia by the fourth century CE.[94] Some chile sources, in addition to using *qie* in the name, also commented on visual similarities, for example, that "it bears fruit resembling the eggplant."[95] The naming and the descriptive comparisons may merely reflect the morphological similarities rather than any overlap in how they were used in cuisine. However, some who made the link may have used less spicy varieties of chiles in ways similar to eggplant—as a vegetable, for color, and for texture. Certainly the contemporary use of bell peppers in Chinese dishes is as a vegetable. The sweet pepper is used in a number of dishes today where it serves as vegetable rather than as a spice; for example, in the dishes "sweet corn with sweet pepper" or "diced chicken with sweet peppers." There are also dishes where chile peppers make up the whole dish; a delicious example being batter-fried spicy chile peppers, a common fare in Dai minority restaurants. As part of promoting regional identities, some localities compile lists of characteristics that distinguish them from other parts of the country. In one of these lists, residents of Shaanxi are described as using only chiles to create a dish—thus using them as vegetables rather than just as flavoring.[96]

Chiles were also preserved in several different manners, often varying by region. In the North, pickling with vinegar was more common. In the South, such as Hunan and Sichuan, preserving chiles with salt was more typical. Such preserved chiles could be eaten alone, served alongside a dish as a garnish, or mixed into a dish as a vegetable ingredient. Preserved chiles retain a great deal of their color, so they could visually enhance a dish when fresh peppers were out of season. Indeed, preserving chiles in salt can actually intensify the red color. In addition, raw and preserved chiles also had positive health impacts. Cooking, pickling, and drying chiles is detrimental to their vitamin C, so raw chiles and those preserved in other ways are higher in that essential vitamin.[97]

The categorization of chiles as vegetables is one of the areas where we can see that the culinary use of chiles moved beyond use as a spice. That so many authors and editors classified chiles as vegetables and described people eating them as vegetables demonstrates that Chinese consumed chiles in ways quite distinct from other flavorings. While pickled cloves of garlic are popular in some regions, garlic is most commonly used as a flavoring, not as a vegetable. The other flavorings for which chiles sometimes served as a replacements—salt, Sichuan pepper, black pepper, and ginger—were rarely eaten by themselves. Thus, among the most typical pungent flavorings, chiles were the only ones that were widely eaten as a vegetable as well as a flavoring.

The integration of chiles by Chinese into their cuisine(s) was the most important avenue for adoption of this foreign plant. Initial use, particularly outside of elite classes, was probably as a substitute for other flavorings. This was at least partially due to economics, chiles being essentially free. In addition, in certain times and places they had been one of the only abundant flavorings available—particularly during crises within the salt industry. If the chile had remained just an economical substitute for other flavorings, however, we could not consider them as a fully integrated component of constructed authenticity. They would have been merely a pale reflection of the flavors they were standing in for, just "deceiv[ing] people's tongues" until the *genuine* flavoring was once again available or affordable.[98] Yet the chile moved well beyond merely being a temporary substitute to becoming "as indispensable in daily cuisine as onion and garlic."[99] By the late eighteenth century a few elite authors, such as Wu Xingqin, whose line of poetry appears as the epigraph to this chapter, began incorporating chiles into literature, an additional example of cultural integration. A mid-nineteenth-century gazetteer underscored its essential role as a domestic crop, emphasizing that "it is the most important vegetable in the garden. It is used as a daily flavoring, not unlike salt."[100] By the mid-nineteenth century the chile pepper was fully indigenized across Inner China; in many places it was consumed daily.

Analysis of the history of the consumption of chiles in China reinforces the importance of regional geographic and cultural differences in understanding history. Chiles were used differently regionally. They occasionally filled in for black pepper more in interior regions, where that imported spice would have been more expensive. Chiles competed most directly with salt in areas where that mineral was scarcest—Guizhou and Guangxi. Association of chiles with ginger occurred primarily in Taiwan. While many uses overlapped across regions, the versatility of chiles allowed locals to fit this introduced plant into unique aspects of their local practices. The chile took on meanings across all of Inner China but also developed others locally. Indeed, by the early twentieth century chile consumption had become a marker for regional identity in several regions, particularly Sichuan and Hunan.

Most of the texts that explicitly refer to chiles being substituted for other flavorings date to the seventeenth or eighteenth centuries, with the latest reference dating to 1877. Thus substitution was no longer particularly common by the early nineteenth century. The excerpts from gazetteers listed in table 2.2 demonstrate that chile use for some, even in the seventeenth and eighteenth centuries, extended well beyond substitution. Of the twelve selections in the table, only one refers to substitution. Ten of the others emphasize its use as a pungent or spicy flavoring in its own right. While the eleventh does not specify the type of flavor, it does state that "during the winter months a little is put in soup, it is also used in food."[101] One of the records also shows the competition between chiles and some of the other pungent flavorings, asserting that "the fruits are much more pungent than *huajiao* [Sichuan pepper]."[102] Such competition between spices demonstrates that chiles were gaining legitimacy on their own account, beyond as a substitute. A similar pattern can be seen in some of the regional names for chiles, such as "surpasses black pepper." In fact, though Sichuan pepper was probably the least expensive flavoring that chiles initially competed with, it was eventually displaced by this interloper in popularity. Chiles were thus not just successful for economic reasons, since they surpassed an inexpensive, indigenous spice. While the pungent foreignness of the chile initially overwhelmed the palates of some elite writers, its ability to pack a flavorful and nutritional punch as vitamin, vegetable, preservative, and spice—freely abundant in the kitchen garden—made for irresistible appeal and widespread acceptance.

3

SPICING UP THE PHARMACOPEIA

[Chiles] miraculously cure all types of hemorrhoids.
—XU WENBI, MEDICAL TEXT, 1771

Medical use of chiles in China began as early as 1621. By 1771 they were described as producing "miraculous" cures. The integration of chiles into traditional Chinese medical classification systems, combined with observations (empirical evidence) of the impact of chile consumption on health, was essential for these adaptations. The importance of this adoption and integration overlapped from medical classifications to influence aspects of culinary uses of chiles as well. Two key aspects of ingredients in Chinese medical systems are the flavor (*wei* 味) and the innate warming or cooling property (*xing* 性). Indeed, Chinese botanical historian Georges Métailié argues that understanding these characteristics for specific products is "fundamental to therapeutics" and "makes it possible for a doctor, once he has made a diagnosis, to choose which products to use as remedies."[1] Given the connections between flavor and health, many items that could be labeled as food or flavoring were also used for medicinal purposes, as seen clearly in the title of the earliest "medical" text to include chiles, *Shiwu bencao* (Pharmacopoeia of edible items). The difficulty of drawing a clear line between cuisine and medicine in Chinese culture was underscored by the eleventh-century medical expert Chen Zhi: "to be good at treatment with medicines does not compare with being good at treatment with food."[2] Indeed, the 1621 edition of the *Shiwu bencao*, in addition to being the earliest medical text to include chiles, is also the earliest source that explicitly placed chiles in cuisine.[3] Furthermore, the preparation of items for medicine sometimes overlapped directly with food preparation. In his medical text of 1771, Xu Wenbi described how to use chiles in a treatment: "To make medicine, chop finely, mix with pork fat and then fry to make a dish (*zuo cai*)."[4] The medicine is actually described as a "dish" of food. For the purposes of analyzing the cultural history of chiles in China, I have placed culinary and medicinal uses into separate chapters, but some of the many links across this artificial divide are emphasized in this chapter as they were in the last.

By the late imperial period, approaches to understanding the body, medicine, food, disease, ailments, and therapies were an intricate web of interconnecting and sometimes contradictory ideas. The well-known historian of traditional Chinese medicine Paul Unschuld has argued that in China, "one encounters, over the last two thousand years, an enormous variety of differently conceptualized systems of therapy, partly overlapping, partly antagonistic, all of which are representative of Chinese culture."[5] Over time, practitioners integrated systems that, at a theoretical level, might be viewed as contradictory or incompatible into a complex regimen of diagnosis and treatment. Unschuld maintains that there are two main paradigms for traditional Chinese medicine: (1) diagnoses and treatments derived from theories about interconnections and correspondences, and (2) diagnoses and treatments derived largely from observed results.[6] Traditional Chinese medicine practitioners, in the late imperial past and into the present, generally engage in both paradigms simultaneously. Thus T. J. Hinrichs and Linda

Barnes, in the introduction to their edited volume *Chinese Medicine and Healing*, argue that "healing . . . is shaped not only by the clean lines of theory but also by the messy contingencies of practice; not only by doctors but also by complex interactions among physicians, patients, and nonphysician caregivers."[7] Eugene Anderson, who has written extensively on food in Chinese culture, emphasizes that the modern villagers he has studied find common experience and practice to be important factors for determining treatment:

> In short, practical experience led Chinese villagers and townsfolk to recognize the value of what only later would be reinterpreted as heat energy, protein and nutrients, and antibiotic "contamination-dispelling" action. Indeed, studies of Chinese medicine that talk only of high theory and neglect practice are getting things backward. Chinese medicine in action privileged practice and empiricism. Theory was useful to explain and interpret, to classify, and to extend logically the procedures used, but common experience was always the first consideration.[8]

Whether a particular practitioner prioritized theory over observation or observation over theory, few if any only endorsed treatments that developed from just one or the other.

It is important to avoid seeing medical theory and lived experience as separate or in conflict. Similarly, whether a particular practitioner was identified as the primary caregiver was often in flux or never even emphasized. Chinese medicine historian Yi-Li Wu emphasizes how families during the Qing consciously employed multiple approaches and techniques when seeking cures:

> The typical pattern, found in medical case records as well as in stories and novels, was that a family would consult all the practitioners they could afford—sometimes sequentially, sometimes

simultaneously—and compare, modify, and reject their recommendations based on the family's own sense of what was appropriate. Unlike today's biomedical physician, who deploys diagnostic and therapeutic technologies to which patients have no access, the Qing physician relied on the unassisted powers of human observation and on medicinal substances that were readily purchased in the marketplace. . . . the practical difference between the activities of a doctor and a layperson could be a matter of degree, not of kind.[9]

While families employed diverse strategies, even individual practitioners would have varied their methods, mixing correlative techniques with empirical practices. Similarly, texts laying out the medicinal uses of chiles reveal that practitioners both placed chiles within the more theoretical correlative or corresponding systems and recorded effects based on empirical observations. The therapies involving the chile pepper that emerged after its introduction fall into both of these paradigms. In this chapter, I begin by examining how authors inserted the chile into the correlative systems and then turn to an analysis of treatments derived from observation. Later authors, identifying some harmful characteristics of chiles, provide another sign of their fuller integration into Chinese culture. Particularly in the modern period, chiles also became an important daily dietary supplement for the overall maintenance of good health. Traditional Chinese medicine is an integral part of Chinese culture. Assimilation of chiles into medicinal practices was an essential component of the naturalization of chiles.

Bencao Texts and Chinese Medicine

Bencao 本草 or *Materia medica* or *Pharmacopeia* are important medical and natural science texts. *Bencao* include far more medical knowledge than just lists of medical ingredients. They typically include a wide range of theories about systems such as *Yinyang* and the Five Phases. They can provide details about diagnosing patients, long sections on pulse readings, detailed descriptions of a wide range of medicinal ingredients, and systems of categorization (taxonomy). Beyond formula books listing medical recipes for specific treatments, they give both historical accounts of past uses of specific ingredients as well as details about the natural history of plants and animals. Though many ingredients come from plants, there are also quite a few from animals and minerals. While medical texts and lists of ingredients predate the use of the term *bencao*, the earliest known reference to the term, as the title of a court position, is from the *Hanshu* (History of the [former] Han) dating to 5 CE. According to legend, the mythical leader Shennong (the "Divine Farmer") invented medicine by eating hundreds of plants in order to observe their effects. During the late imperial period the *Shennong bencao jing* (Shennong's classic bencao) was believed to be the most ancient *bencao*. A number of editions of and many quotations from the text circulated during the Ming, and scholars tried to piece the original work back together. Recent scholarship dates that text to the second to first century BCE, hundreds of years after Shennong's supposed lifetime. Numerous authors used *bencao* in the title of their works, often borrowing heavily from previous *bencao*.[10]

In the twentieth and twenty-first centuries, the most well-known *bencao* is Li Shizhen's (1518–1593) *Bencao gangmu* 本草綱目, published in 1596. *Gangmu* can be translated variously as compendium, detailed outline, or systematic study. Two common translations of the title of Li's work are *Systematic materia medica* and *Compendium pharmacopeia*, both drawing on older traditions for naming collections of medicinal ingredients in the West. For most references in this book, I will stick with the original Chinese of *bencao* since this genre included far more than just lists of ingredients. While Li's work was certainly popular and influential during the late imperial period, it did not gain its current standing until the twentieth century. Li was a native of what is now Hubei province. Like many of his peers, he studied for many years for the civil service exam but never passed the provincial-level exam. He instead followed in the footsteps of both his paternal grandfather and father, pursuing a career in medicine.

In 1547, when Li was around thirty, he began to be troubled by inconsistencies, confusions, and errors within and between the various medical texts he had access to. For example, he felt that a number of ingredients were classified in the wrong category. Ingredients having multiple names and different plants using the same one frustrated him. Thus he struck out on a massive project to align the content of various past texts with personal investigation and experimentation. For the next thirty years he read voraciously, accumulating a list of some eight hundred books. Beginning in 1556 he also traveled extensively, seeking out advice from other medical practitioners, medicine merchants, local healers, herb growers, hunters, woodchoppers, and fishermen. His travels took him around his home province of Hubei, plus Anhui, Beijing, Hebei, Henan, Hunan, Jiangsu, Jiangxi, and Nanjing. In addition to drawing on the rich resources of all this local knowledge, he also experimented on his patients and himself.[11]

Many modern scholars see Li as an extremely important early natural scientist. Joseph Needham describes him as "the prince of pharmacists" and "probably the greatest naturalist in Chinese history."[12] The editors of the modern *Zhonghua bencao* describe his work as "dominating the field of medicine studies for the past 500 years."[13] Carla Nappi, historian of Chinese science and health, asserts that "Li designed his work as a melding of the literatures of medicine and natural history into one monument to his own erudition and to the awesome multivalence of the natural world."[14]

Li's work is important for my book only indirectly, as *Bencao gangmu* does not include the chile pepper. However, a number of late imperial authors refer to other plants in Li's work, arguing that it was actually the chile. Since Li's entries are quite detailed and his descriptions of plants precise, it is possible to definitely state that none of the references to Li's work proffered by later authors actually refers to the chile. Li's work, however, is still a useful reference for my book, for example in my analysis of black pepper in the previous chapter.[15]

The first *bencao* to include the chile pepper was the anonymous *Shiwu bencao* from 1621. This work was the first of any medical text to include the chile, and it was also the first of any work to explicitly place chiles in cuisine. As noted in the previous chapter, *shiwu* translates as "edible items" or "edible things." I translate the full title, *Shiwu bencao*, as *Pharmacopoeia of Edible Items*. The exact text on chiles from the 1621 edition was reproduced in the 1638 and 1642 editions of the *Shiwu bencao*.[16] However, a 1691 edition did not include chiles, demonstrating that the chile still needed to gain ground for wide acceptance in elite texts.[17]

The next important *bencao* for the study of chiles is Zhao Xuemin's (1719–1805) amendments, commentary, and critique of Li Shizhen's work. Zhao's contribution is titled *Bencao gangmu shiyi* (Correction of omissions in [Li's] Bencao gangmu). Zhao specifically stated that he sought to fill in gaps in Li's work. Zhao employed many of the same methods as Li—traveling to talk with local practitioners and relying on regionally published works with small printings or perhaps only hand-copied editions. Less than one hundred years after his death, more than half of the works quoted by Zhao had been lost.[18] Indeed, in his entry for chiles, Zhao cites from eleven texts, of which only four are extant. Zhao supplemented what he found in the other texts with his own experiences using chiles.

A point of significant difference between the two, and a matter where Zhao critiqued Li, was their approach to the use of human bodies in medicine. While Li was not as extreme as some others, he did include a chapter in his *Bencao gangmu* on medical ingredients from people (*ren bu*). This chapter included head hair, hair from a comb, facial hair, pubic hair, dandruff, earwax, knee dirt, finger and toe nails, teeth, tartar, excrement, excrement from a newborn (including meconium), evaporated urine deposit, blood, menstrual blood, placenta, umbilical cord, milk, bone, tears, breath, penis, gallbladder, and flesh.[19] Zhao was adamantly, ethically opposed to the use of human body parts in medicine. As part of his critique of Li on this point, he chose not to include a human section in his work, even rejecting the more benign ingredients such as hair and earwax.[20] Zhao's work contains the longest passage on chiles in any late imperial work. There was a significant lag time between the completion of Zhao's text around 1803, near the end of his life, and when it was actually published in 1871. After Zhao's work was published, it was incorporated into Li's. Subsequent editions of Li's work include Zhao's expansions and thus incorporate a detailed assessment of medical impacts of chiles.[21]

Integration of Chiles into Medical Systems

While most late imperial texts that classified the chile categorized it as a vegetable, there were also a few that identified it as a medicinal ingredient (*yao*). For example, the earliest gazetteers from Guangdong and Guizhou that contain the chile pepper both list it as a medicine.[22] In addition, all the gazetteers I consulted for this study from Quanzhou prefecture in Fujian that list the chile, from the earliest in 1757 through 1929, place it in the medicine category. Thus in some regions the use of chiles for health took precedence over its value as a flavoring.

As we saw in the previous chapter, the Five Phases relational or correlative system draws connections between natural phenomena, flavors, senses, types of *qi* (climate), internal organs (*yin* organs), and various components of the digestive tract (*yang* organs). The five flavors (*wuwei* 五味) in this correspondence or correlative system continue to connect traditional Chinese medicine with food all the way to the present. In the earliest medical text to include chiles, the anonymous author identified the flavor of chiles (foreign peppers) as pungent (*xin* 辛) (table 3.1 lays out some of the correlations within the Five Phases system).[23] Chiles, as a pungent flavoring, are categorized in the metal phase. While some subsequent authors continued to classify chiles as pungent, many chose to label them as spicy (*la* 辣), further evidence of the influence of chiles on the usage and meaning of that term. Within the five flavors, spicy is subsumed under the broader pungent category. Only

TABLE 3.1

Five Phases Correspondences or Correlates (those for chiles highlighted)

Phase	Wood *mu* 木	Fire *huo* 火	Earth *tu* 土	Metal *jin* 金	Water *shui* 水
Direction	East	South	Center	West	North
Color	Green	Red	Yellow	White	Black
Flavor	Sour	Bitter	Sweet	Pungent	Salty
Qi (Climate)	Windy	Hot	Humid	Dry	Cold
Yin organ	Liver	Heart	Spleen	Lungs	Kidneys
Yang organ (Digestive tract)	Gall Bladder	Small intestine	Stomach	Large intestine	Bladder
Sense organs	Eyes	Tongue	Mouth	Nose	Ears
Tissue	Tendons	Blood vessels	Muscle	Skin	Bones

Sources: Nanjing zhongyi xueyuan yijing jiaoyan zu, ed., *Huangdi neijing suwen yishi* (Shanghai: Shanghai kexue jishu, 1981), 36–37, 39; Ted Kaptchuk, *The Web That Has No Weaver: Understanding Chinese Medicine* (New York: Congdon and Weed, 1983), 345.

very spicy chiles, those with high levels of capsaicin (the chemical compound in chiles that makes them spicy), were used in Chinese medical therapies. The sweet or bell pepper, often called the persimmon pepper in late imperial China, is considered sweet, not pungent. Similarly, modern biomedical therapies using chiles also rely on high levels of capsaicin from very spicy chiles.[24] In ancient times the pungent category in China encompassed the onion family (including garlic), ginger, cassia cinnamon, and Sichuan pepper.[25] As we saw in the previous chapter, early culinary use of chiles in China often involved substituting chiles for these and other pungent flavorings. Similarly, some medical texts describe chiles as substitutes for other pungent medicines.

Specific applications of chiles for cures of diseases associated with these characteristics of the Five Phases are found in a number of texts. One of these was by the medical scholar Wang Fu (1692–1759). Wang was a precocious child. His mother read him classic texts as soon as he was able to speak, and he memorized many by the time he was eight. He wrote on both medicine and textual studies.[26] In the preface to his 1758 medical text, Wang Fu, echoing a phrase from the Confucian *Analects*, admonishes his readers to "not be concerned if others do not understand medicine, but instead be concerned if through greater study of medicine you do not gain a more thorough understanding."[27] In his more thorough understanding of how to use chiles medicinally, he observed that "The pungent flavor drains off the lungs" (*xie fei* 瀉肺).[28] Here we see a direct application of the correlation or correspondence between pungency and the lungs. In addition, a symptom often associated with the metal phase and the lungs is coughing.[29] A physiological purpose of coughing is to clear out phlegm. In addition, the capsaicin in chiles can trigger thinning of mucus in the nose, leading to a clearing of the sinuses.[30] Within the Five Phases, the pungent flavor also correlates with dry *qi*. Thus the chile pepper was used to dry out lung ailments. Several sources record the ability of chiles to "expel phlegm" (*qu tan* 去痰), "remove damp" (*chu shi* 除濕), "disperse water damp" (*qu shui shi* 祛水濕) or "cure phlegm caused by damp" (*zhi tan shi* 治痰濕).[31] Zhao Xuemin attests to his own success in employing the combination of the chile's pungency and drying abilities in the diaphragm, an important muscle in respiration: "Its pungent [characteristic] is good for dispersing cold phlegm (*leng tan* 冷痰) that results from accumulated water in the diaphragm. [This cure is really easy], like making water from snow!"[32] Zhao apparently had a great deal of success in capitalizing on these corresponding traits of chiles and passed along his enthusiasm to his readers.

In some cases the pungency of chiles was seen to outperform other pungent plants used in medicine. In his botanical treatise of 1848, Wu Qijun describes how people might need treatment from a pungent flavoring to rectify dietary shortcomings: "Without variety in the diet illnesses can occur. Lesser ones can be treated with ginger and cassia cinnamon. More severe illnesses of the spleen or stomach must be treated with something stronger—the foreign pepper."[33] While the chile may be seen in the quote as more powerful, this does not mean it was always the best option. Suiting treatment to specific ailments and the attributes of the unique patient was also key.

Another important component of Chinese medicine is the *Yin-yang* system or doctrine, built on the ancient system of paired complements in which the two elements, *yin* and *yang*, combine and balance with one another to create a coherent whole. In this system, parts of the body, medicines, foods, diseases, and ailments, in fact most compounds, are dominated by either *yin* or *yang* properties. Thus if someone's body, or a particular part of the body, had too much *yin*, often associated with coolness, then medicine or food dominant in *yang*, or warming properties, would be prescribed.

Thus the innate warming and cooling properties of both medicine and food within the *Yinyang* system are another example of significant overlap between diet and health. In Chinese medicine *yin* and *yang* are not limited to temperature. For example, a *yin* illness could involve depletion or weakness, while a *yang* illness could have symptoms of excess or overexertion. In addition, some parts of the body, including some organs, are considered *yin* while others are *yang*. There is a dialectical relationship between *yin* and *yang*; the one cannot exist without the other. They can balance each other out or even partially destroy or create the other.[34] In terms of temperature, the most common aspect of the *Yinyang* system used in describing the properties of chiles, the simplest form of the system used the two categories cool (*liang* 涼) and warm (*wen* 溫). In this two-category system chile peppers were classified as "warm."[35] In a further refinement of this system, *yin* and *yang* could in turn be subdivided, creating four groupings.[36] This is perhaps best demonstrated concretely using temperature: *YIN-yin* or cold (*han* 寒), *YIN-yang* or cool (*liang* 涼), *YANG-yin* or warm (*wen* 溫), and *YANG-yang* or hot (*re* 熱). In this fourfold system chiles were identified as "hot."[37] A different subschool with six categories, with three different types of *yin* and *yang*, also became popular.[38] Chile peppers in this system were described as "extremely hot (*da re*)."[39] Whether a particular author labeled chiles as "warm," "hot," or "extremely hot," the ways in which the warming properties of chiles were used were quite similar. This heating quality was equally emphasized in cuisine.

As we have seen, the earliest medical text containing chiles, from 1621, classified them as having warming properties.[40] Although this text did not provide any details about how this particular characteristic of chiles could be employed, it was important for the spread and acceptance of chiles that this classification took place relatively early. All subsequent medical texts that contain chiles classified them as either warm, hot, or extremely hot; in addition, many texts in other genres, such as agricultural texts and local gazetteers, also placed chiles within this rubric. Early general categorization allowed later practitioners to record more specific uses of the chile pepper's warming properties. Wang Fu's medical text from 1758, in addition to providing the further details about chile's pungent nature cited above, also included some elaborations on its heating capabilities: "[It has the property of] cold-expelling heat. . . . It has great pungent and warming [properties], and thus can cure those with *yang* wind hemorrhoid sores (*zhilou* 痔瘻). . . . It guides fire to move downward."[41] While the ability of chiles to heat the body is evident to anyone who has eaten spicy ones, Wang also shows how the pungent and warming properties could work in concert to heal particular ailments.

Wang Fu continued his discussion of chiles, adding two additional points about heat, expanding the ability of practitioners or families to employ chiles in their medical practices past treating an imbalance veering toward cold. First, "Even though [the chile] has a hot [characteristic], it can expel heat. *Wu zhuyu* (吳茱萸; *Tetradium ruticarpum*) has the same effect."[42] Wang asserts that the heating property of chiles not only can expel cold but can also use heat to drive out heat (like using fire to fight fire). This is readily observable in the chile pepper's ability to cause people to sweat. The subsequent evaporation of sweat is a cooling process. In addition, Wang points out that this characteristic of chiles is the same as another fruit commonly used in traditional Chinese medicine, *Wu zhuyu*. Wang's readers would probably have been much more familiar with the pharmaceutical uses of *Wu zhuyu* compared to the chile pepper, and showing this overlap in properties made this introduced plant more accessible. Just as chiles were often used as a substitute for other flavors, they could also be used in place of medicines of long repute, thus lending authority to the newer chile.

The warming property of chiles could also be used to heat the body. Zhao cited a now lost text that states: "[Chiles] can warm the core by dispersing cold . . . [and] can cure indigestion [caused by] cold." Zhao himself added that "because its property is hot [it can act as a cold] dispersant by entering the heart and spleen meridians."[43] A modern folk saying underscores the warming property of chiles: "[Eating] three large chiles is as good as wearing a padded cotton jacket."[44] In addition, the warming nature of chiles was used externally to treat skin ailments associated with cold, including cleaning frostbite sores, and bathing itches caused by cold, such as chilblains (see box).[45]

Another important aspect of traditional Chinese medicine was the movement and balance of *qi* within the body. *Qi* is a difficult term to translate as it can carry a variety of meanings in Chinese; it has been variously translated as energy, vitality, life-force, or pneuma. Ted Kaptchuk notes that "we can perhaps think of Qi as matter on the verge of becoming energy, or energy at the point of materializing."[46] Many illnesses were seen as resulting from the disruption of regular *qi* flow throughout the body, usually through either deficiency or blockage. Thus knowledge of which medicines were effective at restoring particular aspects of *qi* flow was an important component of a practitioner's treatments. The fourteenth-century medical author Zou Xuan argued that "physicians must first recognize the causes of an illness and understand in what way the body's own vitalities [*qi*] have become unbalanced."[47] Many aspects of regulating *qi* in the body are connected with either the

TREATMENT FOR CHILBLAINS

Stick peeled skins of the spicy eggplant onto [the chilblains (*dongzhu* 凍瘃)] to achieve healing.

Yinyang or the Five Phases correspondence systems. In the *Yinyang* system, all forms of *qi* are *yang* substances, and *qi* depletion is a *yin* condition, while *qi* blockage is a *yang* condition.[48] Within the Five Phases system, five different types of *qi*, sometimes translated as types of climate, correspond with each of the phases and thus in turn also correlate with each of the five flavors. Pungent flavors, and therefore chiles, correlate with dry *qi*. For example, the ability of chiles to remove phlegm. In addition, by 1621 chiles were being used to "unblock congealed *qi*."[49] Later texts identified chiles as able to "correct earth *qi*" and "open stomach *qi*."[50] The stomach links to the large intestine, the *yang* organ aligned with pungency.

Observed Medical Benefits of the Chile

In addition to linking chiles with these key, long-standing correspondence systems, authors also outlined a number of cures that probably developed primarily from empirical observation of the impacts of chiles on individuals. Within roughly fifty years after introduction, enough observation and experimentation had occurred that chiles were recognized as having medical uses beyond the corresponding *Yinyang*, Five Phases, and *qi* systems.

Some of these observed characteristics of chiles were laid out in the 1621 edition of the *Shiwu bencao*. These properties made chiles an important new ingredient for inclusion in prescriptions. All the noncorresponding traits or characteristics derived from empirical observation or practice described in the *Shiwu bencao* are also identified in modern studies of chiles. While we must be careful about projecting modern biomedical analyses back onto a different cultural milieu, for some of the Chinese medical uses for chiles comparisons with recent biomedical analyses can be illuminating. The author of the *Shiwu bencao* proclaimed that "principally it [aids] with nighttime digestion of food. . . . [In addition it] stimulates the appetite."[51] Capsaicin in spicy chiles causes the mucous membranes in the mouth and stomach to increase production of saliva and gastric juices. Chewing and excretion of saliva are the first steps in digestion. Increased salivation and increased gastric juices stimulate the appetite as well as digestion. In addition, Vitamin A, which chiles are quite high in, is important for the health of epithelial tissues, which include mucous membranes, the lining of the gastrointestinal tract, and the linings of the lungs.[52] This connects back to the Five Phases correlations between pungent medications and the lungs, nose, and large intestine. Appetite stimulation is particularly important when people are eating bland, largely colorless, high starch diets.[53] This certainly would have been the case for the vast majority of Chinese during the late imperial period, when high-starch meals of rice, millet, sorghum, and wheat were commonplace at the lower levels of society. Indeed, it has been estimated that about 90 percent of calories consumed in rural China in traditional times came from cereals and pulses.[54] In addition, chiles "add color and flavor to bland diets, thus relieving their monotony"; furthermore, increased salivation "facilitat[es] the mastication of mealy, starch-based diet."[55] The importance of chiles in stimulating appetite and aiding digestion continued to be emphasized in a variety of texts after 1621.[56]

While all this information about chiles potentially aiding people eating a high-starch diet makes sense for unhealthy people, if lower-class people were starving, appetite stimulation would hardly have been necessary or even beneficial. There is perhaps a class bias among the authors of both the original sources and the modern ones, reflecting their own much more varied diets. On the other hand, other American crops introduced just before the chile, including maize, white potato, and sweet potato, did integrate more high-starch foods into Chinese diets that may have required more flavoring to make them palatable and more easily digested. However, heat and humidity, common throughout much of Inner China in summer time, can inhibit appetites, so chile consumption may indeed have been beneficial for appetite stimulation at times of high temperatures and humidity.[57]

In modern biological analyses of capsaicin, the spicy compound found in chiles, scholars argue for two main evolutionary advantages for the plants. Fruits are designed to attract consumers that will then disperse the seeds. However, if the consumer destroys the seeds, then the plant will not reproduce. High levels of capsaicin prevent mammal consumers, particularly rodents, from eating the chile pods. All mammals react to the spiciness of capsaicin. In an experiment where rodents were offered spicy chiles, nonspicy chiles, and the nonspicy hackberry, they readily consumed the hackberry, completely avoided the spicy chiles, and consumed an intermediate amount of the nonspicy chiles. When rodents were offered only the nonspicy chiles, all consumed seeds were nonviable. Birds, however, are unaffected by capsaicin. In the same study, curved-billed thrashers readily ate up all the spicy chiles, and many of the seeds were viable.[58] Birds are excellent dispersers of seeds. Indeed, Henry Ridley, in his 1930 study of the plant dispersals, observed birds spreading chile seeds.[59] Jean Andrews also noted this difference between mammals and birds and complained about wild turkeys gobbling down her chiltepine chiles.[60] A second evolutionary function of capsaicin is as a defense against fungus. Most of the regions where the chile plant is native are humid. Thus fungus growth on the pods and seeds, which would likely make the seeds nonviable, is a constant threat. Capsaicin, however, has been shown to be an excellent antifungal agent, particularly against a genus of common fungus on chile plants, *Fusarium*.[61] In cultural practice, capsaicin's antifungal attributes certainly helped in Chinese food preservation, including in pickling, sauces, and pastes.

Chiles also have antiseptic or antimicrobial qualities. The earliest record of chiles in Fujian, from 1757 in Quanzhou prefecture, includes the ability to cure some forms of seafood poisoning: "It can detoxify poison (*jie du* 解毒) from aquatic animals (*shuizu* 水族). People who eat too much fish or crab and get diarrhea (*xiexie* 泄瀉) or dropsy (*zhangman* 脹滿) can boil the fruit to make a dose of medicinal broth."[62] Strong antimicrobial properties of chiles have also been observed in modern studies. For example, in one study bacteria killed by chiles included one often occurring in oysters.[63] This antimicrobial property of chiles was taken up most prevalently in Quanzhou prefecture on the coast of Fujian province (see maps 1.1 and 1.2). The emphasis on antiseptic characteristics carried through subsequent gazetteers from Quanzhou prefecture (1763 through 1929), which all assert that chiles "can cure (*zhi*) poisoning from fish (*yu du*)."[64] While many of the Quanzhou gazetteers describe chiles as spicy, and all list "foreign ginger" as an alternative name, none includes any specifics about how chiles were used in food. While it is difficult to separate culinary and medicinal uses of ingredients, the Quanzhou sources do imply a stronger emphasis on medical uses. This was also the only region in China where gazetteers consistently categorized chiles as medicine. Here the chile was integrated into a region with a diet high in seafood as a cure for food poisoning.

The use of chiles to treat diarrhea more generally, not just from seafood poisoning, can be found in several medical texts. Xu Wenbi observed that chiles were "suitable to enter the large intestine to detoxify poisons (*jie du*)."[65] In his compilation, Zhao Xuemin cites four different texts that include treating diarrhea as one of the uses of chile peppers, one of which also specifically refers to the large intestine.[66] (For one prescription, see the box.)[67] While the emphasis on curing diarrhea or detoxifying poisons was noncorresponding, the emphasis on the large intestine actually draws

TREATMENT FOR SEVERE DIARRHEA/DYSENTERY
(*Liji Shuixie* 痢積水瀉)

Take one spicy eggplant, [form it into a] ball, then wrap it inside hot tofu skin and swallow early in the morning; results in cure.

on the corresponding link between pungent and the large intestine in the Five Phases system. Thus we can see here a good example of Unschuld's argument that "the two paradigms should be seen as complementing each other in various ways; they do not exclude each other."[68]

Marta Hanson, a scholar of the history of Chinese medicine, has shown that regional approaches to treatments were common in the late imperial period. She argues that

> literate physicians from the late tenth century onward increasingly explained human variation by differences in regional environment, social status, and bodily attributes. Whether the climate was predominantly cold or hot, dry or damp, fiery or windy mattered clinically because the interior of the human body was a microclimate. Whether the external region was high (mountainous) or low (near sea level), in the northwest or the southeast, north of the Yangzi River or south of it, determined the main climatic factors for that region. . . . From the late fourteenth century on, physicians' geographic conceptions explained divergences in medical doctrines, diagnostic practices, and therapeutic preferences, according to northern and southern medical styles of practice.[69]

Regionalized uses of chiles reflect this aspect of medical theory and practice. People in the Quanzhou region matched the chile's antiseptic qualities with a diet that often contained pathogens.

Malaria and humidity prevalent in other regions were also matched with characteristics of the chile.

The use of chiles to treat malaria is another example of a regional adaptation in their adoption; one that also relied on the observed antiseptic or antimicrobial quality of chiles. A 1766 gazetteer from Guangdong elaborated on their use in treating malaria as well as for relieving inflammatory conditions: "[they] can remove water-borne malaria (*shui zhang*) and disperse rheumatism (*fengshi*). . . . In Guangxi malaria is even more prevalent, and one cannot go a single day without [eating them]."[70] Much later, modern biomedical practitioners have "discovered" that drugs used to prevent or treat malaria, such as Hydroxychloroquine, are also effective in reducing swelling and pain caused by rheumatoid arthritis and lupus.[71] In the malarial areas of Guangdong and Guangxi, chiles were used not just as a treatment after illness occurred, as we saw for "fish poisoning," but as a daily prophylactic against malaria.

The use of chiles as a treatment for malaria extended further north as well. Zhao Xuemin identified chiles as a treatment for malaria after infection near Hangzhou: "A young servant . . . had developed malaria. [He took] myriad medicines without result. In early winter, by chance [he] ate some chile paste. He found this very *palatable*, and *needed* it with every meal. In addition he also used some in a medicinal broth with meals. Before long the malaria was cured."[72] Here we see directly that this remedy was developed through observed results, not through correspondence. The servant's craving for chile paste while he was ailing reflects a phenomenon recognized in Chinese medicine that the body can know what it needs to get back in balance. An ingredient with needed attributes can become craved, leading the patient to consume it. The efficacy of chile paste as a prophylactic was also expressed in the "Chile Paste" poem analyzed in chapter 5. The poet, Wu Xingqin, assured consumers of chile paste that it "wards off malaria, no need to worry."[73] This is the same form for the chiles that Zhao's servant was drawn to after he contracted malaria. Wu's inclusion of this line in his poem implies that the medical use of chiles for malaria was widely known and practiced. In these treatments for both the prevention and cure of malaria, again, local conditions elicited a specific use for chiles.

Another use listed in several texts was for the treatment of hemorrhoids. We have already seen that Wang Fu viewed the pungent and warming properties of chiles as instrumental in curing hemorrhoid sores. Indeed, use of chiles as a treatment for hemorrhoids was apparently quite successful, as we can see in the quote from Xu Wenbi at the beginning of this chapter. Xu's account was reinforced by editors of a series of local gazetteers from Guangxi who similarly proclaimed that chiles "provide a miraculous cure for hemorrhoids" (see box for recipe.)[74] The "miraculous" effects of chiles in treating a fairly common ailment like hemorrhoids likely furthered the acceptance of chiles moving into the nineteenth century.

The capsaicin in chiles also has analgesic properties.[75] This can be seen in a number of over-the-counter creams and ointments now available for topical application for pain relief from arthritis and other joint ailments, as well as shingles.[76] In late imperial China, this aspect of chiles was applied to a range of pains. Zhao Xuemin cited a now lost text whose author claimed that chiles could relieve pain from toothaches.[77] Similarly, chiles were prescribed for relieving pain from snakebites (see box for recipe).[78] In this example, we

---

MIRACULOUS CURE FOR HEMORRHOIDS
(*Zhizhi Dayou Shenxiao* 治痔大有神效)

Eat a dose of three qian [15 grams] of raw chile paste every day.

TREATMENT FOR POISONOUS SNAKEBITES

Chew 11 or 12 raw, spicy eggplant fruits to reduce swelling and stop pain. The small blisters at the wound site will expel a yellow liquid and then heal. When eating this the flavor will be sweet, not spicy. Or masticate and place on the wound to reduce swelling and stop pain.

see a phenomenon recognized in Chinese medicine where, when the body needs a particular substance, potentially intense flavors become subdued. Thus for the snakebite treatment, intense chiles taste "sweet, not spicy." This is similar to the servant with malaria craving chiles and finding them "palatable."

Detrimental Impacts of Chile Consumption

In traditional Chinese medicine, while ingredients have beneficial properties that make them useful for treating particular ailments, those same properties can be detrimental for other conditions. Thus while heat can be useful for removing surplus cold, too much heat can have negative consequences. For example, a *yang* illness might be aggravated by the heat in chiles. The earliest specific example of an author warning about possible negative impacts on health from chiles appeared in 1771.[79] Such warnings can be seen as a sign of the increasing use of chiles in cuisine and medicine.

Some warnings were quite general, such as one for moderation from a Hunan gazetteer from 1876: "Eating too many causes harm."[80] Other examples were more specific about harmful consequences. An earlier Hunan gazetteer, after noting that chiles can "distribute *qi*, and move heat," went on to eventually warn about precise consequences: "Because they are palatable people love to eat them, [but] they are often hurt by them. In Yongzhou they are used when making pickled vegetables, and are invariably used in ordinary food and drink preparation. Thus these [Yongzhou] people have many eye and blood diseases."[81] In the correlative Five Phases system, the chile, as a pungent flavor, is in the metal phase. Metal diminishes or affects wood, the phase for eyes. Zhao Xuemin cited similar warnings in his collection of texts: one author cautioned that chiles can "cause eye illnesses" and that "those with a fiery [constitution] should shun medicine [containing chiles]," and another asserted that "Because [of its ability] to move fire, eating many can lead to dizziness."[82] While many of these affects were probably attributed to chiles based on empirical observations, in terms of the systems discussed above, the negative impacts were probably seen as resulting from too much heat or too much *yang*. Much of Zhao's commentary and his records of other accounts about chiles emphasized a wide range of positive effects, yet these examples of possible ill effects demonstrate that over time practitioners developed a more thorough and nuanced assessment of the impacts of chiles on health, probably largely from empirical observations.

In some cases the warnings seem to completely contradict other sources. However, traditional Chinese medical practitioners always personalized treatments to the individual in a particular place at a specific time. In his 1771 text, Xu Wenbi warned his readers to "avoid eating them raw. [In addition,] eating too many causes tooth aches and swollen lips."[83] As we saw in the section on chiles as vegetables, many people ate chiles raw seemingly without any negative consequences, yet clearly Xu had seen at least a few cases where avoiding raw chiles rectified particular conditions. In his warning about toothaches and swollen lips, Xu emphasized excess and thus was not necessarily contradicting the advice cited above about chiles relieving toothaches. Even though Xu and the editors of the series of Guangxi gazetteers all proclaimed that chiles "miraculously cure every type of hemorrhoids," two authors in now lost works warned that eating chiles can aggravate or even cause hemorrhoids.[84] Again, rather than seeing these authors as contradicting one another, we can see practitioners applying their knowledge differently, or perhaps drawing conclusions from observing different types of patients and different conditions for ailments. It is not useful to look back and proclaim one correct and the others wrong. Instead, we can see that a wide range of authors found chiles common enough to comment on general properties. In addition, all the medical texts and the gazetteers that include negative consequences of consuming chiles also list positive ones as well or at least attribute the negative results to excess. Thus we should read these warnings as a balance to positive uses for the same ailment, and in some cases as a call for moderation.

A final example of a source that includes undesirable effects also provides an example of how the same symptoms can be seen as representative of different conditions; negative or positive impacts could be open to interpretation: "Those who do not eat them often, get burning and swollen lips as soon as [the chiles] enter their mouths. [As the chiles] enter the abdomen and intestines [they can lead to] ulcers in the stomach, which can cause the passing of blood in the stool. This leads those who love to eat them to say that chiles can cleanse the large intestine of fire."[85] In the Five Phases, fire and the movement of blood are associated. This is one of the few pre-twentieth-century sources that commented on the ability of people to build up a tolerance to chiles. So this side effect was one that could be overcome through acclimation. Stomach ulcers, however, were potentially much more serious. The last line, although the author presents it more as an excuse than an alternative interpretation, does actually provide a differing opinion about the source of blood in the stool. Even though these authors cautioned about adverse side effects from chile consumption, their inclusion of such effects indicates greater familiarity with the properties of chiles and probably reflects geographically widespread as well as common consumption. Practitioners were well aware of possible adverse reactions for all well-established items in the Chinese pharmacopeia. Thus inclusion of these negative traits further proved the Chinese naturalization and even authentication of this alien species.

Modern Adaptations

In the twentieth and twenty-first centuries popular accounts of the health effects of chiles continue to abound, while use of chiles in traditional Chinese medicine is limited primarily to dietary restrictions or additions. Thus knowledge about chiles affecting health is available, but practitioners of traditional Chinese medicine tend not to include them in their prescriptions. For example, most modern formularies—handbooks that contain recipes for prescriptions for specific ailments—do not include chile peppers.[86]

The modern *Zhonghua bencao* (1998) contains a great deal of information about chiles, but it is really a resource for scholars of the history of Chinese medicine and for lab researchers of the efficacy of various compounds, rather than for practitioners. The section on chiles includes references to historic sources, a natural history of the plant, detailed chemical analyses of various compounds in the fruit, country-wide output statistics, and the physiological impacts of the chile. The positive health effects include assisting with digestion, aiding in blood circulation, being antifungal, regulating fat oxidation, and aiding the respiratory system. In addition, the editors note that capsaicin can be used as an insecticide.[87] While all these details are included in the ten-volume collection, much of the information seems more designed for inclusion in modern biomedical compounding than in traditional medicines ingested as infusions.

Popular knowledge can be found in a number of genres. A popular song about chiles from Hunan describes several health impacts:

Expel damp *qi*, clear the mind, strengthen the appetite, stimulate the brain. Even more, they are rich in vitamins, and their nutritional value is high. Even though the spiciness makes your whole face sweat, the result will be a victorious cure![88]

A whole litany of positive effects from eating chiles—nutritional, medical, and personal—are worthy of a popular ode whose main focus is more entertainment than education, demonstrating the seamless meshing of chile associations in popular culture. The metaphor of a "victorious cure" draws on symbolism of the fiery nature of chiles affecting people's abilities to wage war, particularly revolution, in the context of the song.

A popular book on connections between spicy flavor and health also lists several effects from chiles. This work specifies that the chemical capsaicin is the source of the medical impacts of chiles. These effects include expelling wind, dispersing cold, activating the blood, expanding the blood vessels in the skin, and directing blood flow to the face.[89] Most of these impacts correspond with effects discussed by late imperial authors. While the specifics of expanding the blood vessels and increasing blood flow to the face were not included in late imperial sources, they fit into the broader category of the warming abilities of chiles.

A personal anecdote helps to reveal the modern emphasis on chiles within the diet rather than in prescriptions. In the mid-1990s, while living in Beijing, I was experiencing skin rashes on my hands, arms, and face. I consulted a traditional Chinese medical doctor for relief from these symptoms. In addition to a typical formula consisting largely of various dried plant parts and a few insect shells to be prepared as an infusion, he quite adamantly advised me to stop eating chiles and to reduce the amount of oil I was consuming. Even though chiles are not used as ingredients in infusion formulas, practitioners are well aware of their impact on health, whether it be an excess that causes too much heat in the skin (part of the correlative system associated with metal and pungency) or as a corrective to balance out excessive climatic moisture in regions such as Hunan and Sichuan.

Although culinary use of chiles dominated their influence on Chinese culture, understanding how they affected health, both positively and negatively, was key to the domestication of this import. Basic categorization, as being heating and pungent, was fundamental to Chinese understanding of how to make use of this newcomer. Just as people used chiles as substitutes for other pungent flavorings in their cooking, they also substituted chiles for other medicinal plants, such as *Wu zhuyu*, for their ability to expel heat, or even as replacements for ginger or cassia cinnamon when something stronger was needed for illnesses in the spleen or stomach.

Inserting the chile into the various traditional medical systems was particularly important for authors of texts that were primarily focused on health. They needed to know where it fit within classifications such as *Yinyang*, the Five Phases, and *qi*. With this knowledge they could then understand how it would work within the body for treating various ailments. While these categorizations were indeed essential, observation of empirical results played an equal or perhaps greater role in the enthusiastic acceptance, indigenization, and even authentication of the chile. Thus the ability of a pungent plant to affect the lungs would be expected because of the Five Phases, but the fact that many experts marveled at how well it expelled moisture from the lungs and diaphragm was certainly a result of observation.

As use of the chile increased, in the late eighteenth century authors began to note some detrimental health impacts from chiles, often from what they deemed was excessive consumption. The listing of harmful effects can be seen as a result of increased observations due to the rising popularization of chiles. Also, as knowledge about the fruit expanded, practitioners began to note differences in the ways it acted regionally or within individuals. This increased understanding allowed practitioners to more carefully craft their use of chiles to the individual patient.

The analysis of the medical uses of chiles in China reinforces recent trends in medical history, demonstrated by authors such as Eugene Anderson, Linda Barnes, T. J. Hinrichs, and Yi-Li Wu, which emphasize the importance of popular healing methods in addition to elite texts that focus on established systems. If traditional medicine in China had consisted only of theories and systems, then the use of chiles as a malaria treatment, an anti-inflammatory, an antiseptic, and an analgesic would possibly have gone unnoticed in the literature. Since all these uses of chiles are highlighted in various texts, including medical ones, we have clear evidence that traditional medicine in practice indeed incorporated popular or observed treatments in combination with the more abstract systems. Even characteristics of chiles that can be seen as falling into systems, such as the Five Phases, were probably augmented by observation. For example, although many pungent flavorings probably aided with digestion and appetite stimulation, this was so regularly emphasized in sources about chiles that it seems that the observed impact heightened the association of chiles with these abilities.

As with culinary uses, medical use was also influenced by regional factors such as climate and environment. In Quanzhou, Fujian, where seafood was widely consumed, the observed antimicrobial characteristic of capsaicin resulted in the chile being used and therefore categorized primarily as a medicinal plant rather than as a flavoring—although probably the flavor was appreciated as well. In malarial areas, particularly Guangdong and Guangxi, chiles were both a cure as well as a preventative treatment. As will be seen in more detail in chapter 6, in the moist, inland regions of Hunan and Sichuan, chiles are seen as an essential part of the diet in order to prevent moisture-related illnesses. Chile consumption became so ubiquitous in these regions that they changed the culture to the extent of becoming cultural identifiers. Although chiles were popular across all of Inner China, the fact that their use could vary from region to region depending on need drove the rapidity with which they became integrated into Chinese culture. The high versatility of the many characteristics and impacts of capsaicin made this outsider local quite quickly.

4

TOO HOT FOR WORDS

Elite Reticence Toward Chile Peppers

The fruit . . . is so spicy it cannot be put in the mouth.
—WANG LU, GARDENING TEXT, 1618

In previous chapters I demonstrated that chiles not only were integrated into preexisting Chinese cultural systems, but their integration also resulted in new practices. Although late imperial sources provide evidence for these changes, it is important to acknowledge that the sources for chiles remain quite thin up to the late nineteenth century. Examining the causes of the limited sources allows us to explore Chinese elite cultural practices from a different angle, thus deepening our understanding of underlying beliefs about elite-class perpetuation, values in scholarship, and interconnections between flavors and spiritual purity.

Two important areas for late imperial elites to express their creativity were poetry and painting. The chile pepper as poetic or pictorial subject encountered nearly impossible hurdles. I have been able to locate only one poem from before the twentieth century and just one higher-quality woodblock print (no actual paintings) with chiles as the subject from the late imperial period. I examine the symbolism of these examples in chapter 5. Beginning in the twentieth century, however, chiles as artistic topics became much more prevalent.

While the spiciness of chiles was a chief characteristic leading to their consumption at Chinese tables, their intensity also made some people reluctant to incorporate them into their diets. This contrast between popular appeal and elite reluctance or avoidance extended through the first two hundred years of the history of chiles in China. We can see these contradictory trends laid out in two pairs of documents—one pair from the seventeenth century and the other from the eighteenth. Broad appeal and acceptance is shown in the earliest medical text to include chiles, from 1621, where the anonymous author observed that "now it is found everywhere. . . . The ground [fruit] is put into food."[1] In contrast, in his gardening text in 1618, Wang Lu asserted that "the fruit . . . is so spicy it cannot be put in the mouth (*bu ke ru kou*)."[2] A similar contrast is evident in two eighteenth-century gazetteers. The editors of a local gazetteer from Shaanxi province in 1755 also emphasized the universality of the chile as a flavoring, asserting, as we have already seen, that chiles had become "as indispensable in daily cuisine as onion and garlic."[3] Yet just a year later, in 1756, an editor of a local-products section of a gazetteer from Jiangxi province described chiles as something to be avoided, something outside the cultural norm—a cultural other. He complained: "When [chiles are] used in flavoring food [the result is] sweat and tears running together, therefore those who use them are very few."[4] While regional (or even individual) variation of chile use certainly affected how they were appropriated and written about, there was more going on in the contrasts between these sources than local or personal difference.

Close attention reveals ways in which some elite authors separated themselves from "others," even as they described lower-class consumption. Thus it is worthwhile revisiting what the sources examined in the earlier chapters reveal about lower-class consumption. Since Ming and Qing officials could not serve in their native provinces, local-products sections of gazetteers were key reference works for officials who came from outside the areas where they were posted. To analyze the subtleties of language choices in local histories, it is important to understand that many local elites and officials stationed from other areas accepted an idealized view that they were part of a country-wide elite that transcended regional differences. While, in reality, there were of course regional differences within the elite and lower classes alike, gazetteers were a genre where certain sections, such as those about well-known residents, emphasized local elites conforming to broad country-wide expectations of upper-class behavior.[5] In contrast, other sections, particularly those on local products and practices, were designed to provide officials with descriptions of nonelite local practices, with the intent that the nonnative officials would develop a better understanding of local conditions, practices, and culture. When the elite editors of gazetteers referred to "local" practices, they typically excluded themselves. They often identified with common elite practices rather than with local cultures. Thus when reading descriptions of chiles in local histories (and other genres as well), the term "local" can usually be read as "nonelite locals." Certainly there were exceptions to this, and surely there were members of the elite in the seventeenth and eighteenth centuries who greatly enjoyed eating chiles. But overall, pre-nineteenth-century sources that describe widespread use refer predominantly to nonelite use. While it was typical for elite authors to ignore the masses across many late imperial genres, it was actually expected that they would write about them in "local" sections of gazetteers because this was helpful for their fellow elites who served as officials.

A major difference between the adoption of chiles in China and that of some of the other American crops was the amount of writing about them. Growing high-caloric crops such as the sweet potato, maize, and peanut was promoted by local elites as well as the government through a variety of detailed written sources.[6] Tobacco appealed to many both as a product and as a cash crop, also resulting in a more voluminous literature than for chiles.[7] For the chile there is a dearth of sources. Sources are thin in overall numbers as well as in the length of those that do exist. Even though gazetteers serve as an important genre for this study, chiles were more absent than present even in these local histories. The longest late imperial discussion of chiles, by far, is only 4½ pages long![8] This scarcity and brevity of sources reveals an overall trend of elite ambivalence or avoidance. Here I explore the likely sources of this reticence, revealing important aspects of elite culture that widespread acceptance and use of the chile, by the mid-nineteenth century, had begun to overcome.

Elite Culinary Reluctance

An obvious genre for analyzing chiles as a flavoring is recipe collections or *shipu* 食譜. However, chiles did not appear in works in this genre until the late eighteenth century. This lack of chiles in recipe books is underlined in a large compilation of recipes dating from the Zhou until the end of the Qing, edited by Liu Daqi. While there could be no recipes containing chiles prior to the late Ming, a large percentage of the works consulted for the compendium date to the late Ming and Qing. The collection contains 3,249 recipes, but only 3 included chile peppers. Those 3 recipes come from two texts, one published in about 1790 and the other in 1916.[9] In addition to those two texts, I have only found chiles in three other Qing recipe collections (all dating to 1863 and later; for a list of recipe collections I consulted for this book, see appendix A).

The paucity of chiles in recipe collections prior to the mid-nineteenth century reflects the general treatment, or rather lack of treatment, of chiles across late imperial genres. Chiles occurred in less than a quarter of all the local gazetteers I examined. In addition, the longest entries on chiles in a gazetteer are only half a page long, with most much shorter. Furthermore, there is an eighty-year gap between the earliest source to include chiles and the earliest gazetteer to include them. Thus although sources attest to the fact that chiles were being used widely, detailed written documentation of their use lagged behind; this was probably at least partially due to a disparity in adoption, with greater early use of chiles among the nonliterate classes.

We can see an elite reluctance toward consuming chiles through close-readings of two different sources where the authors describe local practices yet also insert their own elite class biases. One of the earliest sources to discuss chiles is Wang Lu's gardening treatise *Supplement to the History of Flowers* (1618):

> Appearance of Flowers [chapter]: . . . Vines [category]: . . .
>
> Earth Coral (*di shanhu*): It is produced (*chan*) in all the districts of Fengyang [Prefecture, Anhui]. The fruit is bright red, like coral. It is shaped like the tip of a hanging writing brush. . . . When [the fruits] first come out they are green, later they become red. [Propagation results from] planting the seeds. It is also called spindly sea vine (*hai feng teng*). The fruit has toxins and is so spicy that it cannot be put in the mouth.[10]

Wang, like Gao Lian (the first to write about chiles), was a native of Zhejiang province, but in his commentary on the chile he refers to them being grown in the neighboring, inland area, which would become Anhui province under the Qing. Even though Wang used a different name from Gao for chiles, it is quite likely that chiles spread from coastal Zhejiang to inland Anhui. Wang borrows directly from Gao's text in describing the fruit as shaped like a writing brush, and that the seeds are used for propagation. While Wang did appear to have some firsthand exposure to tasting the fruit, his categorization of the plant as a vine makes it questionable that he had actually seen chile bushes. The black pepper plant is a vine, and Wang may have been correlating flavor with plant type. The alternative name, spindly sea vine, places this misidentification into the name while seeming to correctly identify its overseas origin.[11] Like Gao, Wang gives the impression that he was personally absorbed by the aesthetic appeal of chiles (for more on this, see chapter 5). Even though he concentrated on the appearance of the fruit, he placed the chile plant in his book on flowers, in a chapter on the appearance of flowers—thus by association and categorization highlighting aesthetic appeal. Indeed, his choice to include coral in the name, and then reiterating the comparison in his description, underscores the emphasis on visual appreciation.[12] Polished coral was prized as a semiprecious stone because of its shininess and bright red color. Wang's use of coral in the name and description, like Gao's image of the fruit looking like a writing brush, highlights elite culture, as carved coral would have been nearly nonexistent outside of high-end shops and elite homes.

Given Wang's emphasis on aesthetics, it is possible to interpret the popularity of chile plants throughout Fengyang as resulting from their visual value, but if so, Wang departs from other authors who emphasized decorative qualities of chiles. For example, while Gao emphasized that the fruits "are very pleasing to look at,"[13] Wang is not explicit about their beauty, though he does emphasize that they look like coral. Other authors who focused on aesthetics stressed that people liked to raise them in pots for decoration. The verbs often employed tended to underscore rearing (*xu* 蓄) or planting (*zhi* 植),[14] whereas Wang uses the verb "to produce" (*chan* 產), the same character used in the local-products section of gazetteers. Thus it appears that many farmers were growing chiles (almost certainly for consumption) all across Fengyang prefecture. Remember that two other early seventeenth-century texts recorded fairly widespread cultivation of the chile plant: Wang Xiangjin wrote in 1621 that it was being grown in the North, and the anonymous author of the *Shiwu bencao*, also in 1621, commented that "now it is found everywhere."[15] Wang Lu's account of chiles all across Fengyang can be read as an example of an elite author recording lower-class practice.

Wang concludes his entry with his bias against the intense flavor of chiles. Here he echoes his contemporary in Korea, Yi Su-gwang, who in 1614 had described chiles as toxic and potentially dangerous, even though they were then being "grown everywhere."[16] A product under widespread cultivation in Fengyang was probably being used for more than decoration. Thus the idea that chiles "cannot be put into the mouth" was aloof elite hyperbole that ignored actual lower-class culinary practices.

We can see a similar structure of apparently accurate description of lower-class practices, contradicted by elite bias in a 1756 gazetteer from Jiangxi:

> Vegetables [category]: . . . Peppery eggplant (*jiaoqie* 椒茄): The fruit hangs from the branches [of the plant]. Among [the varieties] some are round and some are pointed. [Because it] resembles the eggplant [*qie*], *qie* is in its name [*jiaoqie*]. Locals (*turen* 土人) call the round ones "chicken heart peppers" (*jixin jiao* 雞心椒) and the pointed ones "goat horn peppers" (*yangjiao jiao* 羊角椒). When used in flavoring food [the result is] sweat and tears running together, therefore those who use them are very few.[17]

A close-reading of this passage reveals a gap between the lower-class growers of the chiles and the elite author. First, the varietal names included in the entry support the interpretation that this source includes some descriptions of local practice. The names listed, "chicken heart peppers" and "goat horn peppers," are metaphors that correlate well with farmers' lived experiences. These were things that farmers would have seen on a regular basis, and their shapes made natural descriptors for delineating the shapes of different types of chiles. These contrast sharply with Gao Lian's writing brush or Wang Lu's coral imagery—metaphors from the scholar's studio. The author's claim that "those who use it are very few" contradicts the fact he had just laid out that locals were growing at least two varieties; they would not have been growing more than one variety of a plant they were not using. Again, since there is no emphasis on aesthetics in this work, it is unlikely that the two varieties were just being grown as decorations. Indeed, "Chicken heart" and "goat horn" do not immediately evoke rhapsodies on beauty. Further, the entry for "peppery eggplant" falls in the vegetable category in the local-products section, suggesting culinary use. The gazetteer compiler's flowing sweat and tears reveals he had clearly not built up any tolerance for this extremely pungent spice. While this could just be the result of his own personal intolerance for the spice, his claim that "those who use it are very few" projected his own intolerance to encompass his fellow elites, ignoring "the locals" who "produced," named, and almost certainly consumed this intense spice.

While biases such as these help explain the lateness of chiles appearing in recipe collections, this delay was exacerbated by the fact that recipe books in the seventeenth and eighteenth centuries tended to reproduce the elite cuisine from the lower Yangzi or Jiangnan region. This cuisine emphasized subtle flavors. Since the Qianlong emperor (r. 1736–1795) strongly favored this culinary tradition, particularly that from Suzhou, literature about food from then and into the nineteenth century reflected this court proclivity. While the Qianlong emperor's taste for Suzhou food dominated his choices regarding Chinese cuisine, his tastes also reflected his Manchu heritage, including a fair amount of roast meat, and he also drank milk in his tea. Manchu cuisine, like Jiangnan cuisine, did not emphasize chiles. Another important aspect of the Qianlong emperor's diet was that his devotion to Buddhism meant that he ate vegetarian meals on festival days.[18] As we will see shortly, Buddhist dietary restrictions included avoiding strong flavors such as chiles. The lack of chiles in written versions of elite cuisine can also be seen in the acclaimed eighteenth-century novel *Honglou meng* (*Dream of the Red Chamber*) by Cao Xueqin. While this work includes a character with chile pepper in her nickname (see chapter 5), none of the many dishes described in the book includes chiles. The main characters in the novel (as well as the author) either are from the Jiangnan area or wholeheartedly endorse that culture. Therefore the recipes in the novel, like those in many of the Qing period recipe books, reflect the subtle flavors of Jiangnan elite cuisine and, unsurprisingly, do not include any chiles. Such a strong flavor was not needed to make the dishes found in recipe collections more palatable. In contrast, however, chiles were potentially important for flavoring the bland, starchy meals of the lower classes. Furthermore, several of the other newly introduced American crops—maize, white potato, and sweet potato—added new high-starch ingredients to the diets of the lower classes. Although chiles first appeared in a recipe collection around 1790, they did not gain consistent presence in recipe collections until the mid-nineteenth century. This shift demonstrates that they were becoming more and more acceptable in elite society over the course of the nineteenth century.

Another likely contributing cause for the lack of elite writing about chiles comes from the fact that several important belief systems in traditional Chinese culture deemphasize strong flavors in foods, either perpetually or at specific times. François Jullien has demonstrated that Chinese elites, in realms as diverse as thought, food, music, and painting, often sought blandness, subtlety, or *dan* 淡. In terms of flavor, Jullien asserts that for many elite authors "all flavor is simply enticing ... being nothing but that immediate and momentary stimulation that is exhausted as soon as it is consumed. But it is necessary to pass beyond such superficial excitations."[19] The first author to write about chilies in China, Gao Lian, as we saw in chapter 1, openly declared his opposition to strong flavors and did not include chiles in the sections of his work on food or medicine.

In Confucian ritual traditions, performers of certain rites needed to purify themselves through fasting and avoidance of particular activities for several days prior to the performance. The fasting generally was not a complete avoidance of food but rather an avoidance of meat and strongly flavored vegetables. Guidance to fasting often included the Chinese character *hun* 葷, which can mean meat, strongly flavored vegetables, or both.[20] According to a second-century commentary on the pre-Qin ritual text the *Yili* (Book of etiquette and ceremony), *hun* refers to pungent vegetables like scallions and the Chinese onion, and eating them interrupts rest.[21] The late Tang author of legendary tales Xue Yongruo (active 821–824) observed that to make your "disposition honest, harmonious, and pure, do not eat pungent *hun*, and regularly seclude [yourself] in a tranquil room."[22] Here Xue modified *hun* with *xin*, pungent. Since *xin* is typically associated with the flavor of plant spices rather than meat, it is likely that Xue was using *hun* as strongly flavored vegetables. In the *History of the Ming Dynasty*, completed in 1735, in the section on abstinence or fasting for rituals, the performers were admonished to "not eat *hun*."[23] While the editors were not specific about whether *hun* meant meat or vegetables or both, in the *Kangxi Dictionary*, which was published in 1716, the definition of *hun* begins with an example of a commentary on the *Record of Rites*, which states that *hun* refers to "pungent vegetables like ginger."[24] The second example in the *Kangxi Dictionary* entry for *hun* is the commentary on the *Yili* cited above.

Buddhist monastic dietary restrictions call for avoidance of meat as well as strongly flavored vegetables at all times. In addition, lay believers, including the Qianlong emperor, often followed these dietary restrictions on specific festival days. In Chinese Buddhist texts the strongly flavored vegetables are generally referred to as the "five *hun*" or the "five pungents" (*xin*). The *Śūraṅgama Sūtra* (*Lengyan jing* in Chinese) is an important Buddhist text "extolled for the profundity of its ideas, the beauty of its language, and its insight into the practice of meditation." In Chinese Buddhist tradition the text was translated from Sanskrit into Chinese in the early eighth century. However, this text was likely first written in Chinese.[25] This Chinese indigenous Buddhist text has been quite influential, particularly within Chan [Zen] Buddhism. The text includes commentary about dietary avoidance of the "five pungents": "garlic, Chinese onion, scallion, garlic chives, and asafetida."[26] Asafetida (*Ferula assa-foetida*) originated in Central Asia; the resin from the root and stem is used in Indian cooking. Thus while garlic, scallion, and asafetida were common in the cuisine of northern India, the birthplace of Buddhism, the inclusion of Chinese onion and garlic chives in this Chinese text was perhaps the result of Chinese adaptation to exclude strong flavorings prevalent in their cuisines. These strongly flavored vegetables were to be avoided because they might stimulate the passions, and also their strong smell was associated with impurity.[27]

Influenced by Buddhist practice, Daoist monastic traditions also called for avoiding the "five *hun*," but these differed somewhat from other lists. The Daoist list had no need to show precedent to Indian traditions, and the list includes vegetables that were all commonly used in Chinese cuisine. Li Shizhen, in his entry for garlic in the *Bencao gangmu*, notes that alchemical practitioners in search of immortality identified the five *hun* as garlic chives, garlic, Chinese chives, rape plant, and coriander.[28] Li goes on to say that Daoists recognized a similar list as the five *hun*: garlic chives, Chinese onion, garlic, rape plant, and coriander.[29] For all these different traditions, the injunctions against particular strongly flavored vegetables derived from the belief that ingestion of these plants interfered with mental focus. Meditation was of course an important part of monastic traditions in Buddhism as well as Daoism. A section on ritual in the *Ming History* explains the goal of abstinence before the performance of Confucian-influenced ritual offerings to ancestors as well as state-level offerings to deities or Confucian sages: "To strictly and carefully focus the mind; if there are any thoughts, they must be of the spirit that is to receive the offering, just as if it is above, or to the left or right; a pure and sincere [mind throughout the ceremony] without a single gap—this is the purpose of abstinence."[30] Although this passage applied to only a few days leading up to a particular ritual, the goal of this abstinence is comparable to the constant abstinence for the contemplative life of Buddhist or Daoist monasticism. Indeed, in his study of official state rituals honoring Confucius, Thomas Wilson's description of the purpose of fasting or abstinence also applies to the other traditions' injunctions as well: "To fast means to abstain from those activities that divide one's concentration when confronted with important matters."[31] There is a fair amount of variation in which specific vegetables were to be avoided, but a common element across all of them is strong or intense flavor. All these lists predate the introduction of chiles. However, if some considered the flavor of garlic, ginger, or coriander to be distracting from concentration, then so much more so would be the intensely spicy chile pepper. Indeed, today it is common for Chinese Buddhist monastics to avoid chiles in addition to various members of the *Allium* family. It is likely that these traditions of avoiding strong flavors, either all the time or for important rituals, in order to foster a clear, focused mind added to the proclivity of elite avoidance of eating and then writing about chiles during the late imperial period.

The Pharmacopeia and the Elusive Search for Precedent

Just as many late imperial authors kept chiles out of their recipes, so too there was a dearth of chiles in late imperial medical texts. I found chile peppers in only thirteen out of more than seventy medical texts (see appendix B). As mentioned previously, the earliest medical text to include chiles was the 1621 anonymous edition of *Shiwu bencao*. In table 4.1 I list all the editions of this work that I consulted so that changes in the editions are visible. The list includes several earlier editions that did not yet include the chile (1550, 1593, and 1620). More telling, however, are the editions published later, in 1624 and 1691, which do not include chiles even though the 1621 edition did. The 1691 edition by Shen Lilong is particularly revealing since two more editions that included chiles preceded it. These two editions, published in 1638 and 1642, included the 1621 entry on chiles verbatim. The lack of chiles in the 1691 edition of the *Shiwu bencao*, as well as in later works, particularly nine texts without chiles published from 1840 to 1869 (see appendix B), demonstrates the difficulty of integrating chiles into medical works, despite the evidence from gazetteers and other medical texts that people were clearly using chiles medicinally.

TABLE 4.1
Selection of Late Imperial Editions of the *Shiwu bencao*
(Pharmacopoeia of edible items)

Year Published	Author	Title	Chilies included
c. 1550	Anonymous [Palace]	*Shiwu bencao*	No
c. 1593	Hu Wenhuan	*Shiwu bencao*	No
1620	Qian Yunzhi	*Shiwu bencao*	No
1621	Anonymous	*Shiwu bencao*	Yes
1624	Zhang Jiebin	*Shiwu bencao*	No
1638	Chen Jiru	*Shiwu bencao*	Yes
1642	Yao Kecheng, attrib.	*Shiwu bencao*	Yes
1691	Shen Lilong	*Shiwu bencao huizuan* [compilation]	No

As with the flavoring sources, it is difficult to pinpoint the exact cause of this bias. Given the intricate connections between food and medicine, though, it seems likely that all the reasons for literati reluctance to consume chiles carried over for medicinal use as well. In addition, quite a few practitioners may have found chiles to be too intense to be used in medical formulas. They might have felt that the powerful spiciness of chiles would overwhelm other ingredients in their prescriptions. Another factor seems to have been the desire on the part of some literati to find an ingredient in a precedent-setting text before fully endorsing its use. While many late imperial authors realized that chiles had been introduced to China fairly recently, some still sought a precedent for chiles in an earlier, respected text. Though many late imperial medical practitioners probably had a favorite, go-to medical text, it is important to emphasize that no single text dominated during the late imperial period. In the twentieth and twenty-first centuries, however, there is a decided bias in favor of Li Shizhen's *Bencao gangmu* as a precedent-setting text. Although late imperial medical authors and practitioners do not appear to have had a strong preference for Li's text, a number of gazetteer editors in the early to mid-nineteenth century did treat the work as authoritative and thus a text to refer to when identifying lesser-known plants.

Li Shizhen's *Bencao gangmu* was first published in 1596. This voluminous work does not include the chile pepper. Despite its absence in Li's text, some later gazetteer authors, probably out of a desire to legitimate a plant that did not have a long pedigree in China, sought to read the chile onto lesser-used plants that Li did discuss.[32] To demonstrate how the lack of chiles in what some perceived as an authoritative text likely contributed to the chile pepper's scarcity in medical texts and other genres, I will trace the entry for "Qin pepper" through a sequence of provincial gazetteers from Yunnan.

There are no entries in either the 1576 or the 1691 edition of the Yunnan provincial gazetteers that might be the chile pepper. The 1736 edition includes the following entry in the section on vegetables: "Qin pepper (*Qinjiao* 秦椒): the common name is spiciness (*lazi* 辣子)."[33] As we have seen, Qin pepper was a name used for both chile peppers and Sichuan peppers. While *lazi* became a fairly common name for chiles later in the eighteenth century, it was also an alternative name for a variety of prickly ash known as *shi zhuyu* (食茱萸), which I translate as "edible prickly ash." This plant was sometimes used as a flavoring but more often medicinally. Its scientific name is *Zanthoxylum ailanthoides*; thus it is in the same genus as Sichuan pepper.[34] Because of the ambiguity of the provincial gazetteer entry from 1736, Jiang Mudong and Wang Siming, in their article on chile peppers, decided that they could not definitively identify this entry as the chile pepper. They actually list an 1894 departmental gazetteer as the earliest explicit written reference to chiles in Yunnan.[35] I present evidence and analysis below showing that the editors of the 1736 edition of the provincial gazetteer linked two alternative or secondary names that were generally associated with two separate plants in order to make it clear to readers that this was an entry for a third, different plant, namely, the recently introduced chile pepper.

The entry does not really make sense unless it refers to the chile pepper. If it did not identify the chile, then it is a reference either to Sichuan pepper or to edible prickly ash. However, while Sichuan pepper (*Zanthoxylum bungeanum*) was often called Qin pepper, there are no known sources that referred to it as *lazi*. Similarly, while edible prickly ash (*shi zhuyu*; *Zanthoxylum ailanthoides*) is sometimes referred to as *lazi*, there are also no known sources that referred to it as *Qinjiao*. In addition, 1736 is close to the same time that *lazi* was first recorded for chile peppers in written sources from other provinces: Hubei in 1754, Guizhou in 1756, Hunan in 1765, and Sichuan in 1758.[36] Further indirect support for the 1736 gazetteer editors identifying chiles can be found within the gazetteer itself. There is a separate entry for Sichuan pepper under the name flower pepper (*huajiao*) in the 1736 gazetteer, so it does seem reasonable that the editors used *Qinjiao* to identify the chile pepper. In addition, the gazetteer does contain other American crops, including the pumpkin, white potato, and peanut.[37] While the presence of other American crops does not prove that chiles were present as well, in the many gazetteers I examined for this book, those that included chiles also list at least one other crop from the Americas. The earliest known sources containing chiles in the neighboring provinces are either earlier or shortly after 1736: Guizhou in 1690, Guangxi in 1733, and Sichuan in 1749 (see map 1.2).[38] It is important to remember that chiles were almost certainly present in all these provinces a number of years, perhaps even a couple of decades, before they were recorded. Thus it is reasonable that chiles were present in Yunnan shortly after they arrived in Guizhou and Guangxi, two likely routes for introduction into Yunnan. It is also reasonable that chiles would have arrived in Yunnan around the same time that they arrived in Sichuan. Finally, a local gazetteer from Yunnan from 1799 definitively identifies chile peppers: "Foreign pepper: another name is Qin pepper, commonly called spiciness."[39] To circumvent any possible ambiguity, the editors added a third name in addition to the same two used in the 1736 provincial gazetteer, one that was never used for anything except chiles. The use of Qin pepper and spiciness (*lazi*) in this entry reinforces the interpretation that the earlier entry in the provincial gazetteer referenced the chile as well.

The editors of the next edition of the Yunnan provincial gazetteer, from 1835, took exception to the wording of the 1736 edition. After reproducing the text from the earlier edition, they went on to argue that "*qinjiao* is just *huajiao*. Spiciness is the edible prickly ash. Li Shizhen has clearly demonstrated this differentiation. The old gazetteer is incorrect."[40] Here the 1835 editors were apparently blinded by what they saw as the necessity to find a precedent or an authority. They sought to point to specific entries in Li's *Bencao gangmu*. Since chiles are not in Li's work, they discounted the entry from the previous gazetteer and insisted that the entry be separated into two other plants, one of which was already included in the 1736 gazetteer under another name. The result of this change in the 1835 edition was that chile peppers were no longer included, and a single entry was illogically delineated into two. There is no doubt that chiles were present in Yunnan by 1799, yet the editors of the 1835 edition of the provincial gazetteer overrode their predecessors, insisting that if a plant was not present in Li's *Bencao gangmu*, then apparently it could not exist!

The editors of the next edition of the gazetteer, from 1894, reproduced the 1835 text verbatim, still demonstrating an unwillingness to identify a plant not present in Li's text.[41] In 1901 another edition was issued, and this time the editors recorded: "Qin pepper:

[according to the] old gazetteer, it is commonly called spiciness."[42] They made no comment about the 1835 or 1894 editions and made no reference to the fact that the "old gazetteer" they were quoting was actually the one from 1736, skipping over the two later editions. Here the editors of the 1901 edition accept this entry as identifying a single plant—the chile pepper. The hurdle of identifying something new without being able to point to an appropriate authority was quite high for some gazetteer editors, particularly during the nineteenth century. Thus we find scholars in Yunnan in 1835 and 1894 essentially denying that anyone was eating chiles there, because they were not in Li's text.

By the late nineteenth century, however, the chile gained a higher profile for those searching for precedent in a medical text. Zhao Xuemin's (c. 1725–c. 1803) *Bencao gangmu shiyi* contains by far the longest late imperial entry on chiles. Even though Zhao finished his work around 1803, it was not published until 1871. As we have seen, after Zhao's work was published it was incorporated into Li's. The earliest reprint of Li's work dating from after 1871 that I have been able to consult dates from 1885 and includes Zhao's augmentations. Subsequent editions of Li's work include Zhao's expansions and thus incorporate a detailed assessment of both the positive and negative medical impacts of chiles on health. Given the high profile of Li's work in the twentieth and twenty-first centuries, the inclusion of chiles in the *Bencao gangmu* via Zhao's emendations furthered the naturalization of chiles as Chinese.

Ironically, even though Zhao explicitly wrote his supplement to Li's work in order to correct errors and omissions, even he was reluctant to state outright that chiles do not appear in the *Bencao gangmu*. He began his entry for "spicy eggplant" (*laqie*) as follows:

People commonly plant it in vegetable gardens. In mid-autumn the mountain people (*shanren* 山人) bring shoulder-poles full of them to

sell at the market to be used in cooking spicy paste and in cleaning frostbite sores. Its uses are extremely varied. However, the [*Bencao*] *gangmu* does not record these uses. Chen Jiongyao (陳炅燡), in
Shiwu yiji (食物宜忌), states that [what Li identified as] edible prickly ash
(*shi zhuyu*) is the spicy eggplant [chile pepper]. Chen is correct.[43]

Instead of stating that Li did not include chiles, Zhao, apparently
in deference to an earlier practitioner, instead argued that *Bencao
gangmu* did not record its *uses*. He deftly used another scholar
(whose text is now lost) to act as an authority in identifying the
chile (spicy eggplant), as being the edible prickly ash, which is of
course included in Li's work. Zhao glosses over the fact that the
edible prickly ash described by Li is certainly not the chile pepper
and so, not surprisingly, does not include any of the symptoms for
which chiles worked so well. Even as he acknowledged that Li's
work was incomplete, Zhao still gave a nod to the importance of
precedent.

If Zhao, the author who wrote more about chiles than any other
during the late imperial period, still sought to find chiles in Li's
work, it is hardly surprising that others pushed back against including them in their works. Across multiple genres—including medical texts, recipe collections, botanical studies, and gazetteers—
chiles had a low profile. Yet the sources that do include chiles prove
geographically widespread distribution as well as diverse uses—
from flavoring to vegetable, from appetite stimulator to miraculous hemorrhoid cure. Thus the limited sources on chiles reflect
biases in literate culture.

While the spicy nature of chiles drew Chinese to incorporate
them into their culture to the level of treating them as native, the
intensity of their spiciness also played a leading role in authors
excluding them from many works. Reticence about chiles for some

elite authors reveals the importance of a number of underlying beliefs. Paternalistic proclivities led many authors and policy makers to encourage the cultivation of newly arrived high-caloric crops such as the sweet potato, maize, and peanut. The low calories of the chile pepper meant that it could not gain the attention of elites in this context. Profit also motivated some authors. For example, many wrote about tobacco because of its perceived health benefits, and perhaps even more so when it became clear that it was a valuable cash crop. The chile, commonly grown in kitchen gardens, would not become an important source of income until the twentieth century, and even then its profitability does not compare to a wide range of cash crops. Elite traditions, which discouraged consumption of strong flavors, combined with the predilection for the delicate flavors of Jiangnan cuisine meant that many late imperial authors avoided both eating and writing about chiles. The spiritual importance of having a clear mind for self-reflection, cultivation, or meditation is exemplified in this rejection of the chile in preference for *dan* or subtle flavors.

Access to literacy and the ability to place oneself within a lineage of scholars were important avenues for elite-class perpetuation. Elites who wanted to be remembered needed to write their way into the future but also needed to demonstrate their ties to the past in order to be accepted and admired. Precedent in writing was thus extremely important, and the chile's newness kept it out of many authors' writings. Precedent demonstrated both knowledge of and access to prior works. As I have argued previously, many late imperial authors sought to place themselves into a lineage of past scholars as a means of both legitimating their scholarship and projecting themselves, through their written works, into the future— reading themselves into the past and writing themselves into the future.[44] It took scholars such as Li Shizhen and Zhao Xuemin to push beyond this requirement of precedent to write about newly introduced plants. Yet even Zhao seems to have been reticent to directly say that chiles were not in Li's work.

Just as elite reticence for chiles had multiple causes, the increasing acceptance of chiles by elite authors beginning in the late eighteenth century, and ever more so across the course of the nineteenth century, also resulted from diverse factors. By the mid-nineteenth century chile pepper usage was so prevalent across all regions of Inner China that it became harder and harder for elite authors to ignore this bright red pod. By about 1790 chiles had worked their way into the first recipe book, breaking through the Jiangnan subtle flavor bias. After 1885 Zhao Xuemin's commentary on chiles was included in Li Shizhen's work, finally granting a degree of precedent for their use medicinally. While gazetteers continued to be an imperfect source for tracing chiles, the inclusion of chiles became more and more common in that genre throughout the nineteenth century. The upward trend in inclusion of chiles in local histories is seen clearly by examining gazetteers from Shandong province.[45] As can be seen in table 4.2, the percentage of gazetteers containing chiles increased dramatically from the mid-nineteenth to the mid-twentieth century. Precedent-setting texts and increased visibility both seem to have played key roles in increased elite attention and acceptance.

Major social changes starting in the mid-nineteenth century had significant impacts on elite attitudes and practices in myriad areas, some of which also probably affected views toward chiles. During the nineteenth century changes in printing, some developed domestically and others brought in by Westerners, resulted in faster printing and cheaper prices. This made works such as Zhao's medical text, particularly as a supplement to Li's *Bencao gangmu*, more

TABLE 4.2

Chiles in Shandong Gazetteers

Years	Total gazetteers consulted	Gazetteers with chiles	Percentage with chiles
1736–1840	70	9	12.9%
1841–1912	59	18	30.5%
1913–1949	57	30	52.6%
Totals	186	57	—

accessible. The first Chinese newspaper, *Shenbao*, began publication in Shanghai in 1872. The circulation of new ideas, particularly from the West and Japan, increased. This in turn affected education, which began to shift away from the Confucian Classics—the mainstay for the traditional civil service exams.

With these changes in culture and education came a decrease in elite focus on fasting. Thus the strong flavor of chiles probably no longer held such a negative position in elite culinary choices. In addition, with the introduction of Western scientific categorization for plants, the need for precedent probably also decreased, leading more writers to engage with this spice. Although we saw earlier writers noting the similarities between chiles and eggplants, by the mid-1920s the scientific categorization of chiles as part of the "eggplant family" (*qieke* 茄科; Solanaceae) became more common.[46] By the 1930s some authors were also including a Latin scientific name for chiles—*Capsicum*—in their descriptions.[47]

Regional identity for elites also increased during the mid-nineteenth century. For example, to suppress the significant Taiping Rebellion, the central Qing government had to give up some of its power and sovereignty, particularly in the area of the military, to regional leaders. These regional leaders recruited men from their own native places to form regional armies, which then played a decisive role in the defeat of the Taipings. Two of the most renowned of these regional army leaders, Zeng Guofan (1811–1872) and his protégé Zuo Zongtang (1812–1885), were both from the chile-loving province of Hunan. These elites expressly emphasized their regional identities. Similarly, restaurants also became spaces for asserting regional identities. Restaurants specializing in regional cuisines became popular in the second half of the nineteenth century in Shanghai. By 1912, dining at Sichuan restaurants in Shanghai, which would have included eating chile peppers, became a mark of status for the city's wealthy.[48] Eating chiles had certainly shifted away from being primarily something for the lower classes. For a number of regions, Sichuan and Hunan in particular, chile consumption became an "identity food."

CHILES AS BEAUTIFUL OBJECTS
AND LITERARY EMBLEMS

If you want to eat chiles, you must not fear spiciness, if you want to become a red soldier, then you must not fear killing.

—REVOLUTIONARY SONG, 1940S

Even from the earliest record in China, chiles were valued beyond their uses in cuisine and medicine. Practices around chiles beyond food and pharmacy ranged from valuing the beauty of the pods hanging on the plant to creating new images that use its spiciness to describe women and revolutionaries. While the chile pepper initially gained a toe-hold in literati appreciation of the bright, shiny pods, it could not break through the barriers of accepted imagery in poetry or painting in significant ways. In contrast, its novelty and its ability to cross class and gender lines allowed it to take on new representations. The chile appealed across class hierarchies—being grown widely in kitchen gardens as well as in elite decorative gardens. It bent gender rules—becoming a symbol for both male revolutionary virility and female passion. Thus over time the metaphoric and emblematic uses of chiles deepened, diversified, and created new symbolic systems. The chile became metaphorically imbued quintessentially as both Chinese and revolutionary—fiery and passionate.

Aesthetics

Elite authors emphasized the visual appeal of chile pods in a number of ways that initially integrated chiles into Chinese conceptions of aesthetics. Red has long been a symbol of fertility and thus a celebratory color in Chinese culture. Traditional bridal gowns were red. Shiny red was particularly popular, be it glossy red silk fabrics or highly polished carved red coral. A few of the general names for chiles emphasize their red color and thus more concretely reflect an emphasis on visual appeal:

Red pepper (*hongjiao* 紅椒)[1]
Coral pepper (*shanhu jiao* 珊瑚椒)[2]
Crimson pepper (*chijiao* 赤椒)[3]

Authors also used colors in their descriptions of chiles. A significant majority of authors simply described chile pods as red (*hong* 紅), but a number of them used other characters, preferring the implications of more nuanced shades of red. A substantial minority of authors referred to ripe chile pods as "crimson" (*chi* 赤).[4] While *chi* is also a fairly common character for "red," it is usually a sharper or more intense color than *hong* and is sometimes described as the color of the sun or the heart.[5] Authors who described chiles as crimson rather than red evoked the beauty of the fruits.

Others chose to describe ripe chile pods as "vermilion red" (*zhuhong* 朱紅). *Zhu* or vermilion was often associated with nobility and particularly the emperor. For example, "vermilion" was the term used to describe the color of special red ink used in commentaries by an emperor; in addition, red robes worn by emperors were always termed "vermilion." Thus the use of *zhu* to describe the color of chiles could project some noble or imperial status onto chiles.

We see this quite explicitly in one varietal name: "Another variety, which is small and pointed, looks like the tip of a writing brush; it is called vermilion (*zhu*) imperial robe brush [pepper]."[6] Furthermore, with the two-character description of the color ("vermilion red"), the greater emphasis on color accentuated the aesthetic appeal of the ripe pods.

In a small number of gazetteers, all from Zhejiang province, editors selected an even less common shade of red to evoke the color of chiles: *chun dan* 純丹 or pure cinnabar.[7] Adding a second, modifying character, meaning pure or unadulterated, emphasized the deepness and intensity of the color. Cinnabar is often associated with Daoist elixirs of immortality and is used in the name for the important meditation focal point and acupuncture point below the navel known as the *dantian* 丹田 or cinnabar field. In addition, the character also forms part of the name for the extremely popular cultivated flower, the peony (*mudan* 牡丹). The choice of a color associated with transcendence and aesthetic beauty in garden spaces emphasized the attractiveness of chile pods.

In China symbols for fertility extended beyond the color red and included plants that bear numerous fruits. Individual chile plants do indeed often bear a large number of pods, which several authors commented on, including an early gardening text from 1690 that described the fruits as "gratifyingly abundant."[8] Fruits with many seeds, especially the pomegranate, were also seen as particularly auspicious in terms of representing the continuation of family lines. The numerous seeds (*baizi* 百子; literally one hundred seeds), symbolize many offspring. The same character *zi* 子, which refers to seeds here, can also mean children. While no sources about chiles make an explicit link between the many seeds in each pod and requests for many children, a number of texts commented on the abundance of chile seeds.[9]

Emphasis on the aesthetic value of chile peppers is evident in the first written account of chiles in China, both directly in the text itself and indirectly through where the author placed his references to chiles within his large work. Gao Lian's complete 1591 description reads: "Foreign pepper: [The plant] has dense growth. The flowers are white. The fruits look just like the worn-out tip of a writing brush. Their flavor is spicy (*la* 辣). Their color is red. They are very pleasing to look at. [Propagation results from] planting the seeds."[10] Although Gao mentioned that the flavor of chiles is spicy, through an examination of the overall layout of his work it becomes clear that he most valued chiles for their aesthetics rather than as a flavoring, vegetable, or medicine. In this way Gao paralleled early Spanish use. Thus shortly after their arrival in China chiles were being enjoyed in the gardens of at least a few of the Jiangnan area elites.

Gao's description of chiles occurs in the sixth section of his *Eight Discourses on Nurturing Life*. This section is titled "Discourse on the Pure Enjoyment of Cultured Idleness." Craig Clunas describes this part as commentary "on a broad range of issues of connoisseurship."[11] The chile pepper is in a section called "Flowering Plants Fit for Vases" within the larger category "On Flowering Plants of the Four Seasons." While the foreign pepper was included in a list of flowering plants, Gao's description makes it clear that it was the red fruits, rather than the white flowers, that he found "very pleasing to look at." The placement of chiles in a discourse devoted to connoisseurship underlines Gao's delight in the fruits' aesthetic appeal. Gao's fifth discourse was on food and drink, while the seventh includes a pharmacological list of ingredients. He did not include chiles in either of these discourses. As we saw in chapter 1, this is not surprising given Gao's statement about strong flavors: "As for those who flavor living creatures (*shengling*) with Sichuan pepper, fragrances or rare delicacies, these are for high officials' sumptuous dinners or for offerings to celestial beings (*tianren*). They are not for a mountain hermit (*shanren*) like me; I make no record of them at all." There is, however, one other passing reference to chiles in Gao's work. The two-character name "foreign pepper" (*fanjiao*) is listed in "An Explanation of Three Categories of Herbaceous and Flowering Plants" within the "Treatise on Daily Peace and Happiness," again underlining the beauty of the plant.[12] Wang Maohua, Wang Cengyu, and Hong Seung Tae, in their article on chiles in East Asia, argue that chiles were initially used in China as a decorative plant, not as a flavoring.[13]

While aesthetic appeal was quickly eclipsed by medical and alimentary uses, references to the beauty of the red, shiny fruit continued in subsequent sources. Wang Xiangjin's *Qun fang pu* (Assembly of perfumes) from 1621 offers a slight amendment to Gao's aesthetic assessment of chiles. Wang was from Shandong, rather than the lower Yangzi area. He passed the *jinshi* exam in 1604, so he traveled at least once to Beijing, and he also served as an official in at least one other province, Zhejiang.[14] Given his travels, it is not possible to determine where he encountered chiles. In the section on vegetables, he included the following entry: "Foreign Pepper: [it] is also called Qin pepper. It has white flowers. The fruits resemble the worn-out tip of a writing brush. They are red in color. When fresh they are pleasing to look at. Their flavor is very spicy. [Propagation results from] planting the seeds."[15] While it is clear that Wang's description was mostly derived from Gao's, Wang added that chiles are "pleasing to look at" when "fresh." He also moved the position of "very" (*shen* 甚) from modifying "pleasing to look at" to modifying "spicy," giving greater importance to the flavor yet retaining the reference to aesthetic appeal.

The earliest known medical text to include chiles, the anonymous edition of the *Shiwu bencao* (The pharmacopoeia of edible items) from 1621, which included both medical and culinary uses of chiles, also emphasized that they could be grown explicitly for visual enjoyment: "People plant them in pots as decorations."[16] Similarly, Huang Zongxi, in his late seventeenth-century collection of miscellaneous writings, included the chile plant in a list of decorative plants being grown in a garden.[17] We also find expressions on the aesthetic appeal of chiles in a number of gazetteer entries:

1776, Zhejiang (coastal, central): "Several can be placed in a pot for pleasure."[18]

1841, Guizhou (inland, southwest): quotes from Gao Lian, "pleasing to look at" and later "they are placed in pots for decoration."[19]

1859, Shandong (coastal, north): "Their color is bright red and they are beautiful."[20]

1867, Hunan (inland, central): "They are shiny and radiant. . . . Many are raised in pots for decoration."[21]

These selections emphasize striking presence, auspicious color, and abundance through multiple plants arranged together.

Refined aesthetic arts held broad appeal among late imperial elites, many of whom cultivated gardens, practiced calligraphy, wrote poetry, and painted. Chile plants certainly made inroads into gardens—catching the eye of the late Ming connoisseur Gao Lian. The threshold of acceptable, traditional subject matter for poetry and painting, however, remained too high for chiles to cross in any impactful way. Late imperial poets typically turned to Tang and Song period poetry for models, which long predate the arrival of chiles in China. Although Chen Dazhang included a short description of the chile plant in *A Collected Overview of Famous Things Passed Down Through Poetry* (1713), there are no poems about chiles in his work, nor did his text motivate numerous poets to expound on chiles in later poems.[22] I have located only one poem about chiles from the late imperial period. Similarly, the most popular Qing painting manual, *Jieziyuan huazhuan* (Manual of the mustard seed garden), first published in 1679 and expanded in 1701, did not include chiles. The most likely place for the chile plant to appear in the collection would have been the section on plants added in 1701. Li Yu (1610–1680) was the publisher of the manual, commissioned by his son-in-law. Li was a well-known dramatist and author of erotic works such as *Rou putuan* (The carnal prayer mat, 1657). He wrote the preface for the painting manual. He also penned a recipe collection, *Xian qing ou ji* (Random notes from a leisurely life), published in 1670. Although his literary predecessor, Tang Xianzu, used the chile in erotic imagery in his opera *The Peony Pavilion* (discussed later in this chapter), the spicy pods did not captivate Li's imagination. Just as the painting manual did not include the chile plant, Li Yu's recipe collection also lacked their spiciness. I have found no examples of chiles in any late imperial paintings. Chiles do occur in a few woodblock prints, but from the perspective of late imperial painters, collectors, and connoisseurs, woodblocks were but a poor substitute for paintings.

In the various botanical texts I consulted for this book, I found only a couple of fairly simple Qing-period woodblock prints, such as the one in figure 2.4, but these images were created for identification purposes and do not emphasize the visual appeal of chiles. The one higher-quality woodblock of the chile plant from the late imperial period, even though it is without color, does highlight the aesthetic value of chiles both in the image itself and via the subject matter of the book in which it appears (see figure 5.1). The late Ming artist Huang Fengchi (fl. 1621–1627) specialized in publishing books of woodblocks on a variety of themes, including Tang poems, trees, flowers, and bamboo. In addition, he published a painting manual. He published the work *Collection of Poems [and Paintings] of Annual Flowers* in 1621. It contains forty-five garden plants,

Figure 5.1 Woodblock print of a chile pepper plant. Huang Fengchi, *Caobenhua shipu* (Collection of poems [and paintings] of annual flowers), 1621, 22a. Item held in the National Library of China. Used with permission.

including the peony, iris, lotus, dianthus, a couple of varieties of lily, morning glory, the Chinese lantern plant, and the foreign [chile] pepper. Each plant is represented visually in a woodblock print, followed by a short descriptive passage in calligraphy on the subsequent page.

For his written description of the foreign pepper, Huang borrowed nearly verbatim from Gao.[23] Therefore he included the same line that chiles are "very pleasing to look at." The image provides a fair amount of detail. He clearly had seen chile plants at various stages of development, including blooming and bearing fruit. While his image is more aesthetically pleasing than simpler ones used primarily for identification, there is an element of taxonomy in his image of the chile plant as well, as he highlights Gao's attention to both the flowers and fruits by including both in his representation.

The image is typical of close-up paintings in general, as well as the other prints in this same work. The chile plant is situated in front of a typical *Taihu* naturally weathered limestone rock often installed in decorative gardens. Bamboo leaves provide background as well. In addition, a beautiful butterfly hovers above the chile plant. While stones, bamboo, and butterflies do carry various connotations in Chinese art, Huang included stones, bamboo, and an insect in many of the pictures in his book, so we should not read too much into their association with chiles.

Bamboo is a common subject in paintings and is often associated with scholars. In addition, both stones and bamboo can be symbols of longevity.[24] The butterfly can be "the emblem of a lover sipping nectar from the calyx of a flower (a female symbol)."[25] Thus there could be an indirect connection between the chile plant and sex, but again, this is not the only plant pictured with a butterfly in his work.

The only pre-twentieth-century poem on chiles is one about chile pepper paste by Wu Xingqin (1729–1803), a line from which I used as the epigraph at the beginning of chapter 2. Wu was born in Jiangsu and held official posts in Sichuan, Hubei, and Zhejiang.[26] It is likely that he developed his love for chiles in either Sichuan or Hubei, as his native Jiangsu and neighboring Zhejiang are known for mild and subtle flavors.

Supple and pointed like a horse's teat,
a red image bursting out in early autumn.
Lovers of spiciness grind with skins on,
thoroughly mix with the appropriate amount of flour.
The seasonal taste, who doesn't want it?
Wards off malaria, no need to worry.
Western Sichuan boasts about betel pepper sauce,
but its pungent fragrance doesn't compare.[27]

Although the image of chiles looking like horse teats may not evoke beauty for many readers, the subsequent idea of chiles as "a red image bursting out" perhaps could inspire a more aesthetic reading. Other elements read more like an encyclopedia entry: providing a recipe for chile paste, pointing out its medicinal use as a prophylactic against malaria, and emphasizing its seasonality. He concludes the poem by emphasizing his enthusiastic preference for chile paste as a flavoring. Although earlier Tang and Song poems could not set a precedent for poems on chiles, it would have been possible for a late Ming or early Qing poet to craft an artful homage to the chile that could have inspired subsequent poems. Unfortunately, Wu's rather pedantic attempt certainly fell far short of becoming an exemplar.

While it is worth examining these two, one-of-a-kind, late imperial works, it is important to emphasize that they are exceptions. The boundaries of tradition in the arenas of painting and poetry proved too steadfast for more than a fleeting sortie by the interloper chile. Meanwhile, in contemporary times popular imagery employing chiles has become much more commonplace. These range from pop songs, to propaganda posters, to souvenirs at a pilgrimage site, to New Year's decorations. The Hunan songs discussed below demonstrate that this upward trend in popular imagery was under way by the mid-twentieth century. I analyze more recent and even more widely disseminated songs in the next chapter on regional identity.

Chiles have appeared in some of the numerous posters erected as part of the ongoing official campaign called China Dream (*Zhongguo meng* 中国梦). This campaign is particularly associated with President Xi Jinping, who in 2013 "encouraged young Chinese people to dare to dream, work assiduously to fulfill the dreams and contribute to the revitalization of the nation."[28] In figure 5.2 chiles are hanging by the door of a house. Text included on the poster to the left of the image (not shown) includes the phrase "Good fortune will arrive at everyone's door." In addition to serving as part of the nationwide campaign, in Kunming in 2017 this poster also

Figure 5.2 "China Dream" propaganda poster on wall in Kunming, Yunnan (detail), 2017.

fulfilled a second purpose, promoting the "Civilized Kunming" (*wenming Kunming* 文明昆明) campaign to have the provincial capital city recognized nationally as a "civilized city." The whole campaign is forward looking and emphasizes change, but the style of the posters is more traditional. The older style seems to endorse the idea that maize and chiles, both American crops, are fully Chinese. The chiles in this poster, in the contexts of these two campaigns, are associated with abundance, prosperity, good fortune, and civilization or culture.

In Xi'an, the capital of Shaanxi province, in 2014 a series of posters installed in subway and pedestrian tunnels depicted "The Eight Great Oddities of Shaanxi [Culture]." The third in the series, titled "Chiles Are a Main Course," depicts a woman preparing a dish of chiles framed by two large bunches of red chiles (see figure 5.3). Lists of regional or provincial oddities are a fairly common, playful way of delineating local cultural identities. For example, boxes of regional snacks that list provincial oddities are available for purchase at many tourist sites and airports. A box of treats from Shaanxi lists ten oddities. The oddities are unnumbered, but the first on the list is "Chiles are a main course." The snack box, like the posters in Xi'an, includes a small image with each oddity. The one for chiles as a main dish is very similar to one in figure 5.3.[29]

The text accompanying the poster in Xi'an included the following competitive claim: "Although Hunanese and Sichuanese can eat spicy [food], [when] old Shaanxiers eat spicy [food] it makes others afraid of spicy noodles!" This is an example of the ubiquity of images and sayings about chiles in places where they have become part of regional identities—a theme pursued in more detail in the next chapter. The competitive aspect of the assertion evokes connotations of fierceness, fortitude, and resolve, similar to themes developed in the next section.

第三怪　辣子是主菜

Figure 5.3 Xi'an government poster *Disan guai* (The third oddity: chiles are a main course), 2014.

In 1995, while conducting fieldwork on pilgrimages to Mount Tai in Shandong province, I observed many pilgrims purchasing small, glass, red chile peppers as souvenirs (see figure 5.4). Although no one provided me with what I felt was a fully satisfactory explanation for the meaning of this souvenir, its popularity speaks to the complete authentication of the chile as people on pilgrimage to one of the holiest sites in China found it perfectly natural to purchase these replica chiles. There are several concrete reasons that these chile souvenirs were so popular at that time. First, they were inexpensive, costing only one yuan. Second, being red and shiny,

Figure 5.4 Glass chile souvenirs on Mount Tai, Shandong, 1995.

they were auspicious. Third, they could be personalized. The man in the photo, the seller, is using a brush to paint the purchaser's name, the date, and the phrase "Mount Tai souvenir" onto the chile. A possible symbolic explanation comes from the fact that the most popular deity on the mountain, the Goddess of Mount Tai, is a fertility goddess. Many of the pilgrims were climbing the mountain in order to pray for a son or grandson at the Goddess's main temple near the peak. The glass chiles look like an uncircumcised penis and might have served as a symbolic prayer asking for a son. However, while this sort of explicit imagery linking the chile and the penis is common in Korea, I have found no similarly explicit references to this parallel in contemporary China.[30]

The aesthetic value of chiles has reached new heights in the early twenty-first century, in the form of cloth or glass strings of chiles popular as New Year's decorations. These decorative strings of chiles play on the phrase "*honghong huohuo* 紅紅火火," literally "red, red, fire, fire," referring to the color and spiciness of chiles (see figure 5.5). The symbolic meaning of the strings of chiles can be translated as a wish or prayer for an "exuberant and affluent life."[31] In addition, both actual strings of chiles and these artificial ones resemble strings of firecrackers.[32] Firecrackers are traditionally set off at

Figure 5.5 Strings of decorative chiles in a restaurant in Kunming, Yunnan, 2017. Photo by Sally Bormann. Used with permission.

New Year's to chase away bad spirits and bad luck. The spicy fire of chiles is a savory echo of the blast of the firecrackers. Chiles have made their mark on an important sacred mountain and the most important holiday of the year. The visual impact of chiles was noted from the beginning of their introduction, but more as an exotic specimen. In current culture, in contrast, chiles have been domesticated and overflow as explosive, fecund multitudes in auspicious decorations.

Fierce Passion

Gendered readings of several different genres of literature reveal how chile pepper imagery both furthered the integration and naturalization of chiles into Chinese cultural practices and created new gender stereotypes. Gendered uses of chiles reveal both common gender tropes as well as some of the inherent ambiguities and inconsistencies in culturally constructed social roles. The earliest literary work to contain a reference to chiles came early in the written history of chiles in China, in Tang Xianzu's canonical drama *Mudan ting* (*The Peony Pavilion*), completed in 1598. His four most well-known operas, including *Peony Pavilion*, are collectively referred to as the "four dreams." Scenes from *Peony Pavilion* remain extremely popular to this day. Tang was born in Jiangxi in 1550, passed the national-level exam in Beijing in 1583, and was first assigned a post in Nanjing. In 1591 he wrote a memorial to the throne criticizing corruption among high officials. This enraged the Wanli emperor, who had him demoted and removed to a more remote post in Guangdong. In 1598 Tang retired from the government, returned home, and took up writing full time until his death in 1616.[33] Given his various travels, it is impossible to pinpoint where he encountered or heard about chiles.

Peony Pavilion focuses on romance, passion, sexual frustration, death, and rebirth. The female protagonist, Du Liniang (translated by literary scholar Cyril Birch as Bridal Du), is an enduring character who has often been held up as a paragon of female passion among readers and in subsequent literary works, such as *Dream of the Red Chamber*. In the preface to his play, Tang waxed eloquently about her passion:

> Has the world ever seen a woman's love to rival that of Bridal Du?
> Dreaming of a lover she fell sick; once sick she became ever worse; and finally, after painting her own portrait as a legacy to the world, she died. Dead for three years, still she was able to live again when in the dark underworld her quest for the object of her dream was fulfilled. To be as Bridal Du is truly to have known love.[34]

The Chinese term *qing*, which Birch translates in the passage above as "love," can also be rendered in English as passion, emotion, or feeling. This sentiment is often contrasted with the term *li*—rationality, reason, or logic. In Chinese literature, *qing* was often associated with women while *li* was often linked to men.

Flower imagery is integral to the work as a whole, from the title, to Bridal Du's dreaming under a flowering apricot tree, to her self-portrait with plum blossoms, to the name of her commemorative shrine, to the relevant scene for our purposes—one where a list of flowers is paired with clever descriptions. In scene 23 Du is in the underworld having her soul judged. Her claims about her death result in the underworld judge summoning the flower spirit from the garden where she had her dream:

> JUDGE: Flower Spirit, this ghost maiden claims to have died of a shock she received when flower petals disturbed her dream in the garden. Is this true?
> FLOWER SPIRIT: It is true. She was tenderly entwined in a dream of a young scholar when a chance fall of petals startled her into wakefulness. Passionate longings brought about her death.[35]

Shortly after this, Tang has the flower spirit name thirty-eight flowers, with the underworld judge replying in an alternating duet. The judge's replies reflect on some nature of each flower, or make a literary reference associated with the flower, or pun on the flower's name, and also "bring out some erotic suggestion."[36] Given the importance of flower imagery throughout the work, all the plant names mentioned in this scene by the flower spirit are described as flowers. For a number of them, however, the judge's lines actually alluded to other parts of the plant. For example, the name "willow flowers" is capped with the phrase "her waist sways and swoops."[37] A common trope describing the movement of women as they walked on their bound feet was to draw on the sinuous and supple movement of the thin branches of weeping willows.

Similarly, while the chile pepper is identified as *lajiao hua* 辣椒花 or spicy pepper flower or chile flower, from the judge's replying line it is likely that Tang was actually referring to the fruit, not the flower: "her welcome is warm."[38] In the original Chinese, Tang uses *re* 熱, heat or hot. This could refer to either the spicy flavor of the fruit or its heating properties in Chinese medicine. While *la* (spicy) would be the logical choice for describing the chile's flavor, since Tang already used *la* in the name of the flower, he would be unlikely to repeat that character in the replying line. While Tang does repeat a character from flower names in the paired replying line three times in the scene, in all three cases the repeated character is used for the end rhyme in the replying line. In this song all the replying end rhymes are "ai," so *la* could not be used as a rhyming character. Thus the lack of the repetition of *la* in the reply neither detracts from nor supports whether Tang was more familiar with chiles as a flavoring or medicine. Regardless of whether Tang played off chiles being used in cuisine or medicine, more important, for this first appearance of chiles in Chinese literature, was that they were used in a sexual innuendo in describing a woman's passion for her lover. In the line "her welcome is warm," Birch translates the character *yin* 陰 as "her," but this character could also have connoted "bodily lust" to a reader or listener.[39] This link between chiles and the passion of Bridal Du marks the beginning of a gender trope connecting chiles with female eroticism.

This use of chiles as a symbol for female fierce passion carried over in the classic eighteenth-century novel *Honglou meng* (*The Dream of the Red Chamber*; also sometimes referred to as *The Story of the Stone*) by Cao Xueqin (c. 1715–c. 1763). Cao even evokes the dreaming imagery from Tang's *Peony Pavilion* with his inclusion of "dream" in his title. Literary analysis of *The Dream of the Red Chamber* is a field of study unto itself (*Hongxue* or Redology). This work on chiles is not a place for in-depth analysis of that work; instead I analyze aspects of the novel to demonstrate how chiles were integrated into literary and gender culture. This is an extremely rich, multivolume work that contains a great deal of commentary on gender roles. A number of characters, both male and especially female, buck gender norms at some level. While the novel certainly critiques some Qing social practices, ultimately it upholds many gender expectations.[40] Many of the young women in the novel live in a garden within the large compound of the elite Jia family where they engage in activities such as poetry competitions, admiration of the plants and flowers in the garden, and even reading romantic literature such as *Peony Pavilion*. While the women in the garden, both elite family members as well as servants, are largely isolated from the male world, one young male, Jia Baoyu, also resides in the garden. Baoyu spends much of his time with women and is often described in ways usually reserved for women. Thus he often crosses gender lines. Similarly, several women in the household, outside of the garden, take on more typically male roles.

The functional head of the family is the matriarch, Grandmother Jia. One of the granddaughters-in-law, Wang Xifeng, was picked by Grandmother Jia to run the extensive household, particularly in the area of finances. Wang Xifeng was brought up like a boy in early childhood and developed into what the matriarch describes as a "family rascal."[41] This was a typically male role. Indeed her given name, Xifeng 熙鳳, is gendered masculine, meaning "splendid male phoenix." As noted in the chapter on flavoring, chiles do not occur in any of the recipes in the novel, nor are they mentioned among the decorative plants in the garden. However, there are two instances in the novel where the spiciness of chile peppers is borrowed to describe personality traits of Wang Xifeng. She is given the epithet or nickname of Feng Lazi 辣子 or Male Phoenix Chile Pepper.[42] *Lazi* can be translated literally as "spiciness" or, in the case of Feng, as "the spicy one," or even as "fierce." However, *lazi* had been used as a primary or secondary name for chile peppers in at least four provinces by the time Cao completed his work.[43] The first entry for *lazi* in the dictionary *Cihai* defines it as "a popular name (*suming*) for chile pepper (*lajiao*)." The second entry initially defines it as "the same as 剌子" (also pronounced *lazi*), which means hard-hearted. The second entry continues, returning to *lazi* with the character for spicy, stating it means "a fierce (*lihai*), or bold and vigorous (*pola* 潑辣) person," and gives the example of the description of Wang Xifeng's nickname from *Dream of the Red Chamber*.[44] The entry for *lazi* 辣子 in *Hanyu dacidian* is very similar to the one in *Cihai*, including the example from novel in the second definition, but does not mention the alternative "hard-hearted" version of *lazi*.[45] Cao Xueqin's choice of using the version of *lazi* with the character for spicy in the novel helped readers to make the association between Wang Xifeng and the chile pepper. Even if Cao Xueqin imagined the epithet as merely provoking images of fierceness, without reference to chiles, subsequent readers have certainly associated the nickname and the character with the chile pepper. An excellent example of a modern reader associating the character of Wang Xifeng with chiles can be seen in the "portrait" of the character painted by the well-known Chinese artist and cartoonist Ye Qianyu (1907–1995).[46] Large calligraphic characters in the upper right of the painting are the name of the character, "Wang Xifeng." Ye's "portrait," on the left side of the painting, represents Xifeng as a fresh, red chile pepper pointing upward. This rather phallic representation of Feng Lazi emphasizes the gender-crossing nature of her character. Incidentally, it also looks a lot like a writing brush! In readings of the novel, then, the intense flavor of the chile is used metaphorically to encapsulate the fiery, fierce, atypically female disposition of Wang Xifeng. While there is an element of critique in the epithet, it is also true that Wang Xifeng was chosen to help keep the Jia family finances under control because of her fiery nature.

Wang Xifeng, or Feng Lazi, can be read as the archetype of a particular type of woman subsequently labeled as *la meizi* 辣妹子, "spicy girl" or "chile girl." Women seen to fit this trope are stereotypically viewed as feisty, sexy, assertive, and willing to bend some female gender norms. They are at once admired and desired but also in its early form spurned for transgressions. Louise Edwards, a scholar of Chinese literature, describes Wang Xifeng as

> lively, humorous, beautiful, and charming but also unrivaled in her cunning cruelty and murderous jealousy. Her importance in the novel is paramount, for it is she, despite her youth, who controls with ruthless efficiency every aspect of the domestic purse. The multiformity of her character evolves from the contradiction between her relatively weak objective status as daughter-in-law and her

undeniable power over the Jia's domestic affairs. Her skillful man-
agement is thereby an object of both praise and suspicion, just as
her confident hold on power elicits respect and disdain.[47]

Although the novel includes complex characters crossing between
a variety of gender roles, ultimately the story upholds the patriar-
chal system and invokes fairly standard moral retribution upon
transgressors, including Wang Xifeng. Edwards argues:

> Blood served as a dual symbol of femininity—at once emphasizing
> woman's weakness and woman's power. Ailments resulting from
> menstrual irregularity dwelt on woman's nature as the "sickly sex,"
> while blood was also symbolic of the reproductive power of the
> young fertile woman. Menstrual blood was both highly polluting
> and representative of a young woman's power and, as evidence
> of its importance, considerable medical attention was given to
> regularity of the menses.
>
> In *Honglou meng* Wang Xifeng's state of health is mentioned
> several times and it is made clear that she suffered a miscarriage
> and subsequently endured chronic hemorrhaging with an uncon-
> trolled loss of menstrual blood . . . [that] symbolizes her inappropri-
> ate relationship to power and her inappropriate connection to
> yang. Her very body manifests the effects of her challenge to con-
> servative Confucian gender imperatives.[48]

While Wang Xifeng was almost certainly not consuming large
quantities of chiles (if any at all), readers of the novel associate the
intense pungency of the pods with the sobriquet for the powerful, youthful, and intense Wang Xifeng. In turn Feng Lazi's personality, power, and ability to move beyond gender norms reflected
back onto the chile pepper as a metaphor for "spicy girls." The

continuation of this spicy girls motif up to the present is examined in chapter 6.

While links between chiles and feisty women are the most common gendered trope associated with chiles, there are also examples of chiles being linked to hypermasculinity, particularly in connection with the revolution. The well-known phrase "without chile peppers there would be no revolution" is attributed to Mao Zedong. The origin of this phrase apparently came from one of the many conversations between Mao and the American journalist Edgar Snow in the Communist Shaanxi base area in 1936. The American medical doctor George Hatem, known as well by his Chinese name Ma Haide, was also present during the particular conversation. Mao's comments about chiles are recorded by Snow and also appear in biographies of Hatem. In *Red Star Over China*, Snow expounded:

> One night at dinner I heard him expand on a theory of [chile] pepper-loving peoples being revolutionaries. He first submitted his own province, Hunan, famous for the revolutionaries it has produced. Then he listed Spain, Mexico, Russia and France to support his contention, but laughingly had to admit defeat when somebody mentioned the well-known Italian love of red pepper and garlic, in refutation of his theory.[49]

Apparently Mao was not particularly knowledgeable about other cultures' cuisines, as French and Russian food is not full of chiles. Clearly he was just choosing countries that had had revolutions or civil wars. Thus, for Mao, those who regularly consumed spicy chiles could become fierce revolutionary fighters. The actual phrase about chiles and revolution appears in Hatem's biography: "Without hot pepper, he said, he could not eat, and without eating he could not make revolution. 'To me,' he quipped, 'no peppers means no revolution.'"[50] While this passage shows that Mao was applying the oft-quoted phrase specifically to himself, today in China the phrase is widely used to describe Mao's view about revolutionaries from Hunan, or even China in general.[51] Even though the gender of the revolutionaries is not specified, the vast majority of Communist fighters during the revolution were male. For men, the ability to consume large quantities of chiles reflected back onto their fighting skills and vice versa. In addition, the CCP, like most Communist organizations, was quite overt in using the color red to represent its cause.

There are a number of references to Mao singing a song about chiles to Snow at some point during the interviews. Snow records a summary of the song that also created a link between chiles and revolution: "One of the most amusing songs of the 'bandits,' incidentally, was a ditty called 'The Hot Red Pepper.' It told of the disgust of the pepper with his pointless vegetable existence, waiting to be eaten, and how he ridiculed the contentment of the cabbages, spinach, and beans with their invertebrate careers. He ends by leading a vegetable insurrection. 'The Hot Red Pepper' was a great favorite with Chairman Mao."[52] The red chile pepper of the song represents the Chinese Communist Party (or even the chile-loving Mao himself), awakening the Chinese people to their oppression and then leading them to a new existence in a postrevolutionary world.

Many of the anti-Japanese and revolutionary songs of the 1930s and 1940s borrowed tunes and even some words from previous folk songs. A prime example of this is the tune for the renowned song "The East Is Red," which began as a popular folk song, evolved into an anti-Japanese song, and later became the piece glorifying Mao.[53] A similar change can be seen in a song from Hunan that includes chiles. The original words could be described as a song about longing, a playful satire of love, or perhaps a male critique of marriage:

> If you want to eat chiles, you must not fear spiciness,
>
> If you want love from a woman, you must not fear silliness.
>
> The knife is propped at the nape of my neck,
>
> Eyebrows won't leap, and eyes won't blink.[54]

The knife at the neck could be a metaphor along the lines of marriage being like a ball and chain. The ability to eat chiles could be seen as preparing the singer for enduring marriage. In addition, the man faces these threats with a stoic resolve. However, this song, like the predecessors of "The East Is Red," evolved into a revolutionary song, which was transcribed in Hunan after 1949:

> If you want to eat chiles, you must not fear spiciness,
>
> If you want to become a red soldier, then you must not fear killing.
>
> The knife is pressed into my throat,
>
> I wouldn't care if my head comes off.[55]

In this revised version, chiles were once again linked to martial ability, but also to revolution. Red soldiers fight for the goal of a new socialist society. Spiciness is linked to a stoic fearlessness. Again, while no gender is specified in the revised version, men are strongly implied, both since a man was the singer in the original version and, more important, because fighting and killing were seen as primarily male activities.

A sign of the widespread adoption and indigenization of an imported object is its symbolic use within the host culture. Chiles have diffused widely throughout Chinese culture in areas such as aesthetics, symbolic decorations, gender tropes, and revolutionary emblems. While initial culinary and medicinal uses of chiles probably started among lower classes and worked their way up, early

Figure 5.6 Strings of decorative chiles hanging along the entrance to an inn in Lijiang, Yunnan, 2017.

Plate 1

Plate 2

Plate 3

Plate 4

Plate 5

Plate 6

Plate 7

Plate 8

第三怪 辣子是主菜

Plate 9

Plate 10

Plate 11

Plate 12

Plate 13

Plate 14

recorded aesthetic appreciation of chiles probably began in elite gardens. By the twenty-first century, however, symbolic chiles as decorations and requests for "exuberance and prosperity" have worked their way widely across classes (see figure 5.6). Although chiles did not make broad inroads into the traditional elite cultural genres of poetry and painting, their evolving symbolism played key roles in changing Chinese culture in areas such as gender tropes and promoting revolutionary spirit. Mao's phrase linking chiles to the success of the revolution and the trope of "spicy girls" demonstrate a thorough integration of the spicy pod into the culture. These unique metaphors reflect the full integration of chiles into Chinese culture.

6

MAO'S LITTLE RED SPICE
Chiles and Regional Identity

The chile pepper has developed into an essence of the Hunan
people, and a totem for Hunan culture.

—YANG XUMING, HUNAN CULINARY SCHOLAR

China has a long, rich history of regional cuisines. These arose
from variations due to a number of factors, including history, influ-
ences from local cultures, regional products, climate, and geography. In many societies, regional identity often includes some culinary components. This is certainly true for China, where records
of regional variation in cuisine date back at least to the fourth century CE, with a geographic text describing Sichuanese as "valuing
flavor" (*xiang ziwei*) and "loving spice" (*hao xinxiang*).[1] In the early
1100s the Northern Song capital had regional restaurants specializing in the local northern style, southern cuisine, and Sichuan
fare.[2] Residents of various regions in Inner China adapted their
use of chiles to mesh with a complex combination of existing practices and their environment. In Taiwan chiles filled a niche similar
to ginger, while in central, inland China chiles were more often
substituted for black pepper, whereas using chiles instead of salt
was more typical in some parts of the Southwest. Again, particular
substitutions would have been more common for a specific region,
but there would have been numerous other uses for chiles in each

of those places as well. Records of such substitutions date back to the late seventeenth century, though written accounts of chiles as distinctive components of particular regional cuisines did not appear until the mid-nineteenth century. Li Huanan's *Xing yuan lu* (Memoir from the garden of awareness) (1750) contains a number of Sichuanese recipes, but none includes chiles. In his 1848 botanical treatise, however, Wu Qijun observed that some regions used chiles differently from others: "Spicy pepper is found everywhere. In Jiangxi, Hunan, Guizhou, and Sichuan it is grown as a vegetable."[3] Here we see the first concrete record of a southern, inland regional association with the chile pepper.

Regional variation in chile use was key in its widespread adoption across Inner China. The importance of such variation is reflected in the numerous regional names for chiles. Names for chiles that were used only locally or regionally constitute 72 percent of the total names found. In contrast, in the late imperial period there is really only one name for black pepper in Chinese (*hujiao*). While regional use of black pepper certainly varied during late imperial times, the sheer number of regional names for chiles demonstrates that this foreign plant had far more regional adaptations.

This chapter begins with a short overview of Chinese regional culinary styles, including examination of chiles generally within those traditions, and then turns to analyzing their role in identity formation for the two regions most associated with chile culinary use—Hunan and Sichuan.

Overview of Chiles in Regional Cuisines

Culinary experts divide Inner China into a varying number of distinct, regional culinary styles; four regions, often labeled with the four cardinal direction points, is common, but so are categorizations with five or eight regions.[4] It is not my intent to attempt to sharply delineate all the regional culinary varieties in China, for, as Eugene Anderson observes, "One person's subregion is another person's region, while a third may not think the area's cooking is distinctive at all."[5] However, prior to delving into the regions where chiles have a high profile, I briefly touch on chile usage in other regions. Both Anderson and Frederick Simoons acknowledge the difficulty in delineating regional cuisines in China, but both settle on the widely used "four great culinary traditions" (*sida caixi*) while acknowledging variation within each region.[6] While scholars sometimes label the four great traditions using the cardinal points, in reality no restaurant owner would use such a label, choosing instead a narrower geographic marker such as Sichuan, Hunan, Beijing, Shanghai, or Canton (Guangzhou). In addition, within any particular region, restaurants typically advertise subregional specialties. For example, in Sichuan a restaurant might promote Chengdu or Chongqing dishes. In this rather rudimentary system, a much smaller area within the region is commonly taken as representative of the whole. Within these four divisions, only the western region is considered to include a high level of spiciness.

Northern cuisine has a major distinction from the other cuisines that is largely due to climate: it is in the cooler and drier North where wheat is grown and rice is not. The area for northern cuisine typically includes Zhili (Hebei), Henan, Shandong, Shanxi, and Shaanxi. In the North Beijing dominates, so *jingcai* or capital cuisine is a common name for this regional style. Noodles are important, and there has been a fair amount of influence from Mongolian, Manchu, and Chinese Muslim cuisines. Writing in the early twentieth century, Xu Ke described northerners as "preferring onions and garlic."[7] A good example of how using just four categories can be misleading is the fact that chiles are prevalent in some Shaanxi cooking even though it is categorized as northern.

The eastern region is dominated by the subtle, Jiangnan elite cuisine favored by the Qianlong emperor. Generally this primarily coastal region includes Jiangsu, Anhui, Zhejiang, and Fujian, with Taiwan sometimes added as a subset of Fujian. Here seafood, vinegar, sugar, and rice are all important. Xu Ke observed that "[Jiang]su people have a taste for sugar."[8] Again, there are of course exceptions: Wu Xingqin, the author of the poem on chile pepper paste discussed in earlier chapters was originally from Jiangsu but was clearly an avid consumer of chiles (although he probably developed his taste for them elsewhere).

Southern cuisine usually includes Guangdong and Guangxi. It is also known as Cantonese cuisine and thus emphasizes the cuisine from the capital of Guangdong, Canton (Guangzhou). Seafood plays a very important role. Cantonese food is often characterized by wide variety and the freshness of ingredients, but lack of spice. Xu depicted the Cantonese as "preferring lightly flavored foods."[9] Again, the cardinal direction categorization falls short, as until the twentieth century Guangxi was essentially landlocked and therefore seafood was less prevalent than in Guangdong, and chiles are fairly common in Guangxi cuisine.

These three regional cuisines—northern, southern, and eastern—are stereotypically not spicy, particularly eastern and southern, and especially in the cores that are representative of the regions. Those with a high tolerance for spice sometimes mock Cantonese speakers for not being able to handle even a modicum of spiciness. In Chinese they are described (usually condescendingly) as *pa la*, literally "afraid of spice." In this phrase *la* or "spicy" is standing in for the chile pepper, *lajiao* or "spicy pepper." Chiles, however, are still important in all these cuisines, even if they are not regional identity markers. For example, fresh chiles in a range of varieties are now available throughout the year in markets in Beijing. The so-called white chile, which is now popular, is a pale yellow variety of *Hangjiao* or Hangzhou chile that is not very spicy. Hangzhou lies in the center of the Jiangnan or eastern culinary region. Hoisin sauce, which is prevalent in Cantonese cooking, often contains a little chile pepper. What contrasts these three regional cuisines from the western region in terms of chiles is not lack of use but less emphasis and a much lower level of spiciness. Northern, eastern, and southern cuisines all employ chiles, but generally cooks in these regions use fewer of them and often choose less spicy varieties, such as the white chile.

Currently, chiles are becoming more prevalent in cuisines across the traditionally nonspicy parts of Inner China—not to the same level as in Hunan or Sichuan, but certainly to a greater degree than even twenty years ago. Several Chinese friends and acquaintances from traditionally non-spice-consuming areas have commented to me that they have a higher tolerance and affinity for chiles than their parents. This is due to a variety of factors, including greater circulation of people for work, dramatic increases in domestic tourism, increasing numbers of restaurants specializing in regional cuisines that include chiles (such as hot pot restaurants), increased availability of regional sauces such as chile paste, and greenhouses that make fresh chiles available year round. Regional differences still hold, especially their perceptions. While Chinese all across Inner China are consuming more chiles, they are not yet identity foods for people outside of the core, inland spicy area.

While the main focus of this chapter is examining and analyzing regions where the chile has become an identity food, it is worth briefly speculating why the typically nonspicy regions did not develop as strong a preference for these pods packed with flavor. The northern region is less humid and is influenced by Mongolian and Manchu cuisines that typically did not employ strong flavoring. Both the eastern or Jiangnan region and the southern or Cantonese region, like the western chile-eating region, are quite humid. Thus it seems that people in the eastern and southern regions would also benefit from the damp-expelling abilities of chiles. Here we have an example of how the environment can be an important contributing factor in some cases but is not a uniform influencer of practice. The humidity of the coast can be different from that of the interior. In addition, access to the ocean made salt readily available in the East and South. Thus in the late Ming, when salt prices increased and in reaction the potential for seeking a substitute increased, places directly on the coast probably did not experience as steep an increase in the price of salt and therefore would have had less pressure to adopt the newly arrived chile as a substitute. In addition, long-established culinary proclivities such as the desire for subtle flavors in the elite-dominated East and for fresh ingredients in the South, made the hurdle for adopting chiles quite high. The emphasis on fresh foods in the South meant less need for preserving foods. As we will see, for Sichuan in particular, preservation methods can impart strong flavors to the food and thus make people more accustomed to such flavors and potentially more open to new, strong flavors.

The western region generally includes Sichuan, Hunan, Hubei, Yunnan, Guizhou, and sometimes Jiangxi. The major characteristic distinguishing this region from the other three is the much greater use of chile peppers. Xu Ke asserted that people from this western region "have a taste for pungent and spicy (*xinla*) items."[10] An important geographic difference is that this whole region is inland, removed from the sea. Climatically much of it is hot and humid in the summer while cool but damp in the winter. As we saw in the chapter on medicine, Chinese classify chiles as having excellent drying capabilities, and they are often seen as an essential component of the diet for those living in humid and damp environments. In addition, chiles are capable of heating the body if it is cold. Perhaps somewhat counterintuitively, chiles can also cool the body if it is warm, by causing the individual to sweat, which in turn cools the body as the sweat evaporates. In addition, long-standing practices employ strong flavorings, particularly in Sichuan.

The provinces where identity is most associated with chile eating are all those from the western culinary region, plus the southern parts of Shaanxi. A modern popular saying playfully pits chile-loving provinces against one another in their love for spiciness. The saying does not lend itself to an elegant English translation. In Chinese, the last part of each line is a word play that changes the position of just three characters: *bu* (not), *pa* (fear), and *la* (spicy food):

> Hunan people don't fear spicy food.
> Guizhou people spicy food don't fear.
> Sichuan people fear nonspicy food.
> Hubei people nonspicy food fear.[11]

In the original Chinese, fearing nonspicy food is more intense than not fearing spiciness, so in this version Sichuan and Hubei people can be seen as requiring more heat than people from Hunan and Guizhou. Needless to say, such claims are widely disputed, and other versions of the saying circulate in different places. For example, another version switches Hunan and Sichuan and drops Hubei completely,[12] a third replaces Hubei with Jiangxi,[13] and another inserts Shaanxi in the final slot.[14] In her book on Hunan cuisine, the version recorded by Fuschsia Dunlop places the Hunanese in the final spot as the greatest lovers of chiles.[15]

Even though Shaanxi falls into what most writers refer to as the nonspicy, northern culinary style, in the southern half of the province, including the capital Xi'an, chile eating is actually quite prevalent. Geographically, this southern area includes the Wei River valley and areas to the south. The earliest source for chiles in Shaanxi (1694) comes from south of the Wei River.[16] Climatically,

Shaanxi is much drier than most of the other chile-eating areas. So chile consumption probably developed for different reasons than for the moister regions to the south. Some people speculate that chiles helped make very popular but potentially bland local dishes such as broad noodles (*biangbiang mian*) and steamed bread (*mantou*) much more palatable.[17] In addition, chile plants are drought tolerant, so in low-water years chiles might have been an even more important source of vitamins A and C. As we saw in figure 5.4, "The Eight Great Oddities of Shaanxi [culture]" includes chiles as the primary ingredient in a dish, rather than just as a seasoning. The popularity of eating chiles in southern Shaanxi was well established by the mid-nineteenth century, as we can see from a local gazetteer: "All the people must eat them [chiles] with every meal!"[18] Thus no single factor, whether cultural or environmental, can explain the degree to which people in a particular region adopted and adapted the chile. Instead, a combination of cultural, environmental, and geographic factors influenced chile pepper use. In addition, Ho Ping-ti made a strong case for some serendipity in the adoption of new crops.[19]

With the economic reforms in the 1980s came increased commercialization and eventually larger grocery stores. This in turn led to the expansion of the availability of regional specialty food items across the country. A number of companies have created important niches for brands and products through promotion of particular spicy regional flavorings, including condiments, sauces, and preserved vegetables. One of the most well-known brands and success stories is that of Tao Huabi's Lao Ganma (Godmother) brand of chile paste. Tao, born to a poor family in a remote village in Guizhou, expanded her business from a noodle stand, to a restaurant, to factories employing more than two thousand workers and producing one of the most popular, nationally recognized, brands of chile paste. An article about her in a journal published by the government All China Women's Federation describes her as "the acknowledged empress of a chili sauce Empire."[20] Through her promotion, a regional adaptation of chiles has gained national attention. Chile paste is a condiment that lends itself well to a wide range of tastes, as individuals can add just as much as they desire.

In an article on the distribution of pungent and spicy flavor in China, Lan Yong analyzed a twelve-volume series of cookbooks published in the 1970s and 1980s, one book for each of twelve regional cuisines. Based on his analysis of the cookbooks in this series, he determined that the area with the greatest use of chile peppers includes the seven provinces mentioned above: Sichuan, Hunan, Hubei, Yunnan, Guizhou, Jiangxi, and Shaanxi (which Lan also delimits to the southern portion). In addition, for this spice-eating area he adds the southern mountainous portion of Anhui and the southern mountainous section of Gansu. In Lan's analysis, Sichuan cuisine stands out as far and away the spiciest of the twelve. Hunan is a fairly distant second but quite a bit higher than third-place Hubei (Yunnan and Guizhou were not included as separate cuisines in the cookbook series).[21] While Lan's analysis is useful for distinguishing some relative rankings in terms of spiciness, his measuring system is rather idiosyncratic, and the recipes in the collections are probably not a perfect match for average consumption. However, the top two provinces for chile consumption that he identifies, Sichuan and Hunan, are indeed the two provinces whose regional identities are most closely associated with chile peppers. Even though the chile is also a food identity for other places in China, such as southern Shaanxi, Guizhou, and Hubei, and the spiciest dish I have eaten in China was from Guizhou, I focus on Sichuan and Hunan as iconic examples largely because the external labeling tends to emphasize these two regions when it comes to chile consumption.

The explicit association of chile eating with regional identities in written sources is a twentieth-century phenomenon. As chiles did not originate in China, their development as authentic components of regional cuisines is, as Fabio Parasecoli has argued, culturally constructed.[22] In addition, Taiwanese historian Lu Yaodong asserts that authenticity (*zhengzong*) for regional cuisines did not develop until it needed to be distinguished from another cuisine.[23] Chiles became a marker for the constructed authenticity of the regional cuisines of Hunan and Sichuan as the modern Chinese nation-state identity was emerging. In the case of chile consumption in Hunan and Sichuan, that constructed authenticity has really only been in the last one hundred years.

Hunan

Chiles arrived in Hunan relatively early, probably in the 1660s–1670s.[24] It is likely that chiles entered Hunan from coastal Guangdong as the date for the earliest source there predates the one for Hunan, while the earliest sources for all the other provinces neighboring Hunan are later (see map 1.2). In addition, the two earliest sources in Hunan both identify chiles as *haijiao* or sea pepper.[25] While it is possible that this name acknowledges the overseas origin of chiles, the only gazetteers that used it are all from the interior, so it is more likely that the name emphasized that chiles were introduced to the interior from the coast; via Guangdong in the case of Hunan (see map 2.2).[26]

While Hunanese are indeed extremely fond of chile peppers, many of them also emphasize that "it's their neighbors in Sichuan and Guizhou who use chiles to painful excess, while they themselves apply the spice with grace and subtlety."[27] This assessment reinforces Lan's finding that Sichuanese consume spicier food than

Hunanese. While there are plenty of Hunan dishes that do not include chiles, a lunch or dinner without chiles in at least one dish is virtually unknown. Even though most Hunanese see the Sichuanese as eating more chiles than they do, chile consumption is still an important marker of Hunan regional identity. Indeed, Yang Xuming, a Hunanese culinary scholar, asserts that "the chile pepper has developed into an essence of the Hunan people and a totem for Hunan culture."[28] Another scholar, Liu Guochu, describes chiles as the "soul of Hunan cuisine."[29] Dunlop, in her book on Hunan cooking, refers to chiles as "the culinary symbol of Hunan province." She also shares the anecdote that "locals even joke that the statue of a blazing red torch that adorns the Soviet-style Changsha [provincial capital] train station is, in fact, meant to represent a chili."[30]

The people living in what is now called Hunan have a long history of using more intense flavorings in their cuisine. The classic poetry collection, *Chuci* (Lyrics of Chu) includes references to several intense flavorings, including mugwort, smartweed, and Sichuan pepper.[31] The poems in the *Chuci* date from the third century BCE through the second century CE. The ancient state of Chu covered a fairly large area that encompassed most of modern-day Hunan, Hubei, and Jiangxi. The ancient residents of this region probably found that the compounds in these plants helped to preserve food in the humid climate. Thus when chiles arrived in Hunan, they fit into an existing culture of strong flavors—albeit perhaps not a cuisine as pungent as ancient Sichuanese food.

Hunanese use all the various forms of chiles described in chapter 2, including fresh, dried, ground, and pickled. Indeed, the 1765 edition of the *Chenzhou Prefectural Gazetteer* notes that "the pod is sliced and used to flavor food in sauces, vinegar, sesame oil, and pickled vegetables."[32] Today chiles preserved in salt is a style of preparing chiles particularly associated with Hunanese cooking.

The name in Chinese for these salted chiles, *duo lajiao* 剁辣椒, literally means chopped chiles, but it is the salt that gives them their distinctive flavoring and color (see recipe in box).[33] The salt preserves them for up to several months so that many of the characteristics of fresh chiles can be enjoyed through the winter. In addition, the process preserves and often intensifies the bright red color. It is a common form of chiles used in many Hunan dishes.

In addition to using chiles as flavoring, Hunanese consume them to counteract the health effects of living in a humid climate.[34] As we saw in chapter 3, within the traditional Chinese medical

HUNAN SALTED CHILES

1000g fresh, facing heaven chiles
170g ginger
1–2 bulbs of fresh garlic
100g salt

Wash and dry chiles.
Cut off stems, then coarsely chop.
Finely chop ginger and garlic.
Mix chopped chiles, ginger, and garlic, then add in salt.
Place in container and seal.
Store for two weeks before using.

STEAMED FISH WITH CHOPPED SALTED CHILES

1 whole lemon sole
1 Tbsp. Shaoxing wine
¾ in. piece fresh ginger
1 whole scallion
½ tsp. black fermented beans
4 Tbsp. chopped salted chiles [*duo lajiao*]
Peanut oil for cooking

system chiles are extremely effective at expelling damp.[35] In addition, in his article on chiles in Hunan, Chen Wenchao argues that "climate is a major cause for Hunan people's particular preference for spicy flavors. Hunan is classified as a continental, subtropical, moist, monsoon climate zone. Atmospheric humidity is high. The summer is scorching hot, while the winter is frigid. Within the human body damp and cold are not easy to expel. Chiles, however, are just right for effectively expelling cold and causing perspiration."[36] Seen as an essential part of a healthy Hunanese diet throughout the year, chiles became part of regional medical treatments adapting to local conditions. Marta Hanson, in her study of epidemics in Chinese medicine, argues that what she calls "'geographic imagination' classified regional variations and assimilated local exceptions into systematic doctrines. The physician could then work out a response that he, and sometimes his colleagues, could follow."[37] Chen also argues that economics, affected by geography, played an important role in the spread of chiles in Hunan:

In earlier times Hunan included many places where transportation for the circulation of commodities was not easy or smooth; [for example,] sea salt and nonlocal seasonal vegetables were difficult to import. In addition, [many residents] had comparatively low purchasing power. Farmers thought of the flavor of chiles as a good and cheap [alternative]. Chiles can be used as a substitute for salt in a variety of dishes and at different levels of cooking. In Hunan, where the growing season is long, chiles are easy to grow. Thus, as soon as chiles entered Hunan they quickly spread throughout [the province].[38]

Thus a synthesis of climatic, geographic, economic, and cultural factors aided in the rise in the importance of chiles in Hunan.

Chiles in Hunan lie at the intersection of food, memory, and identity. The most renowned Hunanese from the recent past, Mao Zedong, is inexorably enmeshed within the identity of Hunanese as consumers of extremely spicy food. In popular accounts, the food Mao ate, hot chile peppers in particular, is linked directly with his identity. According to Hunanese food writer Liu Guochu, Mao even put chile flakes on his watermelon! A commonly repeated story about Mao is that a doctor once recommended that he should cut back on his consumption of chiles, to which Mao rhetorically demanded, "If you are even afraid of chiles in your bowl, how will you dare to attack your enemies!?"[39] Furthermore, he also famously asserted that "no [chile] peppers means no revolution" (for more on this, see chapter 5).[40] Thus the ability to enjoy spiciness became associated with the lack of fear necessary to promote change in China. Mao also teased the German-born Otto Braun, a Comintern agent sent by Moscow to advise the Chinese Communist Party on military manners, for his inability to eat spicy food. In his autobiography Braun wrote that Mao declared that "the food of the true revolutionary is the red pepper," and furthermore, that "he who cannot endure red peppers is also unable to fight."[41] Hunanese military leaders are still valorized as particularly effective, such as Zeng Guofan, or effective and fierce, including Zuo Zongtang and Mao Zedong. One article that emphasizes the link between chiles and recent strong Hunan military leaders states that there is a popular saying, "Throughout their lives Hunan people have three specialties: eating spicy food, reading books and conquering the world." The article goes on to argue that the Hunanese military men "Zeng Guofan, Zuo Zongtang, Huang Xing, Song Jiaoren, Cai E, Mao Zedong, Liu Shaoqi, Ren Bishi, Peng Dehuai, He Long, and Luo Ronghuan . . . all thoroughly exhibit the distinctive 'spicy' disposition of Hunan people."[42] Here chiles are linked with male martial attributes. The ability to eat chiles is linked with bravery, skills on the battlefield, and revolutionary resoluteness. We see a similar association between chiles and revolution in the second of the two popular Hunanese songs analyzed in chapter 5.

Hunan native Zuo Zongtang (1812–1885) is the general referred to in the name of the well-known dish in Chinese American restaurants, General Zuo's [Tso's] chicken. Zuo initially organized a Hunan regional military force under fellow Hunanese Zeng Guofan and used it to success against the Taipings (1850–1864). He subsequently led his Xiang [Hunan] Army against Muslims in Gansu and Xinjiang.

Hunanese chef Peng Chang-kuei first invented the dish General Zuo's chicken in Taiwan in the 1950s. He subsequently brought it to the United States in his restaurant in New York City, where he sweetened the dish for the American palate. The chicken in this dish is breaded and deep fried, then flavored with a sweet and slightly spicy sauce. This extremely popular dish is now a hallmark of "Hunan cuisine" in the United States, where it is even available in some grocery store deli counters. But the general himself never had the opportunity to try his eponymous dish.[43]

Authenticity for Hunan restaurants outside of Hunan emphasizes chiles, but they will often also rely on the chairman for further authenticating their fare. Many restaurants list certain dishes as favorites of Mao, others reference Mao in their names, while some even have busts of him on prominent display. Such busts or images in menus (see figure 6.1) emphasize Mao as an emblematic Hunanese gourmand and a revolutionary leader, and sometimes they also enshrine him like a deity. A Hunan restaurant as a site for a shrine for this revolutionary leader emphasizes the association of Mao with chiles, underscoring the importance of chile consumption for Hunan identity.

Figure 6.1 Mao on frontispiece of the menu from the Financial District Mao Family (Hunan Restaurant), Beijing, 2015.

A playful popular song from the 1990s emphasizes this importance:

辣椒歌	**Chile Pepper Song**
远方的客人，你请坐，	Guest from afar, please sit down and
听我唱个辣椒歌	listen to me sing a chile pepper song.
远方的客人你莫见笑，	Guest from afar, do not mock my
	performance,

湖南人待客爱用辣椒	when Hunanese entertain guests they love to use chiles.
虽说是乡里的土产货,	They can be called a home town local product, and
天天可不能少	day-in, day-out, it cannot be diminished.
要问这辣椒有哪些好?	[You] might ask, what benefits come from these chiles?
随便都能数出几十条	[I] could easily list out dozens:
去湿气, 开心窍,	expel damp qi, clear the mind,
健脾胃, 醒头脑.	strengthen the appetite, stimulate the brain.
更有丰富的维生素, 营养价值高.	Even more, they are rich in vitamins, and their nutritional value is high.
莫看你辣得满头汗, 胜过做理疗!	Even though the spiciness makes your whole face sweat, the result will be a victorious cure!
青辣椒, 红辣椒, 豆豉辣椒, 剁辣椒.	green chile, red chile, Dougu chile [paste], chopped [salted] chiles.
油煎火爆用火烧, 样样有味道.	Quick stir fry with fire, then everything has a wonderful flavor.
莫道辣椒不算菜, 一辣胜佳肴	Without chiles it is not a dish, with spice it is a superb delicacy.
远方的客人, 你莫见笑,	Guest from afar, do not mock my performance,
湖南人实在爱辣椒	Hunanese truly love chiles.
就连说话也带点辣椒味	These linked lines even carry a little chile flavor:
出口哇哇响, 听起火燎燎.	utter crying sounds, hear the firecrackers' bangs.
只要你仔细品品味	[I] only ask you to carefully savor the flavor.

你就会发现这辣椒的后面	You have now discovered the back-
	ground of the chile pepper.
心肠好.	[Now your] heart is attuned.[44]

This song overtly links chiles with regional identity, insisting that "Hunanese truly love chiles," that chiles are "a home town local produce," that "without chiles it is not a dish," and that Hunanese hosts love to entertain guests with chiles. The lyricist, Xie Dingren, is a Hunanese himself. The frame of welcoming guests echoes a well-known line from Confucius about the joy when friends visit from afar. Ironically, traditional Confucian-educated elite often avoided chiles for spiritual purity and mental clarity. The singer insists that the guests need to learn about chiles through the song in order to better appreciate and tolerate them. The song demonstrates that people understand the many positive health impacts from daily consumption of chiles. Like Mao's insistence that chiles are necessary for revolution, the lyricist uses a military metaphor of victory to describe the healing powers of chiles.

The song also presents the most explicit link between strings of New Year's firecrackers and strings of dried chiles in the lyrics and in the video:

These linked lines even carry a little chile flavor:
utter crying sounds, hear the firecrackers' bangs.

While the image for a video on the internet is just the same still photo throughout, the focal point is a large string of chiles hanging at the front of a restaurant.[45] In both the language of the song and the video editor's choice of images, the intense flavor of chiles is linked to the sharp sound of firecrackers.[46] Musically, through dynamics, rising and falling tones, and exclamations from band members, the composer and performers emphasize differences between various forms of chiles that can be used in cooking—red, green, salted, or as a paste. This variety should allow for varying palates among the visitors. While this song is at times joyously irreverent in its aesthetic qualities—including some playful yodeling and trombone glissandos—ultimately it implies concrete, positive impacts from consuming chiles—realigning the tastes and hearts of guests from afar.

As noted at the beginning of this section on Hunan, many Hunanese see themselves as being more subtle in their use of chiles than their neighbors in Guizhou and Sichuan. The song also emphasizes that chiles are perhaps more important for their flavor than their spicy heat, although of course the two aspects are linked. The singer insists that after quick cooking "everything has a wonderful flavor," and he asks the guests "to carefully savor the flavor." Even Mao, like most Hunanese today, did not only eat very spicy dishes. One of his favorite dishes, red-braised pork (*hongshao rou*), is quite mild. This dish is so often associated with Mao that many Hunan restaurants now call it "Mao family red-braised pork."[47] This dish is a good example of how chiles can be used as flavoring without making a dish spicy. In one recipe, despite its mildness, chiles are actually included in two forms: dried and as a paste.[48] Just as culinary styles outside of the so-called spicy zone use chiles for flavoring, Hunanese cooks often seek nuanced flavors from chiles, not merely spice.

While the chile-eating abilities of Hunanese men are seen as important for stimulating revolution, Hunanese women are also often linked with chile peppers. The spicy girl motif, introduced in chapter 5 in reference to the character Wang Xifeng (Chile Pepper Feng) from *Dream of the Red Chamber*, continues up to the present. An article in a publication put out by the All China Women's Federation (ACWF) in 2004 linked Hunanese women with the spiciness of chiles. The ACWF is a bureaucratic body with representation from the local to national levels. It is officially described as "a mass organization that unites Chinese women of all ethnic groups and from all walks of life, and strives for their liberation and development. The mission of ACWF is to represent and uphold women's rights and interests, and to promote equality between women and men."[49] One of the ways the federation goes about fulfilling its mission is through publication of a number of monthly magazines for women, including one in English titled *Women of China*. In 2004 this magazine published an article with the English title "Hunan's 'Spicy' Women." While the article is in English, there is also a Chinese title for the piece: "Hunan nüren: huola ru jiao, rouqing si shui," which translates as "Hunan women: fiery-spicy like chiles, tender like water."[50] Much of the article focuses on these widely held stereotypes of Hunanese women— that they have a fiery disposition but are tender to those whom they love. The authors also include Chinese in a few of the section headings in the article. In one of these they link Hunan women with the "spicy girl" or *la meizi* trope: "'Xiang meizi' de 'la,'" or "The spiciness of Hunan girls."[51] The *mei* in *meizi* translates as "girl" or "younger sister."

The authors explicitly link the generalized character of Hunanese women with chiles in image and text. In the lead photograph for the article the viewer looks in through a window at a woman working; hanging around the outside of the window are numerous strings of red chile peppers. In the text we see some of the same traits that resulted in Wang Xifeng's sobriquet "Chile Pepper Feng," attributed to Hunanese women:

> Hunan girls and local peppers are said to have too much in common—good-looking and appetite-whetting, but not easily digestible. Despite gentle appearances they both actually harbor the elements of heat.

> In China, Hunan girls have the reputation of being generally strong-willed and determined. They are also said to be transparent—they don't conceal their joys and sorrows. When looking for a husband, for instance, they are quite straightforward. They are bold and decisive in their actions. . . .
>
> Women in Changsha, the capital city of Hunan, hold the reputation of being the most typical. They give the impression of being "sharp" and would never act weak and gentle before their husbands.[52]

There is a similar feistiness between this stereotype and Wang Xifeng. In addition, there is a degree of warning to men who might marry a woman from Hunan, just as there was a "sharp" edge to Xifeng. However, the moral critique and retribution present in *Dream of the Red Chamber* are absent in this article. Thus the modern "spicy girl" is assertive, passionate, desirable, and sharp but is not seen as transgressing boundaries.

At the end of the article the authors include short biographies of several well-known Hunanese women. One of these is the renowned pop singer Song Zuying, who is of Miao ethnicity and is known for singing Miao folk songs, popular songs, as well as patriotic songs. One of the songs especially associated with her, particularly since she is from chile-eating Hunan, is "Spicy Girls" (*La meizi*). Song sang this piece three times during the national broadcast of the extravaganza program for celebrating the Chinese New Year in 1995, 1999, and 2009. These annual broadcasts include a variety of singers performing folk and patriotic songs, reaching a huge national audience. The spicy girls of the song are similar to the Hunan women in the article, but with a little more spunk:

辣妹子 *La meizi*	Spicy Girls
哎~~	Aiiii!

辣妹子从小辣不怕	Spicy Girls, from youth, unafraid of spice.
辣妹子长大不怕辣	Spicy Girls, growing up, not afraid of spice.
辣妹子嫁人怕不辣	Spicy Girls, as married women, afraid of unspicy.
吊一串辣椒碰嘴巴	Teasing with a string of chiles as a test of love.
辣妹子从来辣不怕	Spicy Girls, always unafraid of spice.
辣妹子生性不怕辣	Spicy Girls, natural disposition, not afraid of spice.
辣妹子出门怕不辣	Spicy Girls, when they left to be married, afraid of unspicy.
抓一把辣椒 会说话	With a handful of chiles, speak their minds
辣妹子辣 辣妹子辣	Spicy Girls are spicy, Spicy Girls are spicy!
辣妹子辣 妹子 辣辣辣	Spicy Girls, Girls, spicy, spicy, spicy!
辣妹子辣 辣妹子辣	Spicy Girls are spicy, Spicy Girls are spicy!
辣妹子辣哟 辣辣辣	Spicy Girls are spicy, YO! spicy, spicy, spicy!
辣出的汗来汗也辣呀 汗也辣	Even their sweat is spicy, ya! Sweat is spicy too!
辣出的泪来泪也辣呀 泪也辣	Even their tears are spicy, ya! Tears are spicy too!
辣出的火来火也辣呀 火也辣	Even their passion is spicy, ya! Passion is spicy too!
辣出的歌来歌也辣 ~ 歌也辣	Even their songs are spiiiicyyy! Songs are spicy too!
辣妹子说话火辣辣	Spicy Girls speak: fiery, spicy, spicy!
辣妹子做事泼辣辣	Spicy Girls' doings: bold, spicy, spicy!
辣妹子待人热辣辣	Spicy Girls interact: hot, spicy, spicy!
辣椒伴她走天下	Chiles go with them out in the world.
辣妹子辣 辣妹子辣	Spicy Girls are spicy, Spicy Girls are spicy![53]

La meizi could also be translated as "spicy girl" in the singular. I opted for the plural form in my translation in order to emphasize the fact that the song is about a type of woman rather than a specific woman. This interpretation is supported by the MTV-like music video starring Song Zuying.[54] While she is the focal point of the video, she is surrounded by dozens of other spicy girls who all engage in various stages of processing chile peppers and presenting them as offerings in a cave shrine above a river, with erotic overtones.

Whereas Wang Xifeng's nickname borrows the bite of chiles even though she probably did not eat them, in the song the women and chiles are completely interlinked. These women are the way they are because they have been eating chiles since they were children. The power of the chiles and the power of these women are intertwined, going out in the world together, as chiles instigate the power to speak out, to voice their opinions. Female listeners might want to imitate the straightforwardness of the spicy girls—doing, speaking, and interacting. These are active women; there is an edginess in their lives as well as in their diets.

There are indirect links between the earlier revolutionary songs that emphasize men and chiles analyzed in chapter 5 and this song about women and chiles. The red color of chiles connects to the imagery of the Communist Party and therefore to the Chinese Communist victory in the revolution. Song Zuying is also known for singing a number of patriotic songs. The lyricist of "Spicy Girls," She Zhidi, is known for his patriotic and propaganda songs such as "The Party, My Dear Mother" (*Dang a, qin'ai de mama*). Like the lyricist for the Hunan chile song, She Zhidi was also from Hunan. The widely known composer for "Spicy Girls," Xu Peidong, is a vice chairman of the official China Federation of Literary and Art Circles. He too is particularly known for nationalist and patriotic songs, such as "Love My China" (*Ai wo Zhonghua*) and "Wonderful Wind from Asia" (*Yazhou xiongfeng*). The composer and lyricist worked quite nicely together placing a musical emphasis in the line about how the spicy girls' songs are spicy.

In addition to influencing their characters, chiles also alter the spicy girls' bodies. They physically absorb the spiciness, and it comes out in their sweat and tears. These physiological impacts combined with the passion imbued by the chiles result in a portrait of desirable women. Male listeners could certainly find the spicy girls of the song titillating and desirable. They are spicy, bold, fiery, and hot. The song borrows the same word play about fear and spice as occurs in the popular saying that jokes about chile consumption in different provinces discussed at the beginning of this chapter. Here, though, the spicy girls are unafraid of spice earlier in their lives, but the even more intense description of being "afraid of unspicy" does not occur until they are married. In both lines about marriage, the final phrase is the same, "afraid of unspicy." Thus there is an element of warning to potential spouses of spicy girls—their passion will require satisfaction. The message is that if they are not satisfied in their marriages, they will seek out spiciness elsewhere.

From Mao's love of chiles to the lamp on the Changsha train station, from Hunan women being described as spicy girls to revolutionary ability being equated with chile consumption, the chile pepper is an integral element of Hunanese identity. Hunanese so thoroughly integrated this overseas spice into their lives that it is now an indispensable component of their cuisine and is even described as "a totem for Hunan culture."[55] Tourism images for Hunan often emphasize chiles in food or as an important crop. The eye, as well as the palate, is barraged with chiles as markers of place.

Sichuan

Sichuanese today are proud of the importance of flavor in their regional cuisine.[56] The phrase "While China is the place for food, Sichuan is the place for flavor!" (食在中国, 味在四川), commonly cited in reference to Sichuan culture, emphasizes this aspect of local cuisine. The Sichuanese, despite criticisms from outsiders like the Hunanese, emphasize flavor, not just spiciness. This importance is reflected in the fact that in 2010 UNESCO recognized Chengdu, the capital of Sichuan, as a world gastronomic city. A logo for this designation includes a stylized red chile pepper, underscoring the importance of its use in the local cuisine.[57] In addition, because of the agriculturally rich Sichuan plateau, which makes up the center of the province, the region traditionally earned the sobriquet of "Heaven's Storehouse." As noted above, as early as the fourth century CE, Sichuanese culinary preferences have been described as "valuing flavor" and "loving spice."[58]

The exact causes of this prevalence are debated, but geography and climate played key roles. The location and climate of Sichuan meant that it was often necessary to find ways to preserve foods. Food writer Kenneth Lo observes that "because of the region's distance from sea-traders, and the humidity of its climate, the preservation of food became an essential consideration, not only in the storage of ingredients, but also in their preparation. Before the advent of freezing, food was kept by salting, drying, spicing, pickling and smoking. These methods of preservation impart a strong flavor on the food."[59] As was shown in the chapter on medicine, chiles have strong antimicrobial and antifungal properties. In an article on the antimicrobial properties of spices, Jennifer Billing and Paul Sherman conclude that "the probable ultimate reason why humans spice foods is to take advantage of the antimicrobial actions of the plant secondary compounds that give spices their flavors. We hypothesize that, by cleansing foods of pathogens, spice users contribute to their health, survival and reproduction. These then may be the reasons why many people, especially those living in or visiting hot climates, prefer food that is spicy." They emphasize the importance of chiles in cuisines in areas with hot climates, noting their importance as antimicrobials.[60] Thus chiles as preservatives correlate with their ability to kill microbes in food. The antifungal properties of capsaicin were also quite important for preserving food in the humid climate.[61]

In addition to including strong flavors from preservation, Sichuan cuisine has a long tradition of using pungent flavorings such as cassia cinnamon, garlic, ginger, star anise, and, most important,

Sichuan pepper.[62] Although the so-called five spice (*wuxiang*) flavoring is used in other regions, it has a long history in Sichuan. While which five spices are included varies, four are common: Sichuan pepper, star anise, cassia cinnamon, and fennel seed. Other possible flavors include ginger, licorice, clove, and black pepper.[63] Thus when chiles entered Sichuan, they were integrated into a regional culinary system that already used a wide range of strong flavorings and included practices of using spices as preservatives.

Furthermore, like Hunan, Sichuan has a humid climate all year long—hot and humid in the summer, cool and damp in the winter. As noted above for Hunan, many Sichuanese believe that eating chiles helps their bodies to regulate the high humidity and dampness of the local climate.[64] Lo even jokingly proposes that "perhaps one could even add that the hot, strong, salty flavours of Szechuan cooking not only preserve the food but also help to preserve the man!"[65] Prior to the introduction of chiles into Sichuan, it is likely that Sichuanese used other pungent flavorings, such as those in the "five spices," to expel excessive damp. The chile, however, came to be seen as much more effective at this action, and its daily use associated with healthy living in a humid environment.

The likeliest route for the introduction of chiles into Sichuan was via immigrants from Hunan.[66] Over the course of the second half of the seventeenth century, owing to the Manchu conquest of the Ming and suppression of various rebels and uprisings, the population of Sichuan was decimated, perhaps as much as halved.[67] The new Manchu government actively encouraged ethnic Han Chinese to migrate from places like Hunan into Sichuan.[68] The earliest record for chiles in Hunan dates from 1684, which means that chiles likely entered that province in the 1660s–1670s. The immigration of Hunanese into Sichuan would have begun in the late seventeenth century and continued well into the eighteenth century. Thus at least some of the Hunanese immigrants would already have been using chiles in their cooking and probably brought chiles with them when they moved to Sichuan in search of farmland. The earliest record for chiles in Sichuan dates from 1749, not far from Chengdu, in the central, fertile plain of Sichuan.[69] This would put the likely time for introduction of chiles into Sichuan as the 1730s–1740s.

Local Sichuan climate and custom likely influenced the Hunanese immigrants, who over time intensified their use of chiles, diverging in practice from their relatives back in Hunan. Lo argues that the intensely spicy dishes in Sichuan derive from peasants, while banquet-style, milder dishes of the elite show a strong northern influence.[70] While chile peppers of course are not used in every Sichuan dish, and their use varies throughout the large province, in their many forms they are a key ingredient in the cuisine and are also a strong marker of regional identity, what Parasecoli calls an "identity food." Chiles, however, did not make a sustained presence in Sichuan gazetteers until the nineteenth century.

Fu Chongju's *Chengdu tong lan* from 1909 is often referred to as the earliest Sichuan cookbook to include chiles.[71] Some of the condiments and dishes that contain chiles listed in Fu's book include sea pepper powder, sea pepper hot oil, chile (*lazi*) paste, chile sugar, chile-flavored fish, chile-flavored chicken, and numbing-spicy sea cucumber. In addition, Fu lists about a dozen different chile varieties that were available in Chengdu markets.[72] One of the displays at the Interactive Museum of Sichuan Culinary Culture asserts that modern Sichuan cuisine developed between 1861 and 1911. Today chiles are not only integral to Sichuanese cooking, but to overall Sichuan identity. Indeed, another display in the museum proclaims that the introduction of chiles into Sichuan "enabled an epoch-making transformation of Sichuan cuisine."[73]

I have discussed some of the most typical forms of chiles in Sichuan cuisine, including fresh chiles, dried whole chiles, ground dried chiles, and chile oil. In addition, Sichuanese often use preserved chiles, where the preferred method of preservation is "in a solution of salt, sugar, wine and spices," similar to Hunan, and distinctive from eastern cuisine, which favors vinegar as the preserving agent.[74]

A specialty of, and indispensable ingredient for, Sichuan cooking is *douban jiang*, often translated as chile bean paste. It is a fermented paste made from chiles and fava beans. Like the Lao Ganma brand chile paste discussed earlier, commercialized production of *douban jiang* has taken off since the 1980s. Although traditionally it was used and produced throughout all of Sichuan, the *douban jiang* from Pixian, about twenty kilometers northwest of central Chengdu, is considered to be the best. Quite a few Pixian businesses produce their version of this local specialty and market it broadly. Although the increase in commercialization has resulted in much of the paste being aged only for a few months, premium varieties aged for two to three years are available for the more discerning. By the late 1980s, various brands of Pixian *douban jiang* were available throughout China and a few countries abroad. Today exports extend to over forty countries.[75]

Pixian has capitalized on *douban jiang* production and even markets itself as a destination for domestic tourists through factory tours and the recently built Interactive Museum of Sichuan Culinary Culture. Visitors entering the town from Chengdu are greeted by a large sign that localizes the saying about food in China but flavor in Sichuan: "While Sichuan is the place for food, Pixian is the place for flavor!" This important local product is one key way that chiles infuse Sichuan cuisine. A trademark Sichuan dish imbued with Pixian *douban jiang* is mapo doufu (tofu; see list of ingredients in box).[76] Many people see *douban jiang* as such an essential component that it is sometimes referred to as the "soul of Sichuan cooking."[77]

Another important characteristic of Sichuan cuisine, which also distinguishes it from Hunanese cooking, is the combination of Sichuan pepper with chile pepper in many dishes. This distinctive

MAPO DOUFU 麻婆豆腐

Pock-Marked Bean Curd

The recipe, according to legend, was invented during the late Qing dynasty by a woman with small-pox scars on her face. There are many variations on this dish. While it usually contains meat, it is possible to make a vegetarian version.

Ingredients

1 block of bean curd
4 baby leeks
½ cup peanut oil
6 ounces ground beef
2 ½ Tbsp Sichuanese chile bean paste [douban jiang]
1 Tbsp fermented black beans
2 tsp ground Sichuan chiles
1 cup everyday stock
1 tsp white sugar
2 tsp light soy sauce
Salt to taste
4 Tbsp cornstarch mixed with 6 Tbsp water
½ tsp ground roasted Sichuan pepper

combination is referred to as *ma la*, or "numbing and spicy." While this pairing can also be found in neighboring Yunnan, nationwide it is most commonly perceived as a particularly Sichuan culinary element. An oft-repeated phrase in the Sichuan culinary museum is that Sichuanese are "masters of *ma-la*" (*shanyong mala*).[78] According to Dunlop, Hunanese often view the Sichuanese propensity for this combination negatively, as it is one that they use rarely and then only sparingly.[79] Some people jokingly say that the numbing characteristic of Sichuan pepper allows Sichuanese to use even more chiles in their cooking! Mapo doufu includes the *ma-la* combination of flavors, as does the perhaps even more well-known *gongbao jiding*, known more commonly in the United States as kung-pao chicken (see box).[80] There are a range of stories about the origins of this dish. This version was recorded in the Interactive Museum of Sichuan Culinary Culture:

> Ding Baozhen (1820–1886) was a native of Guizhou and during his official career he served as governor of Sichuan. He was very fond of eating chiles quickly stir-fried together with pork or chicken. He was very welcoming of guests and loved to serve them family-style dishes. Because of his fondness for this dish it was named in his honor. The name derives from a posthumous title granted him by the emperor: *Taizi Taibao* 太子太保 or Grand Guardian of the Heir Apparent. The dish name parses as follows: *gongbao* refers to his honorary title and translates as "protector of the palace"; *jiding* means boneless cubes of chicken meat.[81]

Dunlop notes that during the Cultural Revolution, when all things imperial were criticized, the dish was "renamed 'fast-fried chicken cubes' (*hong bao ji ding*) or 'chicken cubes with seared chiles' (*hu la ji ding*) until its political rehabilitation in the 1980s."[82]

Sichuanese restaurants are extremely popular all across China, and indeed around the world. A key trademark of all these restaurants is the liberal use of chiles. A subset of Sichuan restaurants are hot pot establishments—a well-known style of restaurant where patrons cook their food at the table. For those less attuned to Sichuan spiciness, restaurants often use divided pots to accommodate both mild and spicy palates (see figure 6.2).

While the spicy girls motif is not used as broadly to refer to women from Sichuan as it is for Hunan, it is still present. Dunlop observes that "Sichuanese have a reputation for being a little bit spicy themselves, and local women are even known as 'spice girls' (*la meizi*)."[83]

GONGBAO JIDING
宮保雞丁
(Kung-pao Chicken)

Diced, boneless chicken breast 250 g
Peanuts 50 g
White onion 30 g
Chopped garlic to taste
Chopped ginger to taste
Whole dried chiles about 10
Sichuan pepper kernels about 10

Marinade

Chile oil 10 ml
Vegetable oil 10 ml
Corn starch 1 spoonful
Egg white 1
Salt to taste
Soy sauce to taste

Sauce

Sugar 50 g
Vinegar 40 ml
Sichuan-style soy sauce 10 ml
Water ¼ cup
Cornstarch 1 spoonful
Rice wine 10 ml
Salt to taste

The term has also been used in business names. For example, Shancheng lameizi 山城辣妹子 (Mountain city spice girls) is the name of a Chongqing-style Sichuanese restaurant chain in Beijing. In addition, La Meizi is the name of a Chongqing company that produces Sichuanese condiments. Its spicy, pickled mustard tuber is often served in small packets on domestic flights in China.

Figure 6.2 Divided hot pot, Sichuan Hot Pot Restaurant, Xi'an, Shaanxi, 2016.

Historian Hongjie Wang also identifies tropes about Sichuanese, chiles, and revolution, drawing on some of the same ideas Mao played up. In an article about chiles in Sichuan, he argues that "eating spicy food has come to be regarded as an indication of such personal characteristics as courage, valor, and endurance, all essential for a potential revolutionary." Wang includes a photo of a billboard ad for a Sichuan restaurant in the tourist town of Yangshuo, Guangxi, that has the rhyming couplet "No revolution without redness! No happiness without spiciness!" (my translation).[84] Food writer Andrew Leonard similarly emphasizes the chile-eating abilities of Sichuanese, linking it to machismo as well as revolutionary imagery.[85]

Sichuanese have constructed the chile as an identity object. While outsiders may view the level of their use as excessive, Sichuanese themselves emphasize their desire to experience a variety of flavors in their cuisine. At one level one could argue that the introduction of chiles into Sichuan just added one more taste to the palette of Sichuanese cooks. In actuality, however, the chile plays a fundamental role in Sichuan identity. The chile is an inseparable component of Sichuan life, affecting both flavor and health. Zheng Zhu and Zang Xiaoman, in their article on spiciness in Sichuan cooking, ask the rhetorical question: "Without the chile pepper, would there really be something called Sichuan cuisine?"[86]

Chile pepper use significantly altered Hunan and Sichuan. Today consumption of chiles is an important component of local identity. Since the arrival of chiles, the food is much spicier. Culinary tours are becoming fashionable. Tourism promotions for Chinese from other regions often picture chiles and promote visits to sites like the Pixian factories and museums. Many believe that with all the humidity, the daily eating of chiles is necessary for healthy living. The speed at which food went bad in these two areas before refrigeration has resulted in cuisines that use preserved ingredients and, particularly in Sichuan, include strong flavors. The importance of chiles for the regional identities of both Hunan and Sichuan demonstrates how the constructed "authenticity" of this imported plant continues to affect the culture of these areas. The symbolism of "spicy girls" and Mao's revolutionary connections with chiles demonstrate the ability of this pod to transcend food and medicine in their impact on Hunanese and Sichuanese cultures.

CONCLUSION

With a handful of chiles she can speak her mind.
—"SPICY GIRLS," POPULAR SONG

Chinese history is full of people who engaged the American crop *Capsicum annuum* and gave it their own purposes and meanings. Fujianese sailors and traders on the coasts, as well as Shengjing farmers exchanging with Koreans, were among the Chinese introducers of this exotic garden plant, vegetable, spice, and medicine, the earliest likely in the 1570s. While there was elite reticence to see this fruit that was "so spicy it cannot be put in the mouth" as anything but a beautiful garden curiosity that resembled "the worn-out tip of a writing brush," evidence shows this edible plant was "found everywhere" as early as 1621.[1]

The thoroughness of Chinese integration of the chile sprang from the plant's versatility. It provides flavor, spice, medicine, nutrition, and stimulation and induces passion. Chinese from different regions, classes, and genders could all find something compelling and edgy in the chile.

For listeners of Tang Xianzu's Ming dynasty opera *Peony Pavilion* and readers of Cao Xueqin's Qing dynasty *Dream of the Red Chamber*, the chile took on symbolism for female sexual passion, assertiveness, and fierceness. This has expanded more recently into more regional associations with "spicy girls" and masculine revolutionary warriors from Hunan and Sichuan, like international pop star Song Zuying and Mao Zedong.

The mythic, prehistoric leader Shennong, the Divine Farmer, is emblematic of chile's chameleon-like ability to cross over lines and integrate medical systems with practical experience. The *bencao* text attributed to Shennong was seen as an ur-text—the earliest written precedent—for medical practitioners in the late imperial period. Yet Shennong was launched on his medical career through first-hand experimentation with himself as the test-subject. He supposedly ate hundreds of plants in order to observe their effects. Similarly, the chile was integrated into medical structures through identification of characteristics such as heating and pungent, but many of its impressive healing applications came about through observation. The fruit's ability to elicit "miraculous cures" for hemorrhoid sufferers came from observation, not from an analysis of systems.

The chile shifted from obscurity to ubiquity during the late imperial period because Chinese gardeners, farmers, cooks, medical practitioners, and writers integrated the new plant into their cultural contexts, adapting it to fit into existing cultural systems. The visual appeal of chiles allowed them an initial entrée into literati culture, catching the eyes of garden connoisseurs like Gao Lian. Over time, aesthetic valuing expanded across social lines to the point where today bunches of chiles, both real and artificial, appear liberally as decorations and symbols of exuberant, affluent lives.

The unique, intense flavor of capsaicin in chiles attracted disparate attention, but integration into the Chinese medico-culinary systems assured its acceptance and spread. Medically, in addition to aiding with digestion, chiles suited a variety of treatments for illnesses, both therapeutically and preventively. In modern times, people in damp environments consume them avidly as prophylactics to avoid excessive moisture in the body. Substitution of chiles for Sichuan pepper, salt, and black pepper began by the seventeenth century. In some cases, where chiles were a direct substitute, both availability and economics played a role, because families could grow chiles in their own kitchen gardens, essentially for free. This made them a strong competitor of even relatively cheap alternatives, like Sichuan pepper. Names, including "foreign pepper," "foreign ginger," and "surpasses black pepper," reflect this initial phase of replacement. By the mid-eighteenth century chiles were regular ingredients in sauces, pastes, oils, and vinegars. While the names carried over, direct references to substitution stopped after the early nineteenth century, demonstrating the chile's full integration. Just a little earlier, chiles appeared for the first time in a recipe book. About this time, the chile pepper replaced the Sichuan pepper in popularity, becoming the emblematic and ubiquitous *spicy* flavor.

Chiles became common in cooking all across China. Even in regions where the culinary traditions favor nonspicy flavorings, chiles are still popular. Indeed, chiles have even altered the very meaning of the term *la* or "spicy"; it has shifted so that now it primarily refers to the spiciness caused by capsaicin in chiles. With that shift in the meaning of *la* also emerged a more universal or national name for the chile pepper—*lajiao* or spicy pepper. This change occurred as national identity was emerging as an important cultural marker, paralleling other important indicators of China as a nation-state, including a more nationally focused education system, along with newspapers and publishing houses with national audiences.

Climate and culture vary broadly across Inner China. Regional adaptation started immediately upon the chile's arrival. Local conditions influenced naming and use at each point of entry. Versatility was instrumental in the adoption and spread of this plant as locals fit it into their particular environments and cultures. Some places emphasized chiles as vegetables, others as flavoring, and still others as medicine. Using chiles as a substitute for salt was most prevalent in the salt-poor region encompassing Guizhou and Guangxi. Replacing black pepper with chiles occurred inland, removed from the coastal delivery points for the imported South Asian spice. Only in Taiwan did the name "foreign ginger" hold dominant sway. In the warm, seafood-rich environment of central Fujian, chiles served as a cure for food poisoning. In malarial areas, chiles were eaten both as a prophylactic and as a cure. Minorities in several regions quickly integrated chiles into their cultures. They capitalized on their ease of growth, replacing monetized flavorings such as salt. Particularly in mountainous areas, chiles provided a new means of accessing essential vitamins.

Regional identities in the interior, especially for Hunan and Sichuan, are inexorably linked to chile consumption for both flavor and health. The cuisines of those regions similarly are associated with chiles. Hunan and Sichuan restaurants outside of those regions are expected to serve spicy dishes laden with chiles. Hunan restaurants often emphasize Chairman Mao's connection to the province, naming dishes after him or including his portrait or bust as part of the décor. The health benefits of chile consumption in these humid areas advanced the development of chiles into regional identity markers.

Intense chile flavor suited revolutionary symbols. Mao's belief that he personally could not have been a successful revolutionary without eating chiles has transformed into a broader view about chiles helping to feed military actions. Although the gendering of this metaphor is not always explicit, implicitly the violence of revolution is broadly seen as masculine. In addition, in the examples of chile consumption directly linked with specific military leaders and revolutionaries, they are all male. Chile consumption still excites interest around the world because of risk-taking rush and bravado.

While the male gender trope of associating chiles with violence and leadership is important, it is not nearly as prevalent as the female imagery associated with chiles. *La meizi* or "spicy girls" is a trope widely recognized across China. The phrase usually refers to young women from regions where chile consumption is high. It is a marker for spunkiness, independence, and passion. While Bridal Du in *Peony Pavilion* can be seen as the prototype character that linked the chile with passion, the reference is rather fleeting and did not have nearly as large an impact as the reference to Wang Xifeng in *Dream of the Red Chamber*. Wang Xifeng as an example of a *la meizi* is influential all the way to the present. Modern *la meizi*, however, do not carry the baggage of crossing too far in bending gender or moral norms as Wang Xifeng did in the novel. Modern *la meizi* are independent women who exert their right to pursue their passions. In a sense, there is somewhat of a return to some of the traits of Bridal Du, who was assertive to the point of arranging her exit from the underworld to consummate her love. On the other hand, the modern *la meizi* of the song certainly are not going to pine away like Bridal Du; instead they are "fiery," "bold," and "hot" as they go out into the world speaking their minds.[2] The popularity of the "spicy girls" song internationally and as a favorite cover song for amateur groups of women of all ages and regions demonstrates how women outside of Hunan have appropriated the boldness and passionate assertiveness of the chile pepper.

By contrast, the reticence of many late imperial elite toward the chile pepper is telling and suggests power dynamics based on controlling or rejecting this fiery newcomer. The modestly flavored Jiangnan cuisine dominated elite writings on cooking throughout the eighteenth century and into the nineteenth. Long traditions of avoiding strong flavors in order to cultivate spiritual purity and a focused intellect also biased many writers against the extraordinarily pungent chile. The desire of authors to cite precedence was also a factor in the chile pepper's battle to appear in print. Since the chile was an interloper, late imperial authors could not find it in earlier, oft-cited texts. While this was particularly evident in the struggle to be represented in medical texts, it almost certainly contributed to the chile's late appearance in recipe collections as well. Thus we see editors of the Yunnan provincial gazetteer as late as 1894 not including the chile pepper in the products section because it was not included in Li Shizhen's work. People in lower classes, in contrast, were growing multiple varieties of chiles for food and medicine. Rather than employ flowery, elite metaphors to describe chiles, such as writing brushes and coral, they associated chile shapes with their own daily existence—cow horns and chicken hearts.

By the mid- to late nineteenth century much of the elite reticence toward chiles was overcome. As with so many historical changes, there is no single cause; instead multiple factors combined to lead to this overall shift. As chiles became more and more widespread in cooking and medicine, they became harder and harder to ignore. Thus popularity became its own precedent and even a mark of authenticity. By about 1790 chiles had appeared in Tong Yuejian's culinary work *The Harmonious Cauldron*, and many subsequent recipe texts built on his precedent and included chiles in their works. By the late nineteenth century many elite members of society were disillusioned with the Manchu-led Qing dynasty, and some even with the imperial system in general. This is the period where we see the beginnings of advocating for Han-ethnic nationalism. While Jiangnan culture and cuisine remained admired, adherence to court-dominated culinary practices was declining. Zhao Xuemin, who began his supplement to Li Shizhen's work with the desire to fill in gaps, included a great deal of information about the chile. However, although his work was completed in 1803, it was not published until 1871. Thus other authors did not have access to the longest source on chiles from late imperial times until the late nineteenth century. In addition, Western-influenced scientific approaches to various fields, including botany, were taking hold by the early twentieth century. Scholars adopting this approach would not have been as focused on finding precedents in earlier Chinese works. Regional identities that emphasize chile consumption appear in written sources in the late nineteenth and early twentieth centuries. Once those affiliations were strongly established, ignoring the spicy pods became more and more difficult, and less desirable.

From the time of their introduction, probably in the 1570s, until the early twentieth century, chiles went from obscurity to ubiquity in Inner China. Indeed, the chile has become an authentic component of Chinese culture. As Fabio Parasecoli has demonstrated, "authenticity" is a constructed and iterative process: "Tradition and authenticity are the result of the reiteration of highly regulated and ritualized practices, norms and processes that respond to ideals and cultural models, and acquire material reality, visibility, and cultural intelligibility in the very body of each individual."[3] Over the course of those few hundred years, Chinese from many walks of life, from all across China, adapted the chile to fit into existing cultural practices, "norms and processes," particularly in the areas of cuisine, medicine, and gardening. In addition, the increasing utilization of chiles within China led to changes in Chinese culture. The impact of the chile pepper on gender imagery, the very meaning of the term *la*, and regional identities demonstrates the "material reality, visibility, and cultural intelligibility" of this spicy pod. The importance of this nonnative plant, its multiple everyday presence, and its symbolic power all contributed to the chile pepper becoming an authentic part of Chinese identity, and thus an authentic Chinese plant.

From overpowering, dangerous exotic to identity plant providing and infusing Chinese with the native ability to overpower enemies, the history of the chile pepper has been an elusive but compelling story to uncover. The thinness of the historic records on chiles compared to other crops from the Americas parallels their initial use in cuisine. While a dish might have been packed with maize, potatoes, sweet potatoes, or peanuts, only a few chiles were needed to add flavor. However, those few pack a punch, bringing to light the piquancy of the Chinese engagement with the chile. The strings of decorative, or real, New Year's chiles framing front doors and business entrances represent now both warm, welcoming homecoming and the festive fireworks of special celebrations. Chiles have come home yet remain edgy.

APPENDIX A
LATE IMPERIAL RECIPE COLLECTIONS

Date	Title	Author	Chiles
1591	*Yin zhuan fu shi jian*[a]	Gao Lian	No
1670	*Xian qing ou ji*	Li Yu	No
1680	*Shi xian hong mi*	Zhu Yizun	No
1698	*Yang xiao lu*	Gu Zhong	No
1750	*Xing yuan lu*	Li Huanan	No
1790	*Suiyuan shidan*	Yuan Mei	No
c. 1790	Tiao ding ji	Tong Yuejian	Yes
1819	*Bencao zaixin*[b]	Chen Xiuyuan	No
1830	*Qing jia lu*	Gu Lu	No
1863	*Suixiju yinshi pu*	Wang Shixiong	Yes
c. 1883	Suiyuan shidan bu zheng	Xia Zengchuan	No
1907	*Zhong kui lu*	Zeng Yi	Yes
1909	*Chengdu tong lan*	Fu Chongju	Yes
1916	*Qing bai lei chao*[c]	Xu Ke	Yes

[a] *Yin zhuan fu shi jian* was originally published in Gao's larger work *Zunsheng bajian*. This shorter work, a treatise on food and drink, was also published separately.

(continued)

While *Zunsheng bajian* does indeed contain the earliest reference to chiles, since the section containing recipes does not include them, and since that work was published separately, *Yin zhuan fu shi jian* has been included as the earliest recipe collection in this list. Recipe collections from earlier in the Ming were consulted for this study, but none included chiles. Since no studies on chiles in China, including this one, have discovered any sources containing chiles prior to 1591, no recipe collections from prior to that date are listed in this table.

[b] *Bencao zaixin* can also be classified as a medical text, but because it contains some food recipes and also appears in Liu Daqi's *Zhongguo gudian shipu* (Chinese classical recipes) collection, it is included in this list.

[c] Although the *Qing bai lei chao* (Categorized collection of minor Qing matters) is a miscellaneous collection of writings (*biji*), it contains a number of recipes. Indeed, Liu Daqi uses quite a few recipes from *Qing bai lei chao* in his *Zhongguo gudian shipu*, including one of the ones containing chiles.

APPENDIX B
MEDICAL TEXTS CONSULTED

Year published	Author	Title	Chiles included
c. 1550	Anonymous [Palace]	*Shiwu bencao*	No
1565	Chen Jiamo	*Bencao mengquan*	No
1587	Zhang Maochen	*Bencao bian*	No
c. 1590	Ning Yuan	*Shijian bencao*	No
1592	Fang Youzhi	*Shanghan lun tiaobian*	No
1593	Wu Wenbing	*Yaoxing quanbei shiwu bencao*	No
c. 1593	Hu Wenhuan	*Shiwu bencao*	No
1596	Li Shizhen	*Bencao gangmu*	No
c. 1600	Sun Yikui	*Yi zhi xu yu*	No
1602	Wang Kentang	*Zheng zhi zhun sheng*	No
1602	Yang Chongkui	*Bencao zhenquan*	No
1607	Mu Shixi	*Shiwu jiyao*	No
1609	Zheng Quanwang	*Zhangnüe zhinan*	No
1614	Li Zhongli	*Bencao yuanshi*	No

(continued)

Year published	Author	Title	Chiles included
1620	Wu Zhiwang	*Chongding Jiyin gangmu*	No
1620	Qian Yunzhi	*Shiwu bencao*	No
1621	Anonymous	*Shiwu bencao*	Yes
1622	Miao Xiyong	*Pao zhi dafa*	No
1624	Zhang Jiebin	*Shiwu bencao*	No
1624	Miao Xiyong	*Shennong bencao jing shu*	No
1624	Ni Zhumo	*Bencao huiyan*	No
1624	Zhang Jiebin	*Jingyue quanshu*	No
c. 1627	Miao Xiyong	*Xianxing zhai yixue guang biji*	No
1638	Chen Jiru	*Shiwu bencao*	Yes
c. 1640	Zhang Jiebin	*Lei jing*	No
1641	Jiang Yi	*Yao jing*	No
1642	Yao Kecheng, attrib.	*Shiwu bencao*	Yes
1642	Wu Youxing	*Wenyi lun*	No
1644	Jia Suoxue	*Yapin huayi*	No
c. 1644	Li Zhongzi	*Juan bu lei gong pao zhi yao xing jie*	No
1645	Lu Zhiyi	*Bencao cheng ya ban jie*	No
c. 1674	Zhang Zhicong	*Bencao chongyuan*	No
1676	Zhu Benzhong	*Yinshi xuzhi*	No
1679	Zhou Yangjun	*Wenre shu yi quanshu*	No
c. 1684	Fu Qingzhu	*Fu Qingzhu nüke*	No
1690	Wang Ang	*Zengbu bencao beiyao*	No
1691	Shen Lilong	*Shiwu bencao huizuan*	No
1694	Wang Ang	*Zengding bencao beiyao*	No
1695	Zhang Lu	*Ben jing feng yuan*	No
1696	Wang Qixian	*Shiwu xu zhi*	No
1736	Xu Dachan	*Shennong bencao jing baizhong lu*	No
1743	Wu Qian, et al, eds.	*Yi zong jin jian*	No

Year published	Author	Title	Chiles included
1752	Zheng Dianyi	*Wenyi mingbian*	No
1757	Wu Yiluo	*Bencao congxin*	No
1758	Wang Fu	*Yilin zuanyao tanyuan*	Yes
1761	Yan Jie	*Depei bencao*	No
1764	Xu Dachun	*Lantai guifan*	No
1771	Xu Wenbi	*Xinbian shoushi chuanzhen*	Yes
1773	Cao Tingdong	*Laolao hengyan*	No
1773	Huang Gongxiu	*Bencao qiuzhen*	No
1773	Wu Daoyuan	*Li zheng hui can*	No
1778	Li Wenbing	*Jing yan guang ji*	No
1778	Li Wenpei	*Shiwu xiaolu*	No
1783	Dai Tianzhang	*Guang wenyi lun*	No
1785	Yang Jun	*Shanghan wenyi tiaobian*	No
1799	Sun Xingyan, ed.	*Shennong bencao jing* [revised]	No
Pre-1803[a]	Unknown	*Baicao jing*	Yes
Pre-1803[a]	Unknown	*Caiyun baifang*	Yes
Pre-1803[a]	Chen Jiongyao	*Shiwu yiji*	Yes
Pre-1803[a]	Unknown	*Longbo yaoxing kao*	Yes
Pre-1803[a]	Unknown	*Yao jian*	Yes
Pre-1803[a]	Unknown	*Yizong huibian*	Yes
1813	Wu Tang	*Wenxintang wenbing tiaobian*	No
1819	Chen Xiuyuan	*Bencao zaixin*	No
1823	Zhang Mu	*Tiao ji yinshi bian*	No
1840	anonymous	*Bencao huibian*	No
1848	Zhao Qiguang	*Bencao qiuyuan*	No
1849	Taiyiyuan (Imperial Medical Office)	*Yaoxing tongkao*	No

(continued)

Year published	Author	Title	Chiles included
1849	Zou Shu, ed.	*Benjing shuzheng*	No
1850	Shen Youpeng	*Nüke jiyao*	No
1851	Tu Daohe	*Bencao huizuan*	No
1854	Niu Wen'ao	*Bencao minglan*	No
1856	Zhang Renxi	*Yaoxing mengqiu*	No
1863	Fei Boxiong	*Yichun shengyi*	No
1871[b]	Zhao Xuemin	*Bencao gangmu shiyi*	Yes
1885	Li Shizhen and Zhao Xuemin	*Bencao gangmu* with *shiyi* Li's work with Zhao's additions	Yes

[a] Work now lost; cited in Zhao Xuemin, *Bencao gangmu shiyi* (Correction of omissions in the *Bencao gangmu*), 1871. Zhao's work was completed by 1803.

[b] Zhao's work was completed by 1803 but not published until 1871.

NOTES

Introduction

1. Edgar Porter, *The People's Doctor: George Hatem and China's Revolution* (Honolulu: University of Hawai'i Press, 1997), 76.

2. Igor Kopytoff, "Cultural Biography of Things: Commoditization as Process," in *The Social Life of Things: Commodities in Cultural Perspective*, ed. Arjun Appadurai (Cambridge: Cambridge University Press, 1986), 68.

3. Fabio Parasecoli, "Food and Popular Culture," in *Food in Time and Place*, ed. Paul Freedman, Joyce Chaplin, and Ken Albala (Berkeley: University of California Press, 2014), 331–32.

4. Jiang Mudong and Wang Siming, "Lajiao zai Zhongguo chuanbo ji qi yingxiang" (The spread of the chile pepper and its influence in China), *Zhongguo nong shi* 24, no. 2 (2005): 17–27; Wang Maohua, Wang Cengyu, and Hong Seung Tae, "Lüelun lishi shang dongya sanguo lajiao de chuanbo, zhongzhi yu gongyong fajue" (Overview and exploration of the history of chiles in the three East Asian countries, including their spread, cultivation and use), *Zhongguoshi yanjiu* (S. Korea), no. 101 (April 2016): 287–330; Cao Yu, *Zhongguoshi lashi: lajiao zai Zhongguo de sibainian* (The history of spice in

Chinese food: four hundred years of chiles in China) (Beijing: Beijing United, 2019).

5. See, for example, E. N. Anderson, *The Food in China* (New Haven, Conn.: Yale University Press, 1988); Ho Ping-ti, "The Introduction of American Food Plants Into China," *American Anthropologist* 57, no. 2 (1955): 191–201; Thomas Höllmann, *The Land of the Five Flavors: A Cultural History of Chinese Cuisine* (New York: Columbia University Press, 2014); H. T. Huang, *Science and Civilisation in China*, vol. 6: *Biology and Biological Technology, Part 5: Fermentation and Food Science* (Cambridge: Cambridge University Press, 2000); James Lee and Wang Feng, *One Quarter of Humanity: Malthusian Mythology and Chinese Realities, 1700–2000* (Cambridge, Mass.: Harvard University Press, 1999); Sucheta Mazumdar, "The Impact of New World Food Crops on the Diet and Economy of China and India, 1600–1900," in *Food in Global History*, ed. Raymond Grew, 58–78 (Boulder, Colo.: Westview Press, 1999); Georges Métailié, *Science and Civilisation in China*, vol. 6: *Biology and Biological Technology, Part 4: Traditional Botany: An Ethnobotanical Approach* (Cambridge: Cambridge University Press, 2015); Min Zongdian, "Haiwai nongzuowu de chuanru he dui wo guo nongye shengchan de yingxiang" (The introduction of overseas agriculture products and their influence on Chinese agricultural production), *Gujin nongye*, no. 1 (1991): 1–10; Frederick Mote, "Yüan and Ming," in *Food in Chinese Culture: Anthropological and Historical Perspectives*, ed. K. C. Chang, 193–257 (New Haven, Conn.: Yale University Press, 1977); Laura May Kaplan Murray, "New World Food Crops in China: Farms, Food, and Families in the Wei River Valley, 1650–1910," Ph.D. diss., University of Pennsylvania, 1985; Joseph Needham, *Science and Civilisation in China*, vol. 6: *Biology and Biological Technology, Part 1: Botany* (Cambridge: Cambridge University Press, 1986); Frederick Simoons, *Food in China: A Cultural and Historical Inquiry* (Boca Raton, Fla.: CRC Press, 1991); Jonathan Spence, "Ch'ing," in *Food in Chinese Culture: Anthropological and Historical Perspectives*, ed. K. C. Chang, 259–94 (New Haven, Conn.: Yale University Press, 1977); Wang Siming "Meizhou yuanchan zuowu de yinzhong zaipei ji qi dui Zhongguo nongye shengchan jiegou de

yingxiang" (The introduction and cultivation of American crops and their influence on the Chinese agricultural production structure), *Zhongguo nongshi*, no. 2 (2004): 16–27.

6. See *Shiwu bencao* (The pharmacopoeia of edible items) (1621), 16.12b.

7. *Zhen'an xianzhi* (district gazetteer) (Shaanxi) (1755), 7.13a.

8. Song Zuying (singer), Xu Peidong (composer), and She Zhidi (lyricist), "La Meizi" (Spicy girls), in *Jingdian jingxuan* (Collection of classics) (Guangzhou: Guangzhou xinshidai chuban, 1995), track 1.

1. Names and Places

1. Frederick Simoons, *Food in China: A Cultural and Historical Inquiry* (Boca Raton, Fla.: CRC Press, 1991), 169; Edward Schafer, "T'ang," in *Food in Chinese Culture: Anthropological and Historical Perspectives*, ed. K. C. Chang (New Haven, Conn.: Yale University Press, 1977), 93.

2. The earliest use of *laqie* was in the 1671 edition of a Zhejiang local history, *Shanyin xianzhi* [district gazetteer], 7.3a.

3. Wu Zhengyi and Peter H. Raven, eds., *Flora of China*, vol. 17: *Verbenaceae* Through *Solanaceae* (St. Louis: Missouri Botanical Garden, 1994), 313.

4. Wu and Raven, *Flora of China*, 17:313.

5. Inner China designates a geographic area essentially equivalent to the territory of the Ming dynasty (1368–1644) (see map 1.2). Historians of the Qing period created the term to describe the inner provinces of the Manchu-led Qing dynasty (1644–1911), in contrast to the outlying territories that the Manchus added to their empire. The terms "inner" and "outer" are not ideal as they carry connotations that are not always applicable. An alternative for "Inner China," "China proper," however, carries even more bias, so I employ the somewhat more neutral "Inner China."

6. The entry is for January 15, 1493. Christopher Columbus, *The Diario of Christopher Columbus's First Voyage to America 1492–1493*, trans. Oliver Dunn and James E. Kelley, Jr. (Norman: University of Oklahoma Press, 1988), 340–41.

7. The English name for *Capsicum* can be spelled in three ways: chile, chili, and chilli. I have chosen to use chile because it corresponds to

the spelling in Mexico and is the spelling that dominates in culinary writing.

8. Jean Andrews notes that a teacher at the Spanish court, Pietro Martire de Anghiera, also known as Martyr, wrote about chiles in 1493. She implies that he only heard about them from various crew members. Jack Turner implies that Martyr had actually seen and tasted chiles brought back by Columbus. Jean Andrews, *Peppers: The Domesticated Capsicums* (Austin: University of Texas Press, 1995), 3; Jack Turner, *Spice: The History of a Temptation* (New York: Vintage, 2004), 11.

9. Andrews, *Peppers*, 3.

10. Andrews, *Peppers*, 4n.

11. See, for example, Andrew Dalby, *Dangerous Tastes: The Story of Spices* (Berkeley: University of California Press, 2000), 90; John Keay, *The Spice Route, a History* (London: John Murray, 2005), 250; Turner, *Spice*, 12.

12. Henry Ridley, *The Dispersal of Plants Throughout the World* (Ashford, UK: L. Reeve, 1930), 396.

13. Jean Andrews, *The Pepper Trail: History and Recipes from Around the World* (Denton: University of North Texas Press, 1999), 25, 224n25.

14. Andrews, *Peppers*, 5.

15. David Burton, *The Raj at Table: A Culinary History of the British in India* (London: Faber and Faber, 1993), 6.

16. M.A.P. Meilink-Roelofsz, *Asian Trade and European Influence in the Indonesian Archipelago Between 1500 and about 1630* (The Hague: Martinus Nijhoff, 1962), 32, 36, 42.

17. Ridley, *Dispersal of Plants*, 396.

18. Ho Ping-ti, "The Introduction of American Food Plants Into China," *American Anthropologist* 57, no. 2 (April 1955): 192.

19. Chang T'ien-tsê, *Sino-Portuguese Trade from 1514–1644: A Synthesis of Portuguese and Chinese Sources* (New York: AMS, [1934] 1973), 88–91.

20. See William L. Schurz, *The Manila Galleon* (New York: Dutton, 1939), 20–21.

21. Schurz, *Manila Galleon*, 22–23, 25.

22. Carlos Quirino, "The Mexican Connection: The Cultural Cargo of the Manila-Acapulco Galleons," paper presented at the Mexican-Philippine Historical Relations Seminar, New York City, June 21, 1997, http://filipinokastila.tripod.com/FilMex.html.

23. Schurz, *Manila Galleon*, 268; also see Marcy Norton, "Tasting Empire: Chocolate and European Internalization of Mesoamerican Aesthetics," *American Historical Review* 111, no. 3 (June 2006): 660–91.

24. William Adams is the historic person adapted by James Clavell into the main character in his novel *Shōgun* (1975).

25. Marguerite Wilbur, *The East India Company and the British Empire in the Far East* (New York: R. R. Smith, 1945), 81.

26. Roderich Ptak, "Ming Maritime Trade to Southeast Asia, 1368–1567: Visions of a 'System,'" reprinted in Ptak, *China, the Portuguese, and the Nanyang: Oceans and Routes, Regions and Trade (c. 1000–1600)*, vol. 1 (Aldershot, UK: Ashgate Variorum, 2004), 191.

27. Eric Tagliacozzo, "A Sino-Southeast Asian Circuit: Ethnohistories of the Marine Goods Trade," in *Chinese Circulations: Capital, Commodities, and Networks in Southeast Asia*, ed. Eric Tagliacozzo and Wen-Chin Chang (Durham, N.C.: Duke University Press, 2011), 434–37.

28. Ptak, "Ming Maritime Trade," 1:180–81.

29. John D. Langlois, Jr., "The Hung-wu Reign," in *The Cambridge History of China*, vol. 7: *The Ming Dynasty, 1368–1644, Part 1*, ed. Frederick W. Mote and Denis Twitchett (Cambridge: Cambridge University Press, 1988), 168–69.

30. Ptak, "Ming Maritime Trade," 1:187.

31. For excellent study of local gazetteers, see Joseph Dennis, *Writing, Publishing, and Reading Local Gazetteers in Imperial China, 1100–1700* (Cambridge, Mass.: Harvard University Asia Center, 2015).

32. *Tianchang xianzhi* [district gazetteer] [Anhui] (1550), cited and translated in Dennis, *Writing, Publishing, and Reading*, 252.

33. Ho, "The Introduction," 194.

34. *Changshu xianzhi* [district gazetteer] [Jiangsu] (1539), 4.31a. See Ho, "The Introduction," 192. Note that while I am referring to this

gazetteer as being in Jiangsu province, Ming (1368–1644) and Qing (1911–1912) provincial boundaries did not actually correspond completely. However, to show how various crops from the Americas moved within China during both periods, to simplify explanations about movements, and to map out the movement of the chiles in a consistent manner, I have chosen to label places as falling within the Qing provincial boundaries in use in 1820. This also allows me to use the China Historical GIS maps for 1820.

35. Ho, "The Introduction," 192.

36. Ho, "The Introduction," 193.

37. Cited in Ho, "The Introduction," 194.

38. Ho, "The Introduction," 194.

39. Carol Benedict, *Golden-Silk Smoke: A History of Tobacco in China, 1550–2010* (Berkeley: University of California Press, 2011), 7.

40. Yao Lü, *Lu shu* (Book of dew) (1611), j.10.46a [704]. See also Benedict, *Golden-Silk Smoke*, 19.

41. Benedict, *Golden-Silk Smoke*, 2, 19.

42. Jiang Mudong and Wang Siming, "Lajiao zai zhongguo chuanbo ji qi yingxiang" (The spread of the chile pepper and its influence in China), *Zhongguo nong shi* 24, no. 2 (2005): 18–19.

43. In addition to mapping earliest records by province, I also experimented with a larger-scale model, G. William Skinner's macro regions. In addition, I tried mapping out the earliest sources at a more detailed level—prefectures. Since these mapping techniques were less revealing in terms of patterns of introduction and movement, I have chosen not to include them in the book.

44. Ho, "The Introduction," 195.

45. Gao Lian, *Zunsheng bajian* (Eight discourses on nurturing life), in *Siku quanshu zhenben jiuji*, vols. 225–32 (Taibei: Shang wu, [1591] 1979), j.16.27b. This is the earliest source to include chiles I found, and it is also the earliest identified in Chinese studies of chiles, including Jiang and Wang, "Lajiao zai Zhongguo chuanbo ji qi yingxiang," 17; Wang Maohua, Wang Cengyu, and Hong Seung Tae, "Lüelun lishi shang dongya sanguo lajiao de chuanbo, zhongzhi yu gongyong fajue" (Overview and exploration of the history of chiles in the three East Asian countries, including their spread, cultivation

and use), *Zhongguoshi yanjiu* (S. Korea), no. 101 (April 2016): 296; Lan Yong, "Zhongguo gudai xinla yongliao de shanbian, liubu yu nongye shehui fazhan" (The evolution and spread of pungent and spicy ingredients in the development of agricultural society in ancient China), *Zhongguo shehui jingjishi yanjiu*, no. 4 (2000): 17; *Zhongguo nongye baikequanshu* (Encyclopedia of Chinese agriculture) (Beijing: Nongye chubanshe, 1995), 181; and Min Zongdian, "Haiwai nongzuowu de chuanru he dui wo guo nongye shengchan de yingxiang" (The spread of foreign crops and their influence on Chinese agricultural production), *Gujin nongye*, no. 1 (1991): 7.

At the beginning of her article, Hu Yiyin specifically identifies Gao's 1591 work as the earliest record for chiles in Chinese ("Lajiao mingcheng kaoshi" [A philological study of the naming of chile peppers], *Gujin nongye*, no. 4 [2013]: 67). However, later in the article, she also mentions a gazetteer from 1559 as being the earliest to list chiles (73, 74). This is the *Nangong xianzhi* (district gazetteer] [Zhili] (1559). The entry in the vegetable section of this gazetteer only lists the name *lajiao* 辣角 (spicy horn), without any description (1.9b). However, it is in the category of "wild growing" (*ye sheng*) vegetables. It is inexplicable that the first record of an introduced plant would describe it as growing wild. Therefore, this entry almost certainly refers to an indigenous plant. For example, spicy horn is also an alternative name for the native *longkui* 龍葵 or black nightshade (*Solanum nigrum*) that has some edible parts and was also commonly used in traditional Chinese medicine.

46. Shaoxing prefecture, *Shanyin xianzhi* [district gazetteer] [Zhejiang] (1671), 7.3a. See the previous note for a refutation of Hu Yiyin's claim that there is an earlier gazetteer containing chiles.

47. Shiu-ying Hu, *Food Plants of China* (Hong Kong: Chinese University Press, 2005), 659.

48. The biographical information about Gao comes from Craig Clunas, *Superfluous Things: Material Culture and Social Status in Early Modern China* (Urbana: University of Illinois Press, 1991), 14–18.

49. Gao Lian, *Zunsheng bajian*, j.11.1b.

50. The character 畨 *fan*, meaning foreign, is a variant form of 番 *fan*, which was more commonly used for *fanjiao* 番椒.

51. *Taihai caifeng tukao* (Treatise on Taiwan's flora and fauna), in *Taiwan shiliao huibian*, vol. 8 (Beijing: Quanguo tushuguan wenxian suowei fuzhi zhongxin, [1746] 2004), [2.8a] 603.

52. *Taihai caifeng tukao*, [2.8a] 603.

53. Zhang Zhijie, "*Taihai caifeng tukao dian, zhu*" (Annotations to *Taihai caifeng tukao*), in *Zhonghua keji shixuehui congkan*, vol. 1 (Xinbei City: Zhonghua keji shixue hui, 2011), 33n21.

54. Jurgis Elisonas, "Christianity and the Daimyo," in *The Cambridge History of Japan*, vol. 4: *Early Modern Japan*, ed. John Whitney Hall (Cambridge: Cambridge University Press, 1991), 302, 303.

55. Yi Su-gwang, *Jibong yuseol* (Topical discourses of Jibong [Yi]), vol. 2 (Seoul: Euryu munhwasa, [1614] 1994), 635. Similarly, Jiang and Wang, "Lajiao zai Zhongguo chuanbo ji qi yingxiang," 19, cite a modern Korean-language history that concludes that introduction into Korea probably occurred from Japan between 1592 and 1601. Wang, Wang, and Hong, "Lüelun lishi shang dongya sanguo lajiao de chuanbo, zhongzhi yu gongyong fajue," 298, cite an early nineteenth-century Korean source that reports that chiles entered Korea between 1592 and 1618.

56. *Gaiping xianzhi* [district gazetteer] [Shengjing] (1682), *xia*.8b.

57. *Shengjing tongzhi* [provincial gazetteer] (1684), 21.4b.

58. For more on this name, see chapter 2.

59. Jiang and Wang, "Lajiao zai Zhongguo," 19.

60. Qu Dajun, *Guangdong xinyu* (News from Guangdong) (Hong Kong: Zhonghua shuju, [1680] 1974), 371; *Anxi xianzhi* [district gazetteer] (1757) [Fujian], 4.10a–10b.

61. *Yunnan tongzhi* [provincial gazetteer] (1736), 27.3a; Tian Wen, *Qian shu* [Guizhou] (1690), 2.3a; *Guangxi tongzhi* [provincial gazetteer] (1733), 93.28a.

62. *Guangxi fuzhi* [prefectural gazetteer] [Yunnan] (1739), 20.5b.

63. While Jean Andrews included a map showing chiles entering Yunnan from Burma in both editions of her *Peppers* (map on page 7 in both the 1987 and 1995 editions), she did not provide any evidence to support that hypothesis. In a later work she did provide a citation in reference to such a route, but it turns out to be based on Ho's 1955

article, which does not provide any details about the introduction of chiles (Andrews, *The Pepper Trail*, 26).

64. Jiang Xianming, *Gezhong shucai* (All types of vegetables) (Beijing: Nongye chubanshe, 1989), 82.

65. See Min, "Haiwai nongzuowu," 7; Jiang and Wang, "Lajiao zai zhong-guo," 19.

66. *Chongxiu Suzhou xin zhi* [independent prefectural gazetteer] [Gansu] (1737), *ce* 6:11a; *Shanyang xianzhi* [district gazetteer] [Shaanxi] (1694), 3.50a.

67. James Millward, "Chiles on the Silk Road," *Chile Pepper*, December 1993: 36.

68. Ho, "The Introduction," 195.

69. Chiles do not appear in any of the earliest gazetteers for peanuts, sweet potatoes, or maize.

70. See, for example, Ho Ping-ti, *Studies on the Population of China, 1368-1953* (Cambridge, Mass.: Harvard University Press, 1959); Jonathan Spence, "Ch'ing," in *Food in Chinese Culture: Anthropological and Historical Perspectives*, ed. K. C. Chang (New Haven, Conn.: Yale University Press, 1977), 262.

71. Benedict, *Golden-Silk Smoke*, esp. 7–33.

72. *Shiwu bencao* (1621), 16.12b.

73. *Chongxiu Jiashan xianzhi* [district gazetteer] [Zhejiang] (1894), 12.26a.

2. Spicing Up the Palate

1. See David Gentilcore, *Pomodoro!: A History of the Tomato in Italy* (New York: Columbia University Press, 2010), esp. chap. 1.

2. *Zhen'an xianzhi* [district gazetteer] [Shaanxi] (1755), 7.13a.

3. Paul Rozin and Deborah Schiller, "The Nature and Acquisition of a Preference for Chili Pepper in Humans," *Motivation and Emotion*, 4, no. 1 (1980): 99.

4. See Alice Arndt, "Spices and Rotten Meat. Old Saw: 'They Used a Lot of Spices to Disguise Spoiled Meat,'" The Debunk-House, *Food History News*, 2008, https://web.archive.org/web/20180818060609if _/http://foodhistory.news/debunk.html#rotten.

5. This myth has also worked its way into Chinese scholarship on spices. See, for example, Hong Sen, ed., *Lawei meishi yu jianshen* (Spicy flavor in gourmet food for health) (Tianjin: Tianjin keji fanyi chubanshe, 2005), 5.

6. Paul B. Newman, *Daily Life in the Middle Ages* (Jefferson, N.C.: McFarland, 2001), 3. In addition, Paul Freedman points out that meat in fifteenth-century Europe was cheaper than spices, and "trying to improve dubious meat with cloves or nutmeg would have been perverse." Paul Freedman, *Out of the East: Spices and the Medieval Imagination* (New Haven, Conn.: Yale University Press, 2008), 4.

7. *Shiwu bencao* (1621), 16.12b.

8. Nanjing zhongyi xueyuan yijing jiaoyan zu, ed., *Huangdi neijing suwen yishi* (Inner canon of the Yellow Emperor: basic questions section with annotations) (Shanghai: Shanghai kexue jishu, 1981), 36–37, 39.

9. *Shiwu bencao* (1621), 16.12b; *Shanyang xianzhi* [district gazetteer] [Shaanxi] (1694), 3.50a.

10. H. T. Huang, *Science and Civilisation in China*, vol. 6: *Biology and Biological Technology, Part 5: Fermentation and Food Science* (Cambridge: Cambridge University Press, 2000), 92.

11. Hong Sen, *Lawei meishi yu jianshen*, 5–6.

12. H. T. Huang, *Science and Civilisation in China*, 6.5:95. Cassia cinnamon comes from the bark of the *Cinnamomum cassia* tree, which is native to southern China. Ceylon cinnamon comes from the bark of *Cinnamomum verum* (also known previously as *Cinnamomum zeylanicum*), which is native to Sri Lanka (formerly Ceylon). Thus both forms of cinnamon come from trees in the same genus. In China, from ancient times through late imperial times, the native cassia cinnamon was used.

13. Ying-Shih Yü, "Han," in *Food in Chinese Culture: Anthropological and Historical Perspectives*, ed. K. C. Chang (New Haven, Conn.: Yale University Press, 1977), 57.

14. H. T. Huang, *Science and Civilisation in China*, 6.5:96.

15. For early names, see, for example, K. C. Chang, "Ancient China," in *Food in Chinese Culture: Anthropological and Historical Perspectives*, ed. K. C. Chang (New Haven, Conn.: Yale University Press, 1977),

28; H. T. Huang, *Science and Civilisation in China*, 6.5:17–18; and Laura May Kaplan Murray, "New World Food Crops in China: Farms, Food, and Families in the Wei River Valley, 1650–1910," Ph.D. diss., University of Pennsylvania, 1985, 14.

16. Most modern sources identify the scientific name for *jiao, huajiao, Shujiao, Chuanjiao*, and *Qinjiao* as *Zanthoxylum bungeanum*; though different Chinese names are sometimes used interchangeably, they sometimes can distinguish between different varieties of that species. See Shen Liansheng, ed., *Colored Atlas of the Compendium of Materia Medica* (Beijing: Huaxia, 1998), 261; and Wu Zhengyi, Peter Raven, and Hong Deyuan, eds., *Flora of China*, vol. 11: *Oxalidaceae Through Aceraceae* (St. Louis: Missouri Botanical Garden, 2008), 54. A few modern sources identify *huajiao* as *Zanthoxylum simulans* (see Shiu-ying Hu, *An Enumeration of Chinese Materia Medica* [Hong Kong: Chinese University of Hong Kong, 1980], 23), but officially this is recognized as a synonym for *Zanthoxylum bungeanum* (see entry for *Z. simulans* in *The Plant List*, http://www.theplantlist.org/tpl1.1/record/kew-2469033, accessed 3/6/2017). A number of other species of *Zanthoxylum* are also used in cuisine and medicine in China, but they have other names in Chinese, including *yaijiao* 崖椒 (*Zanthoxylum schinifolium*), *manjiao* 蔓椒 (*Zanthoxylum nitidum*), and *shi zhuyu* 食茱萸 (*Zanthoxylum ailanthoides*).

17. Liu Daqi, ed., *Zhongguo gudian shipu* (Chinese classical recipes) (Xi'an: Shaanxi Tourism, 1992); see also Lan Yong, "Zhongguo gudai xinla yongliao de shanbian, liubu yu nongye shehui fazhan" (The evolution and spread of pungent and spicy ingredients in the development of agricultural society in ancient China), *Zhongguo shehui jingjishi yanjiu*, no. 4 (2000).

18. For a study of how the tomato was authenticated into Italian cuisine, see Gentilcore, *Pomodoro!*.

19. H. T. Huang, *Science and Civilisation in China*, 6.5:52.

20. *Hanyu dacidian* (The great Chinese word dictionary), vol. 6 (Shanghai: Hanyu dacidian, 1990), 1206.

21. Li Shizhen, *Bencao gangmu* (Systematic pharmacopeia), in *Yingyin Wenyuange siku quanshu*, vol. 773 (Taibei: Shengwu, [1596] 1983), 32.10a.

22. A total of eight names were used in only two provinces. Of those eight, five occurred in adjacent provinces and are included in the final total for regional names. Four names occurred in only three provinces. Of those four, three occurred where each province was contiguous with at least one of the other two; those three are also included in the final total of regional names.

23. Gao Lian, *Zunsheng*, j.16.27b.

24. *Hanyu dacidian*, 7:1358.

25. Tang Xianzu, *Mudan ting (The Peony Pavilion)* (Beijing: Renmin wenxue, [1598] 1978), 113.

26. Wang Fu, *Yilin zuanyao tanyuan* (Exhaustive essential compilation of the forest of medicine) (N.p.: Jiangsu shuju, [1758] 1897), 2.78b.

27. Wang Xiangjin, *Qun fang pu* (The assembly of perfumes) (Jinan: Qi Lu shushe, [1621] 1997), 1.9a, j.1.7a–b.

28. *Gaiping xianzhi* [district gazetteer] [Shengjing] (1682), xia.8b; *Shenzhou zhi* [independent department gazetteer] [Zhili] (1697), 2.17b; *Shandong tongzhi* [provincial gazetteer] (1736), 24.2b.

29. For the confusion with place names, there are similar sayings concerning the word *di* 地 (place).

30. See Joseph Needham, *Science and Civilisation in China*, vol. 6: *Biology and Biological Technology: Part 1, Botany*. Cambridge: Cambridge University Press, 1986), 311.

31. For example, the following editions of the *Shengjing Provincial Gazetteer* all employ *huajiao* for Sichuan pepper: 1736, 27.4b; 1779, 106.9a; 1852, 27.4b.

32. Chen Jiru, *Zhifu qi shu* (A masterpiece in becoming rich) (c. 1639), 42.

33. *Shanyin xianzhi* [district gazetteer] [Zhejiang] (1671), 7.3a.

34. Gao Lian, *Zunsheng*, j.16.27b.

35. *Shiwu bencao* (1621), 16.12b.

36. *Shanyin District Gazetteer* (1671), 7.3a.

37. Gao Shiqi, *Beishu bao weng lu* (An account of the flowering plants treasured in the Beishu [garden, Hangzhou]) (1690), in *Xuxiu siku quanshu*, 1119:241.

38. *Shiwu bencao* (1621), 16.12b.

39. See E. N. Anderson, *The Food of China* (New Haven, Conn.: Yale University Press, 1988), esp. 156; Andrew Coe, *Chop Suey: A Cultural*

History of Chinese Food in the United States (Oxford: Oxford University Press, 2009), 86–87; Fuchsia Dunlop, *Land of Plenty: A Treasury of Authentic Sichuan Cooking* (New York: Norton, 2001), 53–81; Fuchsia Dunlop, *Revolutionary Chinese Cookbook: Recipes from Hunan Province* (New York: Norton, 2006), 20–29.

40. Tong Yuejian, attrib., *Tiao ding ji* (The harmonious cauldron) (Beijing: Zhongguo fangzhi, [c.1790] 2006), 25, 27, 91, 97, 139. All three recipes in the box are from Tong, 25 and 91.

41. See Cheng Anqi, *La fan tian* (Spiciness crosses the heavens) (Shenyang: Liaoning kexue jishu chubanshe, 2006), 6.

42. *Huangyan xianzhi* [district gazetteer] [Zhejiang] (1877), 32.19a.

43. For gazetteers discussing dried chiles, see *Dading fuzhi* [prefectural gazetteer] [Guizhou] (1850), 58.10a; *Shangyu xianzhi* [district gazetteer] [Zhejiang] (1890), 28.9a. For comparisons of fresh and dried chiles, see Cheng Anqi, *La fan tian*, 4–6; Hong Sen, *Lawei meishi yu jianshen*, 15–19; Danielle Walsh, "When to Use Dried Chilies vs. Fresh vs. Powder vs. Flakes," *Bon Appétit* (March 3, 2014), http://www.bon appetit.com/test-kitchen/cooking-tips/article/how-to-use-chiles.

44. *Chengcheng xianzhi* [district gazetteer] [Shaanxi] (1851), 5.23a.

45. Lan Yong, "Zhongguo gudai xinla yongliao de shanbian," 15.

46. Zheng Zhu and Zang Xiaoman, "Chuancai shi zenyang bian la de?" (How did Sichuan cuisine become spicy?), *Guoxue wenhua*, no. 4 (2009): 57.

47. Tong Yuejian, *Tiao ding ji*, 218.

48. Hong Sen, *Lawei meishi yu jianshen*, 59.

49. Lan Yong, "Zhongguo gudai xinla yongliao de shanbian," 15; H. T. Huang, *Science and Civilisation in China*, 6.5:95–96; Zheng and Zang, "Chuancai shi zenyang bian la de?," 57; and author's database.

50. Tang Xianzu, *Mudan ting*, 113. The earliest gazetteer to use the name *lajiao* is *Guangxi tongzhi* [provincial gazetteer] (1733), 93.28a.

51. For example, Teng Youde, "Sichuan lajiao" (Sichuan chiles), *Lajiao zazhi*, no. 1 (2004); and Zheng and Zang, "Chuancai shi zenyang bian la de?." In Sichuan, the use of *haijiao* seems to refer to introduction from the coast rather than emphasizing an overseas origin. Certainly chiles are viewed as an important "authentic" aspect of Sichuanese identity today. In Taiwan, the name "foreign ginger" is

still common in Taiwanese dialect (*Minnanhua*), although *lajiao* is quite prevalent in Mandarin.

52. Wang Maohua, Wang Cengyu, and Hong Seung Tae, "Lüelun lishi shang dongya sanguo lajiao de chuanbo, zhongzhi yu gongyong fajue" (Overview and exploration of the history of chiles in the three East Asian countries, including their spread, cultivation and use), *Zhongguoshi yanjiu* [S. Korea], no. 101 (April 2016): 313.

53. Zhang Yushu, Watanabe Atsushi, and Yan Yiping, eds., *Jiaozheng Kangxi zidian* (Corrected Kangxi character dictionary), vol. 1 (Taibei: Yiwen yishu guan, 1965), 2838. *La* is listed under a variant form, with the left and right components of the character reversed: 𣐽. This definition is attributed to the second-century-CE text *Shuowen jiezi*.

54. Zhang, Watanabe, and Yan, *Kangxi zidian*, 1:2836.

55. While I examined a number of key twentieth- and twenty-first-century dictionaries, my search was not exhaustive.

56. *Hanyu da zidian* (1993), 1681. The Zhongguo shehuikexueyuan yuyan yanjiusuo's *Xiandai Hanyu cidian* (Modern Chinese dictionary) (Beijing: Shangwu, 2012, 767) has almost the identical definition, including the same ordering for ginger, garlic, and chile pepper.

57. Li Xingjian, ed. *Xiandai Hanyu guifan cidian* (Standardized modern Chinese dictionary) (Beijing: Waiyu jiaoxue yu yanjiu chubanshe, 2004), 776.

58. *Hangzhou fuzhi* [prefectural gazetteer] [Zhejiang] (1686), j.6.23a.

59. *Haining zhouzhi* [departmental gazetteer] [Hangzhou prefecture, Zhejiang] (1776), 2.55a.

60. Wu Xingqin, "Lajiao jiang" (Chile pepper paste), in *Baihua qiangao* (Baihua's [Wu Xingqin] early drafts) (n.p., 1783), 38.9b.

61. Chen Haozi, *Mi chuan hua jing* (Secret transmissions from the mirror of flowers) (1688), 5.43b.

62. Liu Changzhi, "Chen Haozi," in *Zhongguo gudai kexuejia zhuanji*, vol. 2, ed. Du Shiran (Beijing: kexue chubanshe, 1993), 989–91. Jiangnan is the lower Yangzi River delta region.

63. *Taihai caifeng tukao* (1746), 2.8a.

64. Zhang Zhijie, "*Taihai caifeng tukao dian, zhu*" (Annotations to *Taihai caifeng tukao*), in *Zhonghua keji shixuehui congkan*, vol. 1 (Xinbei City: Zhonghua keji shixue hui, 2011), 33.

65. Taishi Kejia xiaochao, https://www.xinshipu.com/zuofa/145688; Taishi lu zhujiao, https://www.xinshipu.com/zuofa/98620; Taishi chao touchou, https://www.xinshipu.com/zuofa/647899, all accessed July 30, 2018.

66. For more on the salt industry, see Tao-chang Chiang, "The Salt Trade in Ch'ing China," *Modern Asian Studies* 17, no. 2 (1983): 197–219; Ray Huang, "Ming Fiscal Administration," in *The Cambridge History of China*, vol. 8: *The Ming Dynasty, 1368–1644*, part 2, ed. Denis Twitchett and Frederick Mote (Cambridge: Cambridge University Press, 1998), 139–44; and Madeleine Zelin, *The Merchants of Zigong: Industrial Entrepreneurship in Early Modern China* (New York: Columbia University Press, 2005), esp. 3–6.

67. This discussion is based on Chiang, "The Salt Trade in Ch'ing China," 205, 198, 197.

68. Tian Wen, *Qian shu* (Account of Qian [Guizhou]), in *Yue ya tang congshu*, vol. 25 (Taibei: Yi wen yin shu guan, [1690] 1965), 2.2b, 2.3a.

69. Arthur W. Hummel, *Eminent Chinese of the Ch'ing Period* (Taibei: Southern Materials, [1943] 1991), 719.

70. Huang, "Ming Fiscal Administration," 143.

71. On the 1620s crisis in the salt industry, see Song Yingxing, *Yeyi* (Unofficial opinions) (Shanghai: Renmin chubanshe, [1636] 1976), 35–38.

72. Chen Wenzhao, "Hunan lajiao fazhan zhuangkuang," *Lajiao zazhi*, no. 2 (2007): 8.

73. *Sizhou fuzhi* [prefectural gazetteer] [Guizhou] (1722), 4.19a; *Guizhou tongzhi* [provincial gazetteer] (1741), 15.53b; *Zheng'an zhouzhi* [departmental gazetteer] [Guizhou] (1818), 3.1b.

74. Laura Hostetler, *Qing Colonial Enterprise: Ethnography and Cartography in Early Modern China* (Chicago: University of Chicago Press, 2001), 101–5.

75. Norma Diamond, "Defining the Miao: Ming, Qing, and Contemporary Views," in *Cultural Encounters on China's Ethnic Frontiers*, ed. Stevan Harrell (Seattle: University of Washington Press, 1995), 95–97.

76. *Guangxi tongzhi* [provincial gazetteer] (1733), 93.28a.

77. Anderson, *The Food of China*, 131.

78. For example, Tian Wen, *Qian shu*, 2.3a.

79. Hu Yiyin, "Lajiao mingcheng kaoshi" (A philological study of the naming of chile peppers), *Gujin nongye*, no. 4 (2013): 71.

80. Wang, Wang, and Hong, "Lüelun lishi shang dongya sanguo lajiao de chuanbo," 309.

81. Cited in Wang, Wang, and Hong, "Lüelun lishi shang dongya sanguo lajiao de chuanbo," 312.

82. Tu Cuizhong, *Sancai zaoyi* (Embellishments on the Sancai encyclopedia) (1689), 31.19a.

83. For example, *Changsha xianzhi* [district gazetteer] [Hunan] (1817), 14.12b. Examples of other varietal names for chiles that grew upward are heavenly peppers (*tian jiao* 天椒), *Shengjing tongzhi* [provincial gazetteer] (1736), 27.4b; pointing to heaven peppers (*zhitian jiao* 指天椒), *Rong xianzhi* [district gazetteer] [Guangxi] (1897), 5.7b; soaring pepper (*chongtian jiao* 沖天椒), *Gejiu xianzhi* [district gazetteer] [Yunnan] (1922), 5.10a; and facing heaven brush (*chaotian bi* 朝天筆), *Chongyin Yong'an xianxuzhi* [Revised district gazetteer] [Fujian] (1834), 9.3a. It is likely that these were just different regional names for the same cultivar, but it is possible that there were two or more distinct varieties.

84. For example, *Guiyang fuzhi* [prefectural gazetteer] [Guizhou] (1852), 47.7a.

85. Dunlop, *Sichuan*, 54.

86. For example, see *Zunyi fuzhi* [prefectural gazetteer] [Guizhou] (1841), 17.6a.

87. See Frederick Simoons, *Food in China: A Cultural and Historical Inquiry* (Boca Raton, Fla.: CRC Press, 1991), 213–16.

88. See Janice E. Stockard, *Daughters of the Canton Delta: Marriage Patterns and Economic Strategies in South China, 1860–1930* (Stanford, Calif.: Stanford University Press, 1989), 41–44.

89. Wu Qijun, *Zhiwu mingshi tukao* (Illustrated treatise on the names and natures of plants) (1848), 6.19b.

90. Zhi Weicheng, *Qingdai puxue dashi liezhuan* (Biographies of masters of textual studies of the Qing dynasty), in *Qingdai zhuanji congkan*, vol. 12, ed. Zhou Junfu (Taibei: Mingwen shuju, [1924] 1986), 677; Qian Shifu, ed., *Qingdai zhiguan nianbiao* (Chronological tables of

Qing period officials), vol. 2 (Beijing: Zhonghua shuju, 1980), 1456–67, 1677–90.

91. Wu Qijun, *Zhiwu mingshi tukao*, 6.19b.

92. *Shanyin xianzhi* [district gazetteer] [Zhejiang] (1671), 7.3a.

93. For example, *Jianchang fuzhi* [prefectural gazetteer] [Jiangxi] (1756), 13.12b; *Jianchang fuzhi* [Jiangxi] (1759), 9.2b.

94. Simoons, *Food in China*, 169.

95. *Chongxiu Suzhou xin zhi* [independent prefecture gazetteer] [Gansu] (1737), *ce* 6.11a.

96. *Disan guai* (The third oddity), poster, Xi'an, Shaanxi, viewed by the author in 2014 (fig. 5.3).

97. Jean Andrews, *Peppers: The Domesticated Capsicums* (Austin: University of Texas Press, 1995), 79–81.

98. Tian Wen, *Qian shu*, 2.3a.

99. *Zhen'an xianzhi* [district gazetteer] [Shaanxi] (1755), 7.13a.

100. *Zunyi fuzhi* [prefectural gazetteer] [Guizhou] (1841), 17.6a.

101. *Haining zhouzhi* [departmental gazetteer] [Zhejiang] (1776), 2.55a.

102. *Shandong tongzhi* [provincial gazetteer] (1736), 24.2b.

3. Spicing Up the Pharmacopeia

1. Georges Métailié, *Science and Civilisation in China*, vol. 6: *Biology and Biological Technology, Part 4: Traditional Botany: An Ethnobotanical Approach*, trans. Janet Lloyd (Cambridge: Cambridge University Press, 2015), 555.

2. Chen Zhi, *Yanglao fengqin shu*, cited and translated in Joseph Needham, Nathan Sivin, and Gwei-Djen Lu, *Science and Civilisation in China*, vol. 6: *Biology and Biological Technology, Part 2: Medicine* (Cambridge: Cambridge University Press, 2000), 79.

3. *Shiwu bencao* (1621), 16.12b.

4. Xu Wenbi, *Xinbian shoushi chuanzhen* (New compilation of the transmitted truths on longevity), in *Xuxiu siku quanshu*, vol. 1030 (Shanghai: Shanghai guji chubanshe, [1771] 2002), 160.

5. Paul Unschuld, *Medicine in China: A History of Ideas* (Berkeley: University of California Press, 1985), 4.

6. Unschuld, *Medicine in China*, 5.

7. Linda Barnes and T. J. Hinrichs, "Introduction," in *Chinese Medicine and Healing: An Illustrated History*, ed. T. J. Hinrichs and Linda Barnes (Cambridge, Mass.: Harvard University Press, 2013), 1.

8. Eugene Anderson, "Folk Nutritional Therapy in Modern China," in *Chinese Medicine and Healing: An Illustrated History*, ed. T. J. Hinrichs and Linda Barnes (Cambridge, Mass.: Harvard University Press, 2013), 260.

9. Yi-Li Wu, "The Qing Period," in *Chinese Medicine and Healing: An Illustrated History*, ed. T. J. Hinrichs and Linda Barnes (Cambridge, Mass.: Harvard University Press, 2013), 170.

10. For more on *bencao*, see Wu Yigu and Song Liren, eds., *Zhonghua bencao* (Chinese bencao), vol. 1 (Shanghai: Shanghai kexue jishu chubanshe, 1998), 5-43; Carla Nappi, *The Monkey and the Inkpot: Natural History and Its Transformations in Early Modern China* (Cambridge, Mass.: Harvard University Press, 2009), 27–32; and Joseph Needham, *Science and Civilisation in China*, vol. 6: *Biology and Biological Technology, Part 1: Botany* (Cambridge: Cambridge University Press, 1986), 220–48.

11. See Li Shizhen, *Bencao gangmu* (Systematic pharmacopeia), in *Yingyin Wenyuange siku quanshu*, vol. 772 (Taibei: Shengwu, [1596] 1983), preface.

12. Needham, *Science and Civilisation in China*, 6.1:308.

13. Wu and Song, *Zhonghua bencao*, 1:33.

14. Nappi, *The Monkey and the Inkpot*, 21.

15. For more on Li Shizhen, see Nappi, *The Monkey and the Inkpot*, esp. chap. 1; Needham, *Science and Civilisation in China*, 6.1:308–21; and Wu and Song, *Zhonghua bencao*, 1:36.

16. Chen Jiru, *Shiwu bencao* (Pharmacopeia of edible items), in *Gugong zhenben congkan*, vol. 366 (Haikou: Hainan chubanshe, [1638] 2000), 433; Yao Kecheng, attrib., *Shiwu bencao* (Beijing: Renmin weisheng chubanshe, [1642] 1994), 965.

17. Shen Lilong, *Shiwu bencao huizuan* (Collected compilation of the pharmacopeia of edible items] (1691).

18. Needham, *Science and Civilisation in China*, 6.1:326.

19. Li Shizhen, *Bencao gangmu*, j. 52.

20. For more on this debate, see Nappi, *The Monkey and the Inkpot*, 130–35.

21. For more on Zhao Xuemin, see Needham, *Science and Civilisation in China*, 6.1:325–28; Wu and Song, *Zhonghua bencao*, 1:41–42.

22. *Yangchun xianzhi* [district gazetteer] [Guangdong] (1687), 14.29b; *Sizhou fuzhi* [prefectural gazetteer] [Guizhou] (1722), 4.19a.

23. *Shiwu bencao* (1621), 16.12b.

24. Jean Andrews, *Peppers: The Domesticated Capsicums* (Austin: University of Texas Press, 1995), 74.

25. H. T. Huang, *Science and Civilisation in China*, vol. 6: *Biology and Biological Technology, Part 5: Fermentation and Food Science* (Cambridge: Cambridge University Press, 2000), 95.

26. Zhi Weichen, *Qingdai puxue dashi liezhuan* (Biographies of masters of textual studies of the Qing dynasty), in *Qingdai zhuanji congkan*, vol. 12, ed. Zhou Junfu (Taibei: Mingwen shuju, [1924] 1986), 196.

27. Wang Fu, *Yilin zuanyao tanyuan* (Exhaustive essential compilation of the forest of medicine) (N.p.: Jiangsu shuju, [1758] 1897), preface.1a.

28. Wang Fu, *Yilin*, 2.79a.

29. Nanjing zhongyi xueyuan yijing jiaoyan zu, ed., *Huangdi neijing suwen yishi* (Shanghai: Shanghai kexue jishu, 1981), 39.

30. Andrews, *Peppers*, 75.

31. Cited in Zhao Xuemin, *Bencao gangmu shiyi* (Correction of omissions in the *Bencao gangmu*), in *Xuxiu siku quanshu*, vol. 995 (Shanghai: Shanghai guji chubanshe, [1803] 2002), 8.72b, 73b; *Jianchang fuzhi* [prefectural gazetteer] [Jiangxi] (1759), 9.3a.

32. Zhao Xuemin, *Bencao gangmu shiyi*, 8.73b.

33. Wu Qijun, *Zhiwu mingshi tukao* (Illustrated treatise on the names and natures of plants) (N.p., 1848), 6.19b–20a.

34. For more on *yinyang*, see Unschuld, *Medicine in China*, 55–58; and Ted Kaptchuk, *The Web That Has No Weaver: Understanding Chinese Medicine* (New York: Congdon and Weed, 1983), 7–15, 40–41.

35. See, for example, the 1621 edition of the *Shiwu bencao*, 16.12b.

36. See Unschuld, *Medicine in China*, 56–57; Kaptchuk, *The Web That Has No Weaver*, 9.

37. See, for example, Xu Wenbi, *Xinbian shoushi chuanzhen*, 160.

38. See Unschuld, *Medicine in China*, 57.

39. See, for example, citations from now lost texts included in Zhao Xuemin, *Bencao gangmu shiyi*, 8.72b.

40. *Shiwu bencao* (1621), 16.12b.

41. Wang Fu, *Yilin*, 2.79a.

42. Wang Fu, *Yilin*, 2.79a. For *Wu zhuyu* as *Evodia rutaecarpa* (a synonym of *Tetradium ruticarpum*), see Shen Liansheng, *Colored Atlas of the Compendium of Materia Medica* (Beijing: Huaxia, 1998), 263; and Shiu-ying Hu, *An Enumeration of Chinese Materia Medica* (Hong Kong: Chinese University of Hong Kong, 1980), 161.

43. Zhao Xuemin, *Bencao gangmu shiyi*, 8.73b.

44. Cited in Hong Sen, ed., *Lawei meishi yu jianshen* (Spicy flavor in gourmet food for health) (Tianjin: Tianjin keji fanyi chubanshe, 2005), 9.

45. Zhao Xuemin, *Bencao gangmu shiyi*, 8.71b, 72b; the recipe for chilblains in the box is from 73a.

46. Kaptchuk, *The Web That Has No Weaver*, 35.

47. Zou Xuan, *Shouqin yanglao xinshu*, cited and translated in Needham, Sivin, and Lu, *Science and Civilisation in China*, 6.6:79.

48. Kaptchuk, *The Web That Has No Weaver*, 41.

49. *Shiwu bencao*, 16.12b.

50. *Dading fuzhi* [prefectural gazetteer] [Guizhou] (1850), 58.10a; *Chongxiu Wuhe xianzhi* [district gazetteer] [Anhui] (1893), 10.9a.

51. *Shiwu bencao* (1621), 16.12b.

52. "Vitamin A," in *Health Encyclopedia* (University of Rochester Medical Center), https://www.urmc.rochester.edu/encyclopedia/content.aspx?contenttypeid=19&contentid=VitaminA, accessed September 9, 2019.

53. Andrews, *Peppers*, 75.

54. Frederick Simoons, *Food in China: A Cultural and Historical Inquiry* (Boca Raton, Fla.: CRC Press, 1991), 63. Pulses are seeds from legumes that are low in oil, such as lentils and chickpeas.

55. Andrews, *Peppers*, 75.

56. See, for example, Wang Fu, *Yilin*, 2.79a; Zhao Xuemin, *Bencao gangmu shiyi*, 8.72b; and *Chiping xianzhi* [district gazetteer] [Shandong] (1935), 9.16a.

57. See C. Peter Herman, "Effects of Heat on Appetite," in *Nutritional Needs in Hot Environments: Applications for Military Personnel in Field*

Operations, ed. Bernadette Marriot (Washington, D.C.: National Academy Press, 1993).

58. Joshua Tewksbury and Gary Nabhan, "Directed Deterrence by Capsaicin in Chillies," *Nature*, no. 412 (2001): 403.

59. Henry N. Ridley, *The Dispersal of Plants Throughout the World* (Ashford, UK: L. Reeve, 1930), 396.

60. Andrews, *Peppers*, 75.

61. Joshua Tewksbury et al., "Evolutionary Ecology of Pungency in Wild Chiles," *Proceedings of the National Academy of Sciences* 105, no. 33 (2008): 11808–11.

62. *Anxi xianzhi* [district gazetteer] [Quanzhou prefecture, Fujian] (1757), 4.10a.

63. Cited in Andrews, *Peppers*, 74.

64. *Quanzhou fuzhi* [prefectural gazetteer] (1763), 19.11b; *Jinjiang xianzhi* [district gazetteer] (1765), 1.53b–54a; *Tong'an xianzhi* [district gazetteer] (1768), 14.21b; *Tong'an xianzhi* [district gazetteer] (1798), 14.21b; *Jinjiang xianzhi* [district gazetteer] (1829), 73.8a; *Maxiang tingzhi* [subprefectural gazetteer] (1893), 12.7a–b; *Tong'an xianzhi* [district gazetteer] (1929), 11.13b.

65. Xu Wenbi, *Xinbian shoushi chuanzhen*, 160.

66. Cited in Zhao Xuemin, *Bencao gangmu shiyi*, 8.72b.

67. The treatment described in the box is cited in Zhao Xuemin, *Bencao gangmu shiyi*, 8.73a.

68. Unschuld, *Medicine in China*, 7.

69. Marta Hanson, *Speaking of Epidemics in Chinese Medicine: Disease and the Geographic Imagination in Late Imperial China* (New York: Routledge, 2011), 25–26.

70. *Enping xianzhi* [district gazetteer] [Guangdong] (1766), 9.10b–11a.

71. For example, see Mayo Clinic, "Drugs and Supplements: Hydroxychloroquine," http://www.mayoclinic.org/drugs-supplements/hydroxychloroquine-oral-route/description/drg-20064216, accessed February 10, 2017.

72. Zhao Xuemin, *Bencao gangmu shiyi*, 8.73b, emphasis added.

73. Wu Xingqin, *Baihua qiangao* (Baihua's early drafts) (1783), 38.9b.

74. Xu Wenbi, *Xinbian shoushi chuanzhen*, 160; *Liuzhou fuzhi* [prefectural gazetteer] (1764), 12.6a; *Liuzhou district gazetteer* (1764), 2.27;

Maping district gazetteer [Liuzhou prefecture] (1764), 2.31a. *Liuzhou fuzhi*, 12.6a, is the source of the hemorrhoid cure in the box.

75. Andrews, *Peppers*, 76.

76. For example, Capsagel, Capsin, Capzasin, Pain Enz, and Zostrix.

77. Cited in Zhao Xuemin, *Bencao gangmu shiyi*, 8.74a.

78. Cited in Zhao Xuemin, *Bencao gangmu shiyi*, 8.72b–73a.

79. Xu Wenbi, *Xinbian shoushi chuanzhen*, 160.

80. *Lingling xianzhi* [district gazetteer] [Hunan] (1876), 1.67a.

81. *Yongzhou fuzhi* [prefectural gazetteer] [Hunan] (1828), 7shang.8b.

82. Cited in Zhao Xuemin, *Bencao gangmu shiyi*, 8.72b, 73b–74a.

83. Xu Wenbi, *Xinbian shoushi chuanzhen*, 160.

84. Cited in Zhao Xuemin, *Bencao gangmu shiyi*, 8.72b, 74a.

85. *Dantu xianzhi* [district gazetteer] [Jiangsu] (1879), 17.7a–b.

86. For example, Geng Junying et al., *Practical Traditional Chinese Medicine and Pharmacology: Herbal Formulas* (Beijing: New World Press, 1991); Li Wenliang and Qi Qiang, eds., *Qianjia miaofang* (Miraculous formulas from myriad experts), 2 vols. (Beijing: Jiefangjun chubanshe, 2016); Peng Huairen, ed., *Zhongyi fangji da cidian* (Dictionary of Chinese medicine formulas), 11 vols. (Beijing: Renmin weisheng, 1993); Quanguo zhongcao yao huibian bianxie zu, ed., *Quanguo zhongcao yao huibian* (Collection of Chinese herb medicines from the whole country), 2 vols. (Beijing: Renmin weisheng, 1988); Daniel Reid, *Chinese Herbal Medicine* (Boston: Shambhala, 1992); Volker Scheid et al., comps. and trans., *Chinese Herbal Medicine: Formulas and Strategies*, 2nd ed. (Seattle: Eastland Press, 2015); *Zhongyi changyong caoyao, Zhongyao, fangji shouce* (Handbook of commonly used plant-based medicine, traditional medicine and formulas for Chinese medicine) (Hong Kong: Yiyao weisheng, 1972); *Zhongyi shijia: zhongyao xue* (Houses of Chinese medicine: studies of Chinese drugs), http://www.zysj.com.cn/lilunshuji/zhongyaoxue/index.html, accessed May 13, 2015.

87. Wu and Song, *Zhonghua bencao*, 7:251–54.

88. He Jiguang (singer), Lu Song (composer), and Xie Dingren (lyricist), "Lajiao ge" (Chile pepper song), *20 shiji Zhonghua getan mingren baiji: He Jiguang* (Collection of the hundred best Chinese singers of the 20th century: He Jiguang) (Beijing: Zhongguo changpian,

1999), track 13. The whole song is reproduced, translated, and analyzed further in chapter 6.

89. Hong Sen, *Lawei meishi yu jianshen*, 9.

4. Too Hot for Words

1. *Shiwu bencao* (1621), 16.12b.
2. Wang Lu, *Huashi zuobian* (Supplement to the history of flowers), in
   Xuxiu siku quanshu, vol. 1117, ([1618] 2002), 23.5b.
3. *Zhen'an xianzhi* [district gazetteer] [Shaanxi] (1755), 7.13a.
4. *Jianchang fuzhi* [prefectural gazetteer] [Jiangxi], (1756), 13.12b.
5. See, for example, Joseph Dennis, *Writing, Publishing, and Reading
   Local Gazetteers in Imperial China, 1100–1700* (Cambridge, Mass.:
   Harvard University Asia Center, 2015), esp. chap. 1.
6. For example, see Ho Ping-ti, "The Introduction of American Food
   Plants Into China," *American Anthropologist* 57, no. 2 (1955): 191–201;
   and Ho, *Studies on the Population of China, 1368–1953* (Cambridge,
   Mass.: Harvard University Press, 1959).
7. See Carol Benedict, *Golden-Silk Smoke: A History of Tobacco in
   China, 1550–2010* (Berkeley: University of California Press, 2011),
   esp. 7–33.
8. Zhao Xuemin, *Bencao gangmu shiyi*, completed around 1803 but not
   published until 1871.
9. The recipes in Liu Daqi's collection with chiles occur on pages 1895,
   1959, and 1970. Two of these come from Tong Yuejian's *Tiao ding ji*
   from c. 1790, and the other comes from Xu Ke's *Qing bai lei chao* from
   1916. While Liu identifies chiles in two recipes in one other source,
   he incorrectly identifies them in the list of ingredients due to punc-
   tuation errors. Both recipes actually call for mustard seed, *jiela* 芥
   辣 (Zhu Yizun, *Shi xian hong mi* (Guide to the mysteries of cuisine)
   (Beijing: Zhongguo shangye, [1680] 1985), 144, 151). Liu instead sep-
   arates the two characters into two ingredients: *jie* as mustard, without
   specifying which part of the plant, and just *la* as chile pepper (Liu
   Daqi, *Zhongguo gudian shipu* (Chinese classical recipes) (Xi'an:
   Shaanxi Tourism, 1992), 821, 1202). In the late seventeenth century,
   however, *la* would have been too vague a term to use in a list of

ingredients. The more direct correlation between *la* and chiles did not occur until the the mid-nineteenth century, and even then it would have been highly unusual to just use that single character to mean chiles in a recipe.

10. Wang Lu, *Huashi zuobian*, 23.5b.

11. Only two other texts include spindly sea vine as a secondary name (none as a primary name): Chen Haozi's botanical work *Michuan huajing* (Secret transmissions from the mirror of flowers) from 1688 (5.43a) quite possibly cites the name from Wang; and Zhao Xuemin's supplement to the *Bencao gangmu* directly quotes Chen's work (8.73a).

12. I have found only three other texts that use coral to describe chiles: Xu Wenbi, in a medical text from 1771, *Xinbian shoushi chuanzhen*, uses it as a color descriptor (160); Zhao Xuemin, *Bencao gangmu shiyi*, cites a now lost text that also used it as a color descriptor (8.73b); and *Yuanzhou fuzhi* [prefectural gazetteer] [Jiangxi] (1860), 10.2a, gives coral pepper as another name.

13. Gao Lian, *Zunsheng*, 16.27b.

14. For example, *Shiwu bencao* (1621), 16.12b; *Ningxiang xianzhi* [district gazetteer] [Hunan] (1867), 25.8a.

15. Wang Xiangjin, *Qun fang pu* (The assembly of perfumes), in *Siku quanshu cunmu congshu bubian*, vol. 80 (Jinan: Qi Lu shushe, [1621] 1997), 1.7a–b, 1.9a; and *Shiwu bencao*, 16.12b.

16. Yi Su-gwang, *Jibong yuseol* (Topical discourses of Jibong), annotated by Nam Man-seong, vol 2 (Seoul: Euryu munhwasa, [1614] 1994), 635.

17. *Jianchang fuzhi* [prefectural gazetteer] [Jiangxi] (1756), 13.12b.

18. Joanna Waley-Cohen, "The Quest for Perfect Balance: Taste and Gastronomy in Imperial China," in *Food: A History of Taste*, ed. Paul Freedman (Berkeley: University of California Press, 2007), 124–26.

19. François Jullien, "The Chinese Notion of 'Blandness' as a Virtue: A Preliminary Outline," trans. Graham Parkes, *Philosophy East and West*, 43, no. 1 (1993): 107.

20. *Hanyu da cidian* (The great Chinese word dictionary), vol. 9 (Shanghai: Hanyu dacidian, 1992), 490. Hun 葷 includes the grass radical.

21. Zheng Xuan. "Yili jiao" (Commentary on the *Yili*), in *Shisan jing* (The thirteen classics], 1815 ed., 75–1, in Hanji quanwen ziliao ku, http://hanchi.ihp.sinica.edu.tw/ihp/hanji.htm. *Cong* 蔥 is *Allium fistulosum*, often translated as scallion but also known as the bunching onion; *xie* 薤 is *Allium chinense*, usually translated as Chinese onion.

22. Cited in *Hanyu dacidian*, 9:490.

23. Zhang Tingyu et al., eds., *Ming shi* (History of the Ming dynasty), in Hanji quanwen ziliao ku, 47.1239, http://hanchi.ihp.sinica.edu.tw/ihp/hanji.htm.

24. Zhang Yushu, Watanabe Atsushi, and Yan Yiping, eds., *Jiaozheng Kangxi zidian* (Corrected Kangxi character dictionary), vol. 1 (Taibei: Yiwen yishu guan, 1965), 1:2373.

25. James Benn, "Another Look at the Pseudo-Śūraṃgama sūtra," *Harvard Journal of Asiatic Studies* 68, no. 1 (2008): 57.

26. *Lengyan jing* (*Śūraṅgama Sūtra*), j. 8, 925, Zhonghua dianzi Fodian xiehui (Chinese Buddhist Electronic Text Association), CBETA.org. The "five pungents" (*wuxin*) in the sūtra are (1) *dasuan* 大蒜 or garlic (*Allium sativum*); (2) *gecong* 茖蔥, another name for *xie* 薤 or Chinese onion (*Allium chinense*); (3) *cicong* 慈蔥 or scallion (*Allium fistulosum*); (4) *lancong* 蘭蔥, another name for *jiu* 韭 or garlic chives (*Allium tuberosum*); and (5) *Xingqu* 興渠 or asafetida (*Ferula assa-foetida*).

27. See John Kieschnick, "Buddhist Vegetarianism in China," in *Of Tripod and Palate: Food, Politics, and Religion in Traditional China*, ed. Roel Sterckx (New York: Palgrave Macmillan, 2004), 191–92.

28. Li Shizhen, *Bencao gangmu* (Systematic pharmacopeia), in *Yingyin Wenyuange siku quanshu*, vol. 773 (Taibei: Shengwu, [1596] 1983), 26.20a. Lianxing jia 鍊形家 are identified as *fangshi* or alchemists or magicians in the *Hanyu da cidian*, 9:932.

29. Li Shizhen, *Bencao gangmu*, 26.20a. Li uses the term generic term *Daojia* for Daoists.

30. Zhang Tingyu et al., *Ming shi*, 47:1239–40.

31. Thomas Wilson, "Sacrifice and the Imperial Cult of Confucius," *History of Religions* 41, no. 3 (2002): 272.

32. For example, the *Lingui xianzhi* [district gazetteer] from Guangxi from 1802 claims that Li identified the chile as edible prickly ash (*shi zhuyu* 食茱萸, 12.8b). The *Guiyang fuzhi* [prefectural gazetteer]

[Guizhou] from 1852 asserts that the chile is listed as earth pepper (*dijiao* 地椒) in the *Bencao gangmu* (47.7a). However, in Li's work these two plants are clearly not the chile but instead two different plants in the same genus as Sichuan pepper (32.10a, 20b–22a).

33. *Yunnan tongzhi* [provincial gazetteer] (1736), 27.3a.

34. Shen Liansheng, ed., *Colored Atlas of the Compendium of Materia Medica* (Beijing: Huaxia, 1998), 263.

35. Jiang Mudong and Wang Siming, "Lajiao zai zhongguo chuanbo ji qi yingxiang" (The spread of the chile pepper and its influence in China), *Zhongguo nong shi* 2, no. 24 (2005): 18, 22.

36. *Changyang xianzhi* [district gazetteer] [Hubei] (1754), 6.20b; *Pingyuan zhouzhi* [departmental gazetteer] [Guizhou] (1756), 14.24b; *Chenzhou fuzhi* [prefectural gazetteer] [Hunan] (1765), 15.12a; Duan Rulin, *Chunan miaozhi* [Sichuan] (1758), 15.

37. *Yunnan provincial gazetteer* (1736), 27.2a, 3a–b.

38. Tian Wen, *Qian shu* (Account of Qian [Guizhou]), in *Yue ya tang congshu*, vol. 25 (Taibei: Yi wen yin shu guan, [1690] 1965), 2.3a; *Guangxi tongzhi* [provincial gazetteer] (1733), 93.28a; *Dayi xianzhi* [district gazetteer] [Sichuan] (1749), 3.32a.

39. *Ningzhou departmental gazetteer* [Yunnan] (1799), 1.13b. This gazetteer apparently now exists only as a single copy held in the University of Washington Library, so Jiang and Wang did not have access to it.

40. *Yunnan tongzhi* [provincial gazetteer] (1835), 67.14a.

41. *Yunnan tongzhi* [provincial gazetteer] (1894), 67.14a.

42. *Yunnan tongzhi* [provincial gazetteer] (1901), 56.6a.

43. Zhao Xuemin, *Bencao gangmu shiyi*, 8.71b. Chen's work is now lost.

44. Brian Dott, *Identity Reflections: Pilgrimages to Mount Tai in Late Imperial China* (Cambridge, Mass.: Harvard University Asia Center, 2004), chap. 3.

45. I thoroughly examined a whole series of gazetteers from Shandong, including all editions from the Republican period as well as those from the Qing dynasty.

46. For example, *Yangxin xianzhi* [district gazetteer] [Shandong] (1926), 7.4a.

47. For example, *Yinxian tongzhi* [district gazetteer] [Zhejiang] (1933), *bowu zhi* 3:13a.

48. Mark Swislocki, *Culinary Nostalgia: Regional Food Culture and the Urban Experience in Shanghai* (Stanford, Calif.: Stanford University Press, 2009), 75–80, 152.

5. Chiles as Beautiful Objects and Literary Emblems

1. See, for example, *Pi xianzhi* [district gazetteer] [Sichuan] (1762), 2.5b.
2. *Yuanzhou fuzhi* [prefectural gazetteer] [Jiangxi] (1860), 10.2a. For earth coral (*di shanhu* 地珊瑚), see Wang Lu, *Huashi zuobian* (Supplement to the history of flowers), in *Xuxiu siku quanshu*, vol. 1117 (Shanghai: Shanghai guji chubanshe, [1618] 2002), 23.5b.
3. Qin Wuyu, *Wenjian banxiang lu* (1793), *ren*.20b.
4. See, for example, *Shanyang xianzhi* [district gazetteer] [Shaanxi] (1694), 3.50a; Wang Fu, *Yilin zuanyao tanyuan* (Exhaustive essential compilation of the forest of medicine) (N.p.: Jiangsu shuju, [1758] 1897), 2.79a; *Baixiang xianzhi* [district gazetteer] [Zhili] (1766), 10.*wuchan*.7a; *Yanzhou fuzhi* [prefectural gazetteer] [Shandong] (1770), 5.8a.
5. *Hanyu da zidian* (The great Chinese character dictionary) (Chengdu: Sichuan ci shu chubanshe, 1993), 1461.
6. *Jianning xianzhi* [district gazetteer] [Fujian] (1759), 6.13b.
7. See *Hangzhou fuzhi* [prefectural gazetteer] (1686), 6.23a; *Haining zhouzhi* [departmental gazetteer] (1776), 2.55a; *Tongxiang xianzhi* [district gazetteer] (1882), 7.4b; *Hangzhou fuzhi* [prefectural gazetteer] (1898), 78.5a; *Hangzhou fuzhi* (1916), 38.5a.
8. Gao Shiqi, *Beishu bao weng lu* (An account of the flowering plants treasured in the Beishu [garden, Hangzhou]), in *Xuxiu siku quanshu*, vol. 1119 (Shanghai: Shanghai guji chubanshe, [1690] 2002), 29b. Also see *Jiaxing fuzhi* [prefectural gazetteer] [Zhejiang] (1878), 33.24a which cites Gao Shiqi; and *Gaozhou fuzhi* [prefectural gazetteer] [Guangdong] (1885), 7.3a.
9. See, for example, *Chenzhou fuzhi* [prefectural gazetteer] [Hunan] (1765), 15.12a; Qin Wuyu, *Wenjian banxiang lu*, *ren*.21a; *Xuxiu Tongcheng xianzhi* [district gazetteer] [Anhui] (1827), 22.2b; *Shanghai xianzhi* [district gazetteer] [Jiangsu] (1872), 8.11b.
10. Gao Lian, *Zunsheng bajian*, 16.27b.

11. Craig Clunas, *Superfluous Things: Material Culture and Social Status in Early Modern China* (Urbana: University of Illinois Press, 1991), 18. The translations of Gao's larger discourse titles are from Clunas.

12. Gao Lian, *Zunsheng bajian*, j.11.1b, 7.37b.

13. Wang Maohua, Wang Cengyu, and Hong Seung Tae, "Lüelun lishi shang dongya sanguo lajiao de chuanbo, zhongzhi yu gongyong fajue" (Overview and exploration of the history of chiles in the three East Asian countries, including their spread, cultivation, and use), *Zhongguoshi yanjiu* [S. Korea], no. 101 (April 2016): 297.

14. Zhang Qigan, *Mingdai qian yimin shi yong* ([Biographies] of 1,000 poets from the Ming dynasty), vol. 67 (Taibei: Mingwen shuju, [1929] 1986): 73.

15. Wang Xiangjin, *Qun fang pu* (The assembly of perfumes), vol. 80 (Jinan: Qi Lu shushe, [1621] 1997), 1.9a.

16. *Shiwu bencao* 1621, 16.12b.

17. Huang Zongxi, *Nanlei wending* (Writings of Nanlei [Huang Zongxi]), in *Zhongguo jiben guji ku* [digital collection] (Beijing: Beijing Ai Rusheng shuzi huaji shu yanjiu zhongxin, [c. 1695] 2009), 139.

18. *Haining zhouzhi* [departmental gazetteer] [Zhejiang] (1776), 2.55a.

19. *Zunyi fuzhi* [prefectural gazetteer] [Guizhou] (1841), 17.6a.

20. *Qingzhou fuzhi* [prefectural gazetteer] [Shangdong] (1859), 32.4b.

21. *Ningxiang xianzhi* [district gazetteer] [Hunan] (1867), 25.8a.

22. Chen Dazhang, *Shichuan mingwu jilan* (A collected overview of famous things passed down through poetry), in *Yingyin Wenyuange siku quanshu*, vol. 86 (Taibei: Shengwu, [1713] 1983), 12.12a.

23. Huang Fengchi, *Caobenhua shipu* (Collection of poems [and paintings] of annual flowers) (1621), 22b. Huang added one character to Gao's text, using 儼如 *yanru* instead of just 儼 *yan* to mean "look just like."

24. See Wolfram Eberhard, *A Dictionary of Chinese Symbols* (London: Routledge, 1983), 277; C.A.S. Williams, *Outlines of Chinese Symbolism & Art Motives* (New York: Dover, [1941] 1976), 33

25. Eberhard, *Dictionary of Chinese Symbols*, 52; see also Williams, *Outlines of Chinese Symbolism*, 51–52.

26. Zhang Huizhi et al., eds., *Zhongguo lidai renming dacidian* (Dictionary of Chinese historical names), vol. 1 (Shanghai: Shanghai guji, 1999), 1065.

27. Wu Xingqin, *Baihua qiangao* (Baihua's (Wu Xingqin) early drafts) (N.p., 1783), 38.9b. Betel pepper (*jujiang* 蒟醬; *Piper betle*) is a relative of black pepper. It is much more common in South and Southeast Asia (including Taiwan) than in Sichuan or Yunnan. In the most common use, a betel leaf is used to wrap an areca nut to form "betel nut," which is chewed for its stimulant effects.

28. "Youth Urged to Contribute to Realization of 'Chinese Dream,'" Xinhua, May 5, 2013, http://www.chinadaily.com.cn/china/2013-05/04/content_16476313.htm.

29. A "Shaanxi ten great oddities (*shi daguai*)" gift box was given to me in 2017. Similar gift boxes listing "The 18 oddities of Yunnan" were widely available at tourist sites throughout Yunnan in 2017.

30. I have found only one late imperial source that describes a particular variety of chile as being "shaped like a human penis." Qin Wuyu, *Wenjian banxiang lu*, ren.21a.

31. "Honghong huohuo," Baidu baike.com, https://baike.baidu.com/item/%E7%BA%A2%E7%BA%A2%E7%81%AB%E7%81%AB/5684388, accessed July 28, 2018.

32. Fuschia Dunlop also identifies the visual connection between strings of chiles and firecrackers in her book *Land of Plenty: A Treasury of Authentic Sichuan Cooking* (New York: Norton, 2001), 15.

33. Cyril Birch, "Preface to the Second Edition," in *Peony Pavilion*, trans. Cyril Birch, 2nd ed. (Bloomington: Indiana University Press, 2002), ix.

34. Tang Xianzu, translated by Birch in "Preface to the Second Edition," ix.

35. Tang Xianzu, *Mudan ting* (*The Peony Pavilion*) (Beijing: Renmin wenxue, 1978), 112; Birch, *Peony Pavilion*, 130.

36. Birch, *Peony Pavilion*, 130.

37. Tang, *Mudan ting*, 113; Birch, *Peony Pavilion*, 131.

38. Tang, *Mudan ting*, 113; Birch, *Peony Pavilion*, 131. Birch translates the flower name indefinitely as "pepper flower." However, I have not found any examples from late imperial sources where *lajiao* was used

to name any other plant than the chile. So a specific translation as "spicy pepper flower" or "chile flower" is justified.

39. The original Chinese for the judge's reply is 把陰熱窄 (Tang, *Mudan ting*, 131). For *yin* as "bodily lust," see Louise Edwards, "Women in *Honglou meng*: Prescriptions of Purity in the Femininity of Qing Dynasty China," *Modern China* 16, no. 4 (1990): 415.

40. The later sections of the novel are often seen as having been revised or even written by Gao E, the editor and publisher of the first printed edition. Thus Cao Xueqin may not have intended some of the karmic retributions in the last third of the novel.

41. Cao Xueqin, *Honglou meng* (*Dream of the Red Chamber*) (Beijing: Zhonghua shuju, [1760] 1985), *hui* 3.27.

42. Cao Xueqin, *Honglou meng* 3.27, 75.844.

43. *Yunnan tongzhi* [provincial gazetteer] (1736), 27.3a; *Pingyuan zhouzhi* [departmental gazetteer] [Guizhou] (1756), 14.24b; *Changyang xianzhi* [district gazetteer] [Hubei] (1754), 6.20b; *Yichuan xianzhi* [district gazetteer] [Shaanxi] (1754), 3.20b.

44. *Cihai, suoyin ben* (Ocean of words—condensed, one-volume edition) (Shanghai: Shanghai cishu, 1999), 2387–88.

45. *Hanyu dacidian*, 11.492.

46. Unfortunately I was unable to obtain permission to reproduce Ye's painting.

47. Louise Edwards, "Representations of Women and Social Power in Eighteenth Century China: The Case of Wang Xifeng," *Late Imperial China* 14, no. 1 (1993): 35.

48. Edwards, "Representations," 39, 40.

49. Edgar Snow, *Red Star Over China* (New York: Modern Library, 1938), 75.

50. Edgar Porter, *The People's Doctor: George Hatem and China's Revolution* (Honolulu: University of Hawai'i Press, 1997), 76.

51. See, for example, Wen Ermao, "Mao Zedong de yinshi guan: bu chi lajiao bu geming," *Renmin wang*, November 21, 2010 (published by People's Daily), http://history.people.com.cn/GB/198593/13272886.html.

52. Snow, *Red Star Over China*, 75–76. Despite much searching, I have been unable to track down the original Chinese lyrics for this song.

53. See the archived website for the documentary *Morning Sun*: "The East Is Red: Transformation of a Love Song," https://web.archive.org /web/20190830210213/http://www.morningsun.org/east/song.swf.

54. Wen Ermao, "Mao Zedong de yinshi guan."

55. Xiao San, ed., *Geming minge ji* (Beijing: Zhongguo qingnian chubanshe, 1959), 158.

6. Mao's Little Red Spice

1. Chang Qu, *Hua yang guo zhi* (Geographical treatise on the states south of Mount Hua), in *Yingyin Wenyuange siku quanshu*, vol. 463 (*Taibei: Shengwu*, [c. 316] 1983), 3.1b.

2. Meng Yuanlao, *Dongjing menghua lu* (A dream of splendors past in the Eastern Capital) (Zhongguo zhexueshu dianzihua jihua, [1147] 2006), j. 4, *shidian*, https://ctext.org/wiki.pl?if=gb&chapter=804 903&remap=gb.

3. Wu Qijun, *Zhiwu mingshi tukao* (Illustrated treatise on the names and natures of plants) (N.p. 1848), 6.19b.

4. On regions, see Eugene N. Anderson, *The Food of China* (New Haven, Conn.: Yale University Press, 1988), 159–86; Kenneth Lo, *Chinese Provincial Cooking* (London: Elm Tree, 1979); Frederick Simoons, *Food in China: A Cultural and Historical Inquiry* (Boca Raton, Fla.: CRC Press, 1991), 43–57; and Mark Swisocki, *Culinary Nostalgia: Regional Food Culture and the Urban Experience in Shanghai* (Stanford: Stanford University Press, 2009), 9–11.

5. Anderson, *The Food of China*, 159.

6. Anderson, *The Food of China*, 160; Simoons, *Food in China*, 45.

7. Xu Ke, *Qing bai lei chao* (Categorized collection of minor Qing matters), vol. 13 (Beijing: Zhonghua shuju, [1916] 1984–1986), 6238.

8. Xu Ke, *Qing bai lei chao*, 13:6239.

9. Xu Ke, *Qing bai lei chao*, 13:6238–39.

10. Xu Ke, *Qing bai lei chao*, 13:6238.

11. In Chinese:

   湖南人不怕辣 *Hunanren bu pa la*
   贵州人辣不怕 *Guizhouren la bu pa*

四川人怕不辣 *Sichuanren pa bu la*
湖北人不辣怕 *Hubeiren bu la pa*

"Zhongguo shei zui bu pa la," *Zhongguo lajiao*, no. 4 (2002): 23. While *pa* in this context could be translated as "cannot stand" or "is unaccustomed to," *pa* does also mean "fear," and that more intense meaning meshes well with the intense flavor of chiles.

12. In Chinese:

四川人不怕辣 *Sichuanren bu pa la*
贵州人辣不怕 *Guizhouren la bu pa*
湖南人怕不辣 *Hunanren pa bu la*

Found in Huo Ke, "Lajiao Hunan," *Shengtai wan xiang*, no. 8 (2003): 78; Yang Xuming, "Hunan lajiao wenhua de neihan jiqi zhenghe kaifa celüe" (The culture of chiles in Hunan as well as the development of their integration), *Hengyang shifan xueyuan xuebao* 34, no. 5 (2013): 171; and Zheng Zhu and Zang Xiaoman, "Chuancai shi zenyang bian la de?" (How did Sichuan cuisine become spicy?), *Guoxue wenhua*, no. 4 (2009): 58.

13. "Quanguo chila nengli paihang bang," http://www.baike.com/wiki /全国吃辣能力排行榜, accessed March 22, 2015.

14. "Shaanxi shi daguai" (The ten great oddities of Shaanxi [culture]), https://baike.baidu.com/item/陕西十大怪, accessed September 26, 2019.

15. Fuschia Dunlop, *Revolutionary Chinese Cookbook: Recipes from Hunan Province* (New York: Norton, 2006), 10.

16. *Shanyang xianzhi* [district gazetteer] [Shaanxi] (1694), 3.50a.

17. "Shaanxi shi daguai."

18. *Chengcheng xianzhi* [district gazetteer] [Shaanxi] (1851), 5.23a.

19. Ho Ping-ti, "The Introduction of American Food Plants Into China," *American Anthropologist* 57, no. 2 (1955): 195.

20. "Chili Sauce Empress," *Women of China*, January 13, 2011, http:// www.womenofchina.com.cn/html/people/1163-1.htm.

21. Lan Yong, "Zhongguo yinshi xinla kouwei de dili fenxi ji qi chengyin yanjiu" (A study of the contributing factors for the geographic distribution of pungent and spicy flavors in food and drink in China),

Renwen dili 16, no. 5 (2001): 84–88. The cookbook series used by Lan is *Zhongguo caipu*, 12 vols. (Beijing: Zhongguo caizheng jingji chubanshe, 1975–1982). The twelve regional cuisines represented in the series are Anhui, Beijing, Fujian, Guangdong, Hubei, Hunan, Jiangsu, Shaanxi, Shandong, Shanghai, Sichuan, and Zhejiang.

22. Fabio Parasecoli, "Food and Popular Culture," in *Food in Time and Place*, edited by Paul Freedman, Joyce Chaplin, and Ken Albala (Berkeley: University of California Press, 2014), 332.

23. Lu Yaodong, *Duda nengrong: Zhongguo yinshi wenhua sanji* (The stomach's almighty capacity: notes on the culture of Chinese food and drink) (Taibei: Dongda tushu, 2001), 48.

24. Introduction probably occurred a couple of decades prior to the first written record: *Shaoyang xianzhi* [district gazetteer] [Hunan] (1684), 6.11b.

25. *Shaoyang xianzhi*, 6.11b; *Baoqing fuzhi* [prefectural gazetteer] [Hunan] (1685), 13.29a.

26. The gazetteers that used the name *haijiao* are from Guizhou, Hubei, Hunan, Shaanxi, Shanxi, Sichuan and Yunnan. See map 2.2.

27. Dunlop, *Revolutionary Chinese Cookbook*, 12.

28. Yang Xuming, "Hunan lajiao wenhua," 172.

29. Liu Guochu, *Xiangcai shengyan* (The grand banquet of Hunan cuisine) (Changsha: Yuelu shushe, 2004), 19.

30. Dunlop, *Revolutionary Chinese Cookbook*, 10, 21.

31. *Chuci* (Lyrics of Chu), Zhongguo zhexueshu dianzihua jihua, [3rd c. BCE–2nd c. CE] (2006), "qijian," https://ctext.org/chu-ci/qi-jian/zh.

32. *Chenzhou fuzhi* [prefectural gazetteer] [Hunan] (1765), 15.12a.

33. The recipe is from "Hunan duolajiao jiang de zuofa," https://www.douban.com/group/topic/93842840/, accessed June 28, 2019; the second list of ingredients is part of a recipe available in Dunlop, *Revolutionary Chinese Cookbook*, 167–69.

34. See Yang Xuming, "Hunan lajiao wenhua," 172; and Dunlop, *Revolutionary Chinese Cookbook*, 12.

35. For example, see Zhao Xuemin, *Bencao gangmu shiyi* (Correction of omissions in the *Bencao gangmu*), in *Xuxiu siku quanshu*, vols. 995 (Shanghai: Shanghai guji chubanshe, [1803] 2002), 8.72b, 73b; *Jianchang fuzhi* [prefectural gazetteer] [Jiangxi] (1759), 9.3a.

36. Chen Wenchao, "Hunan lajiao fazhan zhuangkuang" (The situation of the development of chile peppers in Hunan), *Lajiao zazhi*, no. 2 (2007): 8.

37. Marta Hanson, *Speaking of Epidemics in Chinese Medicine: Disease and the Geographic Imagination in Late Imperial China* (New York: Routledge, 2011), 14.

38. Chen Wenchao, "Hunan lajiao fazhan zhuangkuang," 8.

39. Liu Guochu, *Xiangcai shengyan*, 21.

40. Cited in Edgar Porter, *The People's Doctor: George Hatem and China's Revolution* (Honolulu: University of Hawai'i Press, 1997), 76.

41. Otto Braun, *A Comintern Agent in China, 1932–1939*, trans. Jeanne Moore (Stanford, Calif.: Stanford University Press, 1982), 55.

42. "Hunan ren yisheng zhizuo sanjianshi: chila, dushu, datianxia" (Throughout their lives Hunan people have three specialties: eating spicy food, reading books and conquering the world) (2017), https://kknews.cc/history/8xxyq94.html.

43. See Dunlop, *Revolutionary Chinese Cookbook*, 117–19; Andrew Coe, *Chop Suey: A Cultural History of Chinese Food in the United States* (Oxford: Oxford University Press, 2009), 242–43. There is also a fun documentary, *The Search for General Tso* (2014), directed by Ian Cheney.

44. He Jiguang (singer), Lu Song (composer), and Xie Dingren (lyricist), "Lajiao ge" (Chile pepper song)," in *20 shiji Zhonghua getan mingren baiji: He Jiguang* (Collection of the hundred best Chinese singers of the 20th century: He Jiguang) (Beijing: Zhongguo changpian, 1999), track 13. Song Zuying covered this song on a 1990 album with only slight variations in the lyrics: *Zhongguo Hunan minge* (Hunan folk songs) (Guangzhou: Guangdong Zhujiang yinxiang chubanshe, 1990), track 2.

45. Online video version: He Jiguang, Lu Song, and Xie Dingren, "Lajiao ge" (Chile pepper song), https://www.youtube.com/watch?v=VQX4iUCmRwM, accessed June 4, 2017.

46. Dunlop also makes the visual connection between strings of chiles and firecrackers in her book on Sichuan cuisine. Fuschia Dunlop, *Land of Plenty: A Treasury of Authentic Sichuan Cooking* (New York: Norton, 2001), 15.

47. Dunlop, *Revolutionary Chinese Cookbook*, 78; and *Manla Xiangcai* (Fiercely spicy Hunan cooking), DVD (Shenzhen: Zhongying yinghua, 2012).

48. *Manla Xiangcai*.

49. All China Women's Federation, http://www.womenofchina.cn /about.htm, accessed June 6, 2015.

50. Yao Huoshu and Christina Lionnent, "Hunan's 'Spicy' Women," *Women of China* (English monthly), September 2004, 26.

51. Yao and Lionnent, "Hunan's 'Spicy' Women," 29. In this passage Xiang refers to Hunan.

52. Yao and Lionnent, "Hunan's 'Spicy' Women," 29.

53. Song Zuying (singer), Xu Peidong (composer), and She Zhidi (lyricist), "La meizi" (Spicy girls), *Jingdian jingxuan* (Collection of classics) (Guangzhou: Guangzhou xinshidai chuban, 1995), track 1. Lyrics reproduced with permission from the lyricist She Zhidi.

54. See, for example, https://www.youtube.com/watch?v=rGKIGQ4l 7qE or http://v.youku.com/v_show/id_XMTkxMjg1NzM2.html.

55. Yang Xuming, "Hunan lajiao wenhua," 172.

56. Although the city of Chongqing and the immediately surrounding counties were made into a separate political jurisdiction in 1997, culturally most people still consider it to be part of Sichuan. Thus for this study Chongqing is included as part of Sichuan.

57. UNESCO, "Chengdu, China: UNESCO Food Capital," http://www .unesco.org/new/zh/culture/themes/creativity/creative-cities-net work/gastronomy/chengdu/, accessed August 14, 2018.

58. Chang Qu, *Hua yang guo zhi*, 3.1b.

59. Lo, *Chinese Provincial Cooking*, 196.

60. Jennifer Billing and Paul Sherman, "Antimicrobial Functions of Spices: Why Some Like It Hot," *Quarterly Review of Biology* 73, no. 1 (March 1998): 30, 25.

61. See Joshua Tewksbury et al., "Evolutionary Ecology of Pungency in Wild Chilies," *Proceedings of the National Academy of Sciences* 105, no. 33 (2008): 11808–11.

62. See Lo, *Chinese Provincial Cooking*, 197; Dunlop, *Land of Plenty*, 15–19; Simoons, *Food in China*, 52; Anderson, *Food of China*, 167-69; Zheng and Zang, "Chuancai shi zenyang bian la de?," 57.

63. For the "five spice" flavoring, see Dunlop, *Land of Plenty*, 356; and H. T. Huang, *Science and Civilisation in China*, vol. 6: *Biology and Biological Technology, Part 5: Fermentation and Food Science* (Cambridge: Cambridge University Press, 2000), 95.

64. See Dunlop, *Land of Plenty*, 16; Lo, *Chinese Provincial Cooking*, 197; Teng Youde, "Sichuan lajiao" (Sichuan chiles), *Lajiao zazhi*, no. 1 (2004): 7.

65. Lo, *Chinese Provincial Cooking*, 197.

66. See Anderson, *The Food of China*, 131.

67. See Diana Lary, *Chinese Migrations: The Movement of People, Goods, and Ideas Over Four Millennia* (Lanham, Md.: Rowman and Littlefield, 2012), 77–78; Frederic Wakeman, Jr., *The Great Enterprise* (Berkeley: University of California Press, 1985), 1109n; and Zheng and Zang, "Chuancai shi zenyang bian la de?," 56.

68. See Lary, *Chinese Migrations*, 78.

69. *Dayi xianzhi* [district gazetteer] [Sichuan] (1749), 3.32a.

70. Lo, *Chinese Provincial Cooking*, 196.

71. See Jiang Mudong and Wang Siming, "Lajiao zai zhongguo chuanbo ji qi yingxiang" (The spread of the chile pepper and its influence in China), *Zhongguo nong shi* 2, no. 24 (2005): 21; Zheng and Zang, "Chuancai shi zenyang bian la de?," 58; Endymion Wilkinson, *Chinese History: A New Manual* (Cambridge, Mass.: Harvard University Asia Center, 2013), 457.

72. Fu Chongju, *Chengdu tong lan* (Guide to Chengdu) (Chengdu: Ba shu, [1909] 1987), 260, 261, 279, 288, 293–99, 304–15, 340.

73. "Xiandai Chuancai de fazhan dingxing" (The development and formation of modern Sichuan cuisine) and "Lajiao" (Chile peppers), information signs in the Interactive Museum of Sichuan Culinary Culture, Pixian, Sichuan, viewed August 2015.

74. Dunlop, *Land of Plenty*, 56.

75. "Pixian douban de maoyi" (Trade in Pixian chile bean paste), information sign in the Interactive Museum of Sichuan Culinary Culture, Pixian, Sichuan, viewed August 2015.

76. For the full recipe, see Dunlop, *Land of Plenty*, 313–14.

77. Shuijing Yueguang [pseud.], *Shuijing Yueguang: Chuanwei biji* (Shuijing Yueguang's Notes on Sichuan flavors) (Hangzhou: Zhejiang kexue jishu, 2014), 17.

78. For example, "Chuancai zhi wei" (Flavors of Sichuan cuisine) and "Chuancai meili" (The enchantments of Sichuan cuisine)," information signs in the Interactive Museum of Sichuan Culinary Culture, Pixian, Sichuan, viewed August 2015.

79. Dunlop, *Revolutionary Chinese Cookbook*, 127.

80. The list of ingredients in the box is from Shuijing Yueguang, *Shuijing yueguang: Chuanwei biji*, 52.

81. Summarized from "Gongbao jiding" (Kung-pao chicken), information sign in the Interactive Museum of Sichuan Culinary Culture, Pixian, Sichuan, viewed August 2015.

82. Dunlop, *Land of Plenty*, 238.

83. Dunlop, *Land of Plenty*, 15.

84. Hongjie Wang, "Hot Peppers, Sichuan Cuisine and the Revolutions in Modern China," *World History Connected* 12, no. 3 (October 2015), https://worldhistoryconnected.press.uillinois.edu/12.3/wang.html.

85. Andrew Leonard, "Why Revolutionaries Love Spicy Food: How the Chili Pepper Got to China," *Nautilus*, no. 35, April 14, 2016, http://nautil.us/issue/35/boundaries/why-revolutionaries-love-spicy-food.

86. Zheng and Zang, "Chuancai shi zenyang bian la de?," 56.

Conclusion

1. Wang Lu, *Huashi zuobian* (Supplement to the history of flowers]) in *Xuxiu siku quanshu*, vol. 1117 (Shanghai: Shanghai guji chubanshe, [1618] 2002), 23.5b; Gao Lian, *Zunsheng bajian* (Eight discourses on nurturing life), in *Siku quanshu zhenben jiuji*, vol. 230 (Taibei: Shang wu, [1591] 1979), 16.27b; *Shiwu bencao* (1621), 16.12b.

2. Song Zuying (singer), Xu Peidong (Composer), and She Zhidi (lyricist), "La meizi" (Spicy girls), in *Jingdian jingxuan* (Collection of classics) (Guangzhou: Guangzhou xinshidai chuban, 1995), track 1.

3. Fabio Parasecoli, "Food and Popular Culture," in *Food in Time and Place*, ed. Paul Freeman, Joyce Chaplin, and Ken Albala (Berkeley: University of California Press, 2014), 332.

BIBLIOGRAPHY

The earliest source for chiles for each province is marked with an *.

Gazetteers

Anhui

*Earliest: see Wang Lu, *Huashi zuobian*, 1618.

Chongxiu Wuhe xianzhi 重修五河縣志 (Wuhe revised district gazetteer), 1893.

Fanchang xianzhi 繁昌縣志 (Fanchang district gazetteer), 1826.

Xuxiu Tongcheng xianzhi 續修桐城縣志 (Tongcheng revised district gazetteer), 1827.

Fujian

Chongyin Yong'an xian xuzhi 重印永安縣續誌 (Yong'an revised district gazetteer), 1834.

Jianning xianzhi 建寧縣志 (Jianning district gazetteer), 1759.

QUANZHOU PREFECTURE

Anxi xianzhi 安溪縣志 (Anxi district gazetteer), 1757.
Jinjiang xianzhi 晉江縣志 (Jinjiang district gazetteer), 1765.
Jinjiang xianzhi 晉江縣志 (Jinjiang district gazetteer), 1829.
Maxiang tingzhi 馬巷廳志 (Maxiang subprefectural gazetteer), 1893.
Quanzhou fuzhi 泉州府志 (Quanzhou prefectural gazetteer), 1763.
Tong'an xianzhi 同安縣志 (Tong'an district gazetteer), 1768.
Tong'an xianzhi 同安縣志 (Tong'an district gazetteer), 1798.
Tong'an xianzhi 同安縣志 (Tong'an district gazetteer), 1929.

Gansu

Chongxiu Suzhou xin zhi 重修肅州新志 (Newly revised Suzhou independent prefectural gazetteer), 1737.

Guangdong

*Earliest: see Qu Dajun, *Guangdong xinyu*, 1680.
Enping xianzhi 恩平縣志 (Enping district gazetteer), 1766.
Gaozhou fuzhi 高州府志 (Gaozhou prefectural gazetteer), 1885.
Yangchun xianzhi 陽春縣志 (Yangchun district gazetteer), 1687.

Guangxi

Guangxi tongzhi 廣西通志 (Guangxi provincial gazetteer), 1733.
Lingui xianzhi 臨桂縣志 (Lingui district gazetteer), 1802.
Liuzhou xianzhi 柳州縣志 (Liuzhou district gazetteer), 1764.
Rong xianzhi 容縣志 (Rong district gazetteer), 1897.

Guizhou

*Earliest: see Tian Wen, *Qian shu*, 1690.
Dading fuzhi 大定府志 (Dading prefectural gazetteer), 1850.
Guiyang fuzhi 貴陽府志 (Guiyang prefectural gazetteer), 1852.
Guizhou tongzhi 貴州通志 (Guizhou provincial gazetteer), 1741.

Pingyuan zhouzhi 平遠州志 (Pingyuan departmental gazetteer), 1756.
Sizhou fuzhi 思州府志 (Sizhou prefectural gazetteer), 1722.
Zheng'an zhouzhi 正安州志 (Zheng'an departmental gazetteer), 1818.
Zunyi fuzhi 遵義府志 (Zunyi prefectural gazetteer), 1841.

Henan

*Xiuwu xianzhi 修武縣志 (Xiuwu district gazetteer), 1840.

Hubei

*Changyang xianzhi 長陽縣志 (Changyang district gazetteer), 1754.
Fang xianzhi 房縣志 (Fang district gazetteer), 1866.
Hubei tongzhi 湖北通志 (Hubei provincial gazetteer), 1921.
Laifeng xianzhi 來鳳縣志 (Laifeng district gazetteer), 1866.
Yunxi xianzhi 鄖西縣志 (Yunxi district gazetteer), 1777.

Hunan

Baojing xianzhi 保靖縣志 (Baojing district gazetteer), 1871.
Baoqing fuzhi 寶慶府志 (Baoqing prefectural gazetteer), 1685.
Changsha xianzhi 長沙縣志 (Changsha district gazetteer), 1817.
Chenzhou fuzhi 辰州府志 (Chenzhou prefectural gazetteer), 1765.
Fenghuang tingzhi 鳳凰廳志 (Fenghuang subprefectural gazetteer), 1824.
Lingling xianzhi 零陵縣志 (Lingling district gazetteer), 1876.
Longshan xianzhi 龍山縣志 (Longshan district gazetteer), 1818.
Ningxiang xianzhi 寧鄉縣志 (Ningxiang district gazetteer), 1867.
Qianzhou tingzhi 乾州廳志 (Qianzhou subprefectural gazetteer), 1877.
*Shaoyang xianzhi 邵陽縣志 (Shaoyang district gazetteer), 1684.
Yongzhou fuzhi 永州府志 (Yongzhou prefectural gazetteer), 1828.

Jiangsu

Changshu xianzhi 常熟縣志 (Changshu district gazetteer), 1539. [Does not include chiles.]
Dantu xianzhi 丹徒縣志 (Dantu district gazetteer), 1879.

Shanghai xianzhi 上海縣志 (Shanghai district gazetteer), 1872.
*Zhili Taicang zhouzhi 直隸太倉州志 (Taicang independent departmental gazetteer), 1802.

Jiangxi

Fengxin xianzhi 奉新縣志 (Fengxin district gazetteer), 1871.
*Jianchang fuzhi 建昌府志 (Jianchang prefectural gazetteer), 1756.
Jianchang fuzhi 建昌府志 (Jianchang prefectural gazetteer), 1759.
Jianchang fuzhi 建昌府志 (Jianchang prefectural gazetteer), 1872.
Yuanzhou fuzhi 袁州府志 (Yuanzhou prefectural gazetteer), 1860.

Shaanxi

Chengcheng xianzhi 澄城縣志 (Chengcheng district gazetteer), 1851.
Hannan xuxiu junzhi 漢南續修郡志 (Hannan revised prefectural gazetteer), 1924.
Hanzhong xuxiu fuzhi 漢中續修府志 (Hanzhong revised prefectural gazetteer), 1814.
*Shanyang xianzhi 山陽縣志 (Shanyang district gazetteer), 1694.
Xuxiu Ningqiang zhouzhi 續修寧羌州志 (Ningqiang revised departmental gazetteer), 1832.
Yichuan xianzhi 宜川縣志 (Yichuan district gazetteer), 1754.
Zhen'an xianzhi 鎮安縣志 (Zhen'an district gazetteer), 1755.

Shandong

Chiping xianzhi 茌平縣志 (Chiping district gazetteer), 1935.
Qingzhou fuzhi 青州府志 (Qingzhou prefectural gazetteer), 1859.
*Shandong tongzhi 山東通志 (Shandong provincial gazetteer), 1736.
Yangxin xianzhi 陽信縣志 (Yangxin district gazetteer), 1926.
Yanzhou fuzhi 兗州府志 (Yanzhou prefectural gazetteer), 1770.

Shanxi

*Jiexiu xianzhi 介休縣志 (Jiexiu district gazetteer), 1696.

Shengjing (Liaoning)

Gaiping xianzhi 蓋平縣志 (Gaiping district gazetteer), 1682.
Shengjing tongzhi 盛京通志 (Shengjing provincial gazetteer), 1684.
Shengjing tongzhi 盛京通志 (Shengjing provincial gazetteer), 1736.
Shengjing tongzhi 盛京通志 (Shengjing provincial gazetteer), 1779.
Shengjing tongzhi 盛京通志 (Shengjing provincial gazetteer), 1852.

Sichuan

Dayi xianzhi 大邑縣志 (Dayi district gazetteer), 1749.
Pi xianzhi 郫縣志 (Pi district gazetteer), 1762.

Taiwan

*Earliest: see *Taihai caifeng tukao*, 1746.

Yunnan

Gejiu xianzhi 個舊縣志 (Gejiu district gazetteer), 1922.
Guangxi fuzhi 廣西府志 (Guangxi prefectural gazetteer), 1739.
Ningzhou zhi 寧州志 (Ningzhou departmental gazetteer), 1799.
Xu Yunnan tongzhi gao 續雲南通志稿 (Draft revision of the Yunnan provincial gazetteer), 1901.
Yunnan tongzhi 雲南通志 (Yunnan provincial gazetteer), 1736.
Yunnan tongzhi 雲南通志 (Yunnan provincial gazetteer), 1894.
Yunnan tongzhi gao 雲南通志稿 (Draft of the Yunnan provincial gazetteer), 1835.

Zhejiang

*Earliest: see Gao Lian, *Zunsheng bajian*, 1591.
Haining zhouzhi 海寧州志 (Haining departmental gazetteer), 1776.
Hangzhou fuzhi 杭州府志 (Hangzhou prefectural gazetteer), 1686.
Hangzhou fuzhi 杭州府志 (Hangzhou prefectural gazetteer), 1898.
Hangzhou fuzhi 杭州府志 (Hangzhou prefectural gazetteer), 1916.

Huangyan xianzhi 黃巖縣志 (Huangyan district gazetteer), 1877.
Jiaxing fuzhi 嘉興府志 (Jiaxing prefectural gazetteer), 1878.
Shangyu xianzhi 上虞縣志 (Shangyu district gazetteer), 1890.
Shanyin xianzhi 山陰縣志 (Shanyin district gazetteer), 1671.
Tongxiang xianzhi 桐鄉縣志 (Tongxiang district gazetteer), 1882.
Yinxian tongzhi 鄞縣通志 (Yinxian complete [district] gazetteer), 1933.

Zhili (Hebei)

Baixiang xianzhi 柏鄉縣志 (Baixiang district gazetteer), 1766.
Nangong xianzhi 南宮縣志 (Nangong district gazetteer), 1559. [Does not include chiles.]
*Shenzhou zhi 深州志 (Shenzhou independent department gazetteer), 1697.
Shuntian fuzhi 順天府志 (Shuntian prefectural gazetteer), 1886.

Other Works

Anderson, Eugene N. "Folk Nutritional Therapy in Modern China." In *Chinese Medicine and Healing: An Illustrated History*, ed. T. J. Hinrichs and Linda Barnes, 259–63. Cambridge, Mass.: Harvard University Press, 2013.

——. *The Food of China*. New Haven, Conn.: Yale University Press, 1988.

Andrews, Jean. *Peppers: The Domesticated Capsicums*. New ed. Austin: University of Texas Press, 1995.

——. *The Pepper Trail: History and Recipes from Around the World*. Denton: University of North Texas Press, 1999.

Arndt, Alice. "Spices and Rotten Meat. Old Saw: 'They Used a Lot of Spices to Disguise Spoiled Meat.' " The Debunk-House, Food History News, 2008. Archived at https://web.archive.org/web/20180818060609if_/http://foodhistory.news/debunk.html#rotten

Barnes, Linda, and T. J. Hinrichs. "Introduction." In *Chinese Medicine and Healing: An Illustrated History*, ed. T. J. Hinrichs and Linda Barnes, 1–4. Cambridge, Mass.: Harvard University Press, 2013.

Bencao huibian 本草彙編 (A revised pharmacopeia). In *Zhongguo bencao quanshu*, vol. 139. Beijing: Huaxia chubanshe, [1840] 1999.

Benedict, Carol. *Golden-Silk Smoke: A History of Tobacco in China, 1550–2010*. Berkeley: University of California Press, 2011.

Benn, James A. "Another Look at the Pseudo-*Śūraṃgama sūtra*." *Harvard Journal of Asiatic Studies* 68, no. 1 (2008): 57–89.

Billing, Jennifer, and Paul Sherman. "Antimicrobial Functions of Spices: Why Some Like It Hot." *Quarterly Review of Biology* 73, no. 1 (March 1998): 3–49.

Birch, Cyril, trans. *The Peony Pavilion*. 2nd ed. Bloomington: Indiana University Press, 2002.

Burton, David. *The Raj at Table: A Culinary History of the British in India*. London: Faber and Faber, 1993.

Cao Tingdong 曹庭棟. *Laolao hengyan* 老老恒言 (On longevity). Shanghai: Shanghai shudian, [1773] 1981.

Cao Xueqin 曹雪芹. *Honglou meng* 紅樓夢 (*Dream of the Red Chamber*). Beijing: Zhonghua shuju, [1760] 1985.

Cao Yu 曹雨. *Zhongguoshi lashi: lajiao zai Zhongguo de sibainian* 中国食辣史：辣椒在中国的四百年 (The history of spice in Chinese food: four hundred years of chiles in China). Beijing: Beijing United, 2019.

Chang, K. C. "Ancient China." In *Food in Chinese Culture: Anthropological and Historical Perspectives*, ed. K. C. Chang, 25–52. New Haven, Conn.: Yale University Press, 1977.

——. "Introduction." In *Food in Chinese Culture: Anthropological and Historical Perspectives*, ed. K. C. Chang, 1–21. New Haven, Conn.: Yale University Press, 1977.

Chang Qu 常璩. *Hua yang guo zhi* 華陽國志 (Geographical treatise on the states south of Mount Hua). In *Yingyin Wenyuange siku quanshu*, vol. 463. Taibei: Shengwu, [c. 316] 1983.

Chang, T'ien-tsê. *Sino-Portuguese Trade from 1514–1644: A Synthesis of Portuguese and Chinese Sources*. New York: AMS, [1934] 1973.

Chen Dazhang 陳大章. *Shizhuan mingwu jilan* 詩傳名物集覽 (A collected overview of famous things passed down through poetry). In *Yingyin Wenyuange siku quanshu*, vol. 86. Taibei: Shengwu, [1713] 1983.

Chen Haozi 陳淏子. *Michuan huajing* 秘傳花鏡 (Secret transmissions from the mirror of flowers). In *Xuxiu siku quanshu*, vol. 1117. Shanghai: Shanghai guji chubanshe, [1688] 2002.

Chen Jiamo 陳嘉謨. *Bencao mengquan* 本草蒙筌 (Enlightened pharma-copoeia). In *Xuxiu siku quanshu*, vol. 991. Shanghai: Shanghai guji chubanshe, [1565] 2002.

Chen Jiru 陳繼儒. *Shiwu bencao* 食物本草 (Pharmacopeia of edible items). In *Gugong zhenben congkan*, vol. 366. Haikou: Hainan chubanshe, [1638] 2000.

——. *Zhifu qi shu* 致富奇書 (A masterpiece in becoming rich). In *Zhong-guo jiben guji ku* [digital collection]. Beijing: Beijing Ai Rusheng shuzi huaji shu yanjiu zhongxin, [c. 1639] 2009.

Chen Wenchao 陈文超. "Hunan lajiao fazhan zhuangkuang 湖南辣椒发展状况" (The situation of the development of chile peppers in Hunan). *Lajiao zazhi*, no. 2 (2007): 8–9.

Chen Xiuyuan 陳修園. *Bencao zaixin* 本草再新 (Newly revised pharma-copoeia). Shanghai: Qun xue shu she, [1819] 1931.

Cheney, Ian. *The Search for General Tso*. Wicked Delicate Films. DVD. Oley, Penn.: Bullfrog films, 2014.

Cheng Anqi 程安琪. *La fan tian* 辣翻天 (Spiciness crosses the heavens). Shenyang: Liaoning kexue jishu chubanshe, 2006.

Chiang, Tao-chang. "The Salt Trade in Ch'ing China." *Modern Asian Studies* 17, no. 2 (1983): 197–219.

"Chili Sauce Empress." *Women of China*. January 13, 2011. http://www .womenofchina.com.cn/html/people/1163-1.htm.

Chuci 楚辭 (Lyrics of Chu). Zhongguo zhexueshu dianzihua jihua [3rd c. BCE–2nd c. CE]. 2006. https://ctext.org/chu-ci/qi-jian/zh.

Cihai, suoyin ben 辞海-缩印本 (Ocean of words—condensed, one-volume edition). Shanghai: Shanghai cishu, 1999.

Clunas, Craig. *Superfluous Things: Material Culture and Social Status in Early Modern China*. Urbana: University of Illinois Press, 1991.

Coe, Andrew. *Chop Suey: A Cultural History of Chinese Food in the United States*. Oxford: Oxford University Press, 2009.

Columbus, Christopher. *The* Diario *of Christopher Columbus's First Voy-age to America 1492–1493*, trans. Oliver Dunn and James E. Kelley, Jr. Norman: University of Oklahoma Press, [1493] 1988.

Counihan, Carole, and Penny Van Esterik. "Introduction to the Third Edition." In *Food and Culture: A Reader*, ed. Carole Counihan and Penny Van Esterik, 1–16. New York: Routledge, 2013.

Dai Tianzhang 戴天章. *Guang wenyi lun* 廣瘟疫論 (A broad discussion of pestilences). In *Xuxiu siku quanshu*, vol. 1003. Shanghai: Shanghai guji chubanshe, [1783] 2002.

Dalby, Andrew. *Dangerous Tastes: The Story of Spices*. Berkeley: University of California Press, 2000.

Dennis, Joseph. *Writing, Publishing, and Reading Local Gazetteers in Imperial China, 1100–1700*. Harvard East Asia Monographs, no. 379. Cambridge, Mass.: Harvard University Asia Center, 2015.

Diamond, Norma. "Defining the Miao: Ming, Qing, and Contemporary Views." In *Cultural Encounters on China's Ethnic Frontiers*, ed. Stevan Harrell, 92–115. Seattle: University of Washington Press, 1995.

Dott, Brian R. *Identity Reflections: Pilgrimages to Mount Tai in Late Imperial China*. Harvard East Asia Monographs, no. 244. Cambridge, Mass.: Harvard University Asia Center, 2004.

Duan Rulin 段汝霖. *Chunan miao zhi* 楚南苗志 (Miao album for Southern Chu [Sichuan]). In *Zhongguo jiben guji ku* [digital collection]. Beijing: Beijing Ai Rusheng shuzi huaji shu yanjiu zhongxin, [1758] 2009.

Dunlop, Fuchsia. *Land of Plenty: A Treasury of Authentic Sichuan Cooking*. New York: Norton, 2001.

——. *Revolutionary Chinese Cookbook: Recipes from Hunan Province*. New York: Norton, 2006.

Eberhard, Wolfram. *A Dictionary of Chinese Symbols*. London: Routledge, 1983.

Edwards, Louise. "Representations of Women and Social Power in Eighteenth Century China: The Case of Wang Xifeng." *Late Imperial China* 14, no. 1 (1993): 34–59.

——. "Women in *Honglou meng*: Prescriptions of Purity in the Femininity of Qing Dynasty China." *Modern China* 16, no. 4 (1990): 407–29.

Elisonas, Jurgis. "Christianity and the Daimyo." In *The Cambridge History of Japan*, vol. 4: *Early Modern Japan*, ed. John Whitney Hall, 301–72. Cambridge: Cambridge University Press, 1991.

Fang Youzhi 方有執. *Shanghan lun tiao bian* 傷寒論條辨 (Discussion and debate on typhoid). In *Yingyin Wenyuange siku quanshu*, vol. 775. Taibei: Shengwu, [1592] 1983.

Fei Boxiong 費伯雄. *Yichun shengyi* 醫醇勝義 (Enriching the meaning of the purity of medicine). In *Xuxiu siku quanshu*, vol. 1006. Shanghai: Shanghai guji chubanshe, [1863] 2002.

Freedman, Paul. *Out of the East: Spices and the Medieval Imagination.* New Haven, Conn.: Yale University Press, 2008.

Freedman Paul, Joyce Chaplin, and Ken Albala, eds. *Food in Time and Place.* Berkeley: University of California Press, 2014.

Fu Chongju 傅崇矩. *Chengdu tong lan* 成都通覽 (Guide to Chengdu). Chengdu: Ba shu, [1909] 1987.

Fu Qingzhu 傅青主. *Fu Qingzhu nüke* 傅青主女科 (Fu Qingzhu on gynecology). N.p.: Hubei chongwen shuju, [c. 1684] 1869.

Gao Lian 高濂. "Cao hua pu 草花譜" (Treatise on herbaceous flowering plants). In *Zunsheng bajian*, by Gao Lian. In *Siku quanshu zhenben jiuji*, vol. 230. Taibei: Shang wu, [1591] 1979.

——. "Yin zhuan fu shi jian 飲饌服食牋" (On food and drink). In *Zunsheng bajian*, by Gao Lian. In *Siku quanshu zhenben jiuji*, vol. 229. Taibei: Shang wu, [1591] 1979.

*——. *Zunsheng bajian* 遵生八牋 (Eight discourses on nurturing life). In *Siku quanshu zhenben jiuji*, vol. 225–32. Taibei: Shang wu, [1591] 1979. [Earliest record for chiles in Zhejiang.]

Gao Shiqi 高士奇. *Beishu bao weng lu* 北墅抱瓮錄 (An account of the flowering plants treasured in the Beishu [garden, Hangzhou]). In *Xuxiu siku quanshu*, vol. 1119. Shanghai: Shanghai guji chubanshe, [1690] 2002.

Geng Junying, Huang Wenquan, Ren Tianchi, and Ma Xiufeng. *Practical Traditional Chinese Medicine and Pharmacology: Herbal Formulas.* Beijing: New World Press, 1991.

Gentilcore, David. *Pomodoro!: A History of the Tomato in Italy.* New York: Columbia University Press, 2010.

Gu Lu 顧祿. *Qing jia lu* 清嘉錄 (A record of clear praise). Beijing: Zhongguo shangye, [1830] 1989.

Gu Zhong 顧仲. *Yang xiao lu* 養小錄 (Guide to nurturing life). In *Congshu jicheng chubian*, vol. 1475. Beijing: Zhonghua shuju, [1698] 1985.

Guo Lin 郭麐. *Chu yuan xiao xia lu* 樗園銷夏錄 (Record of the summer market of Ailanthus garden). In *Zhongguo jiben guji ku* [digital collection]. Beijing: Beijing Ai Rusheng shuzi huaji shu yanjiu zhongxin, [1820] 2009.

Hanson, Marta E. *Speaking of Epidemics in Chinese Medicine: Disease and the Geographic Imagination in Late Imperial China*. New York: Routledge, 2011.

Hanyu dacidian 漢語大詞典 (The great Chinese word dictionary). 12 vols. Shanghai: Hanyu dacidian, 1988–1993.

Hanyu dazidian suoyin ben 漢語大字典-縮印本 (The great Chinese character dictionary—condensed, one-volume edition). Chengdu: Sichuan ci shu chubanshe, 1993.

He Jiguang 何纪光 (singer), Lu Song 鲁颂 (composer), and Xie Dingren 谢丁仁 (lyricist). "Lajiao ge 辣椒歌" (Chile pepper song). In *20 shiji Zhonghua getan mingren baiji: He Jiguang* 20世纪中华歌坛名人百集: 何纪光 (Collection of the hundred best Chinese singers of the 20th century: He Jiguang), track 13. Beijing: Zhongguo changpian, 1999. Online video version accessed June 4, 2017. https://www.youtube.com/watch?v=VQX4iUCmRwM.

He Qing 何青 and An Di 安狄. "Lajiao yu Zhongguo lajiao wenhua 辣椒与中国辣椒文化" (The chile pepper and Chinese chile pepper culture). *Lajiao zazhi*, no. 2 (2004): 46–48.

Herman, C. Peter. "Effects of Heat on Appetite." In *Nutritional Needs in Hot Environments: Applications for Military Personnel in Field Operations*, ed. Bernadette Marriot, 178-213. Washington, D.C.: National Academy Press, 1993.

Hinrichs, T. J., and Linda Barnes, eds. *Chinese Medicine and Healing: An Illustrated History*. Cambridge, Mass: Harvard University Press, 2013.

Ho, Ping-ti. "The Introduction of American Food Plants Into China." *American Anthropologist* 57, no. 2 (1955): 191–201.

——. *Studies on the Population of China, 1368–1953*. Cambridge, Mass.: Harvard University Press, 1959.

Höllmann, Thomas O. *The Land of the Five Flavors: A Cultural History of Chinese Cuisine*, trans. Karen Margolis. New York: Columbia University Press, 2014.

Holtzman, Jon D. "Food and Memory." *Annual Review of Anthropology* 35 (2006): 361–78.

Hong Sen 红森, ed. *Lawei meishi yu jianshen* 辣味美食与健身 (Spicy flavor in gourmet food for health). Tianjin: Tianjin keji fanyi chubanshe, 2005.

Hostetler, Laura. *Qing Colonial Enterprise: Ethnography and Cartography in Early Modern China*. Chicago: University of Chicago Press, 2001.

Hu, Shiu-ying. *An Enumeration of Chinese Materia Medica*. Hong Kong: Chinese University of Hong Kong, 1980.

——. *Food Plants of China*. Hong Kong: Chinese University Press, 2005.

Hu Wenhuan 胡文煥. *Shiwu bencao* 食物本草 (Pharmacopeia of edible items). c. 1593.

Hu Yiyin 胡乂尹. "Lajiao mingcheng kaoshi 辣椒名称考释" (A philological study of the naming of chile peppers). *Gujin nongye*, no. 4 (2013): 67–75.

Huang Fengchi 黃風池. *Caobenhua shipu* 草本花詩譜 (Collection of poems [and paintings] of annual flowers). 1621.

Huang Gongxiu 黃宮繡. *Bencao qiuzhen* 本草求眞 (A truthful pharmacopeia). In *Xuxiu siku quanshu*, vol. 995. Shanghai: Shanghai guji chubanshe, [1773] 2002.

Huang, H. T. *Science and Civilisation in China*. Vol. 6: *Biology and Biological Technology, Part 5: Fermentation and Food Science*. Cambridge: Cambridge University Press, 2000.

Huang, Ray. "Ming Fiscal Administration." In *The Cambridge History of China: The Ming Dynasty, 1368–1644 Part 2*, vol. 8, ed. Denis Twitchett and Frederick Mote, 106–71. Cambridge: Cambridge University Press, 1998.

Huang Zongxi 黃宗羲. *Nanlei wending* 南雷文定 (Writings of Nanlei [Huang Zongxi]). In *Zhongguo jiben guji ku* [digital collection]. Beijing: Beijing Ai Rusheng shuzi huaji shu yanjiu zhongxin, [c. 1695] 2009.

Hummel, Arthur W. *Eminent Chinese of the Ch'ing Period*. 2 vols. Taibei: Southern Materials, [1943] 1991.

"Hunan ren yisheng zhizuo sanjianshi: chila, dushu, datianxia 湖南人一生只做三件事: 吃辣、讀書、打天下" (Throughout their lives Hunan people have three specialties: eating spicy food, reading books, and conquering the world). November 18, 2017. https://kknews.cc/history/8xxyq94.html.

Huo Ke 霍克. "Lajiao Hunan 辣椒湖南" (The chile in Hunan). *Shengtai wan xiang* 生态万象, no. 8 (2003): 78–79.

Jia Suoxue 賈所學. *Yaopin huayi* 藥品化義 (Rules for medicine ingredients). In *Xuxiu siku quanshu*, vol. 990. Shanghai: Shanghai guji chubanshe, [1644] 2002.

Jiang Mudong 蔣慕东 and Wang Siming 王思明. "Lajiao zai Zhongguo chuanbo ji qi yingxiang 辣椒在中国传播及其影响" (The spread of the chile pepper and its influence in China). *Zhongguo nong shi* 24, no. 2 (2005): 17–27.

Jiang Xianming 蔣先明. *Gezhong shucai* 各种蔬菜 (All types of vegetables). Beijing: Nongye chubanshe, 1989.

Jiang Yi 蔣儀. *Yao jing* 藥鏡 (Mirror of medicines). In *Siku quanshu cunmu congshu bubian*, vol. 42. Jinan: Qi Lu shushe, [1641] 1997.

Jieziyuan huazhuan 芥子園畫傳 (Manual of the Mustard Seed Garden). N.p., 1679.

Johnson, David, Andrew J. Nathan, and Evelyn S. Rawski, eds. *Popular Culture in Late Imperial China*. Berkeley: University of California Press, 1985.

Jullien, François. "The Chinese Notion of 'Blandness' as a Virtue: A Preliminary Outline," trans. Graham Parkes. *Philosophy East and West*, 43, no. 1 (1993): 107–11.

Kaptchuk, Ted. *The Web That Has No Weaver: Understanding Chinese Medicine*. New York: Congdon and Weed, 1983.

Keay, John. *The Spice Route, a History*. London: John Murray, 2005.

Kieschnick, John. "Buddhist Vegetarianism in China." In *Of Tripod and Palate: Food, Politics, and Religion in Traditional China*, ed. Roel Sterckx, 186–212. New York: Palgrave Macmillan, 2004.

Kopytoff, Igor. "Cultural Biography of Things: Commoditization as Process." In *The Social Life of Things: Commodoties in Cultural Perspective*, ed. Arjun Appadurai, 64–92. Cambridge: Cambridge University Press, 1986.

Lan Yong 蓝勇. "Zhongguo gudai xinla yongliao de shanbian, liubu yu nongye shehui fazhan 中国古代辛辣用料的嬗变流布与农业社会发展" (The evolution and spread of pungent and spicy ingredients in the development of agricultural society in ancient China). *Zhongguo shehui jingjishi yanjiu*, no. 4 (2000): 13–23.

———. "Zhongguo yinshi xinla kouwei de dili fenbu ji qi chengyin yanjiu 中国饮食辛辣口味的地理分布及其成因研究" (A study of the contributing factors for the geographic distribution of pungent and spicy flavors in food and drink in China). *Renwen dili* 16, no. 5 (2001): 84–88.

Langlois, John D., Jr. "The Hung-wu Reign." In *The Cambridge History of China*, vol. 7: *The Ming Dynasty, 1368–1644, Part 1*, ed. Frederick W. Mote and Denis Twitchett. Cambridge: Cambridge University Press, 1988.

Lary, Diana. *Chinese Migrations: The Movement of People, Goods, and Ideas Over Four Millennia*. Lanham, Md.: Rowman and Littlefield, 2012.

Lee, James, and Wang Feng. *One Quarter of Humanity: Malthusian Mythology and Chinese Realities, 1700–2000*. Cambridge, Mass.: Harvard University Press, 1999.

Lengyan jing 楞嚴經 (Śūraṅgama Sūtra). Zhonghua dianzi Fodian xiehui 中華電子佛典協會 (CBETA [Chinese Buddhist Electronic Text Association]). CBETA.org.

Leonard, Andrew. "Why Revolutionaries Love Spicy Food: How the Chili Pepper Got to China." *Nautilus*, no. 35, April 14, 2016. http://nautil.us/issue/35/boundaries/why-revolutionaries-love-spicy-food.

Li Guoying 李国英. "Lajiao, lajiao chanye, lajiao wenhua 辣椒,辣椒产业, 辣椒文化" (The chile pepper, chile pepper production, and chile pepper culture). *Tan suo yu qiu shi*, no. 9 (2002): 20–21.

Li Huanan 李化楠. *Xing yuan lu* 醒园录 (Memoir from the garden of awareness). In *Congshu jicheng chubian*, vol. 1474. Beijing: Zhonghua shuju, [1750] 1991.

Li Shizhen 李時珍. *Bencao gangmu* 本草綱目 (Systematic pharmacopeia). In *Yingyin Wenyuange siku quanshu*, vol. 772–74. Taibei: Shengwu, [1596] 1983.

Li Shizhen 李時珍 and Zhao Xuemin 趙學敏. *Bencao gangmu (he shiyi)* 本草綱目(和拾遺) (The systematic pharmacopeia with correction of omissions). Hefei: Zhangshi wei gu zhai, 1885.

Li Wenbing 李文炳. *Jing yan guang ji* 經驗廣集. Beijing: Zhongyi guji, [1778] 2009.

Li Wenliang 李文亮 and Qi Qiang 齐强, eds. *Qianjia miaofang* 千家妙方 (Miraculous formulas from myriad experts). 2 vols. Beijing: Jiefangjun chubanshe, 2016.

Li Wenpei 李文培. *Shiwu xiaolu* 食物小錄 (A small record on edible items). In *Zhongguo bencao quanshu*, vol. 108. Beijing: Huaxia chubanshe, [1778] 1999.

Li Xingjian 李行健, ed. *Xiandai Hanyu guifan cidian* 现代汉语规范词典 (Standardized modern Chinese dictionary). Beijing: Waiyu jiaoxue yu yanjiu chubanshe, 2004.

Li Yu 李漁. *Xian qing ou ji* 閒情偶寄 (Random notes from a leisurely life). Shanghai: Shanghai guji, [1670] 2000.

Li Zhongli 李中立. *Bencao yuanshi* 本草原始 (The original pharmacopeia). In *Xuxiu siku quanshu*, vol. 992. Shanghai: Shanghai guji chubanshe, [1614] 2002.

Li Zhongzi 李中梓. *Juan bu lei gong pao zhi yao xing jie* 鐫補雷公炮製藥性解. In *Xuxiu siku quanshu*, vol. 990. Shanghai: Shanghai guji chubanshe, [c. 1644] 2002.

Liu Changzhi 刘昌芝. "Chen Haozi 陈淏子." In *Zhongguo gudai kexuejia zhuanji*, vol. 2, ed. by Du Shiran 杜石然, 989–91. Beijing: kexue chubanshe, 1993.

Liu Daqi 劉大器, ed. *Zhongguo gudian shipu* 中國古典食譜 Chinese classical recipes). Xi'an: Shaanxi Tourism, 1992.

Liu Guochu 刘国初. *Xiangcai shengyan* 湘菜盛宴 (The grand banquet of Hunan cuisine). Changsha: Yuelu shushe, 2004.

Lo, Kenneth. *Chinese Provincial Cooking*. London: Elm Tree, 1979.

Lu Yaodong 逯耀東. *Duda nengrong: Zhongguo yinshi wenhua sanji* 肚大能容: 中國飲食文化散記 (The stomach's almighty capacity: notes on the culture of Chinese food and drink). Taibei: Dongda tushu, 2001.

Lu Zhiyi 盧之頤. *Bencao cheng ya ban jie* 本草乘雅半偈. In *Yingyin Wenyuange siku quanshu*, vol. 779. Taibei: Shengwu, [1645] 1983.

Luo Guihuan 罗桂环. "Laizi yixiang de zuowu: lajiao 来自异乡的作物: 辣椒 (Crops from foreign lands: the chile pepper). *Kexue yuekan*, no. 12 (2002): 1078–80.

Manla Xiangcai 蛮辣湘菜 (Fiercely spicy Hunan cooking). DVD. Shenzhen: Zhongying yinghua, 2012.

Mayo Clinic. "Drugs and Supplements: Hydroxychloroquine." Accessed February 10, 2017. http://www.mayoclinic.org/drugs-supplements/hydroxychloroquine-oral-route/description/drg-20064216.

Mazumdar, Sucheta. "The Impact of New World Food Crops on the Diet and Economy of China and India, 1600–1900." In *Food in Global History*, ed. Raymond Grew, 58–78. Boulder, Colo.: Westview, 1999.

Meng Yuanlao 孟元老. *Dongjing meng hua lu* 東京夢華錄 (A dream of splendors past in the Eastern Capital). Zhongguo zhexueshu dianzihua jihua, [1147] 2006. https://ctext.org/wiki.pl?if=gb&chapter=804903&remap=gb.

Métailié, Georges. *Science and Civilisation in China*, vol. 6: *Biology and Biological Technology, Part 4: Traditional Botany: An Ethnobotanical Approach*, trans. Janet Lloyd. Cambridge: Cambridge University Press, 2015.

Miao Xiyong 繆希雍. *Pao zhi dafa* 炮炙大法 (Fundamental principles of pharmaceuticals). Beijing: Renmin weisheng, [1622] 1956.

——. *Shennong bencao jing shu* 神農本草經疏 (Commentary on *Shennong's classic pharmacopeia*). In *Yingyin Wenyuange siku quanshu*, vol. 775. Taibei: Shengwu, [1624] 1983.

——. *Xianxing zhai yixue guang biji* 先醒齋醫學廣筆記 (Miscellaneous notes on alertness, fasting, and medicine). Hong Kong: Wanye chuban, [c. 1627] 1977.

Millward, James. "Chiles on the Silk Road." *Chile Pepper*, December 1993: 34–36, 41–42.

Min Zongdian 闵宗殿. "Haiwai nongzuowu de chuanru he dui wo guo nongye shengchan de yingxiang 海外农作物的传入和对我国农业生产的影响" (The introduction of overseas agriculture products and their influence on Chinese agricultural production). *Gujin nongye*, no. 1 (1991): 1–10.

Mote, Frederick W. "Yüan and Ming." In *Food in Chinese Culture: Anthropological and Historical Perspectives*, ed. K. C. Chang, 193–257. New Haven, Conn.: Yale University Press, 1977.

Mu Shixi 穆世錫. *Shiwu jiyao* 食物輯要 (Summary of edible items). In *Zhongguo bencao quanshu*, vol. 63. Beijing: Huaxia chubanshe, [1607] 1999.

Murray, Laura May Kaplan. "New World Food Crops in China: Farms, Food, and Families in the Wei River Valley, 1650–1910." Ph.D. dissertation, University of Pennsylvania, 1985.

Nanjing zhongyi xueyuan yijing jiaoyan zu 南京中医学院医经教研组, ed. *Huangdi neijing suwen yishi* 黄帝内经素问译释 (Inner canon of the

Yellow Emperor: basic questions section with annotations). Shanghai: Shanghai kexue jishu, 1981.

Nappi, Carla. *The Monkey and the Inkpot: Natural History and Its Transformations in Early Modern China.* Cambridge, Mass.: Harvard University Press, 2009.

Needham, Joseph. *Science and Civilisation in China*, vol. 6: *Biology and Biological Technology, Part 1: Botany.* Cambridge: Cambridge University Press, 1986.

Needham, Joseph, Nathan Sivin, and Gwei-Djen Lu. *Science and Civilisation in China*, vol. 6: *Biology and Biological Technology, Part 2: Medicine.* Cambridge: Cambridge University Press, 2000.

Newman, Paul B. *Daily Life in the Middle Ages.* Jefferson, N.C.: McFarland, 2001.

Ni Zhumo 倪朱謨. *Bencao huiyan* 本草彙言 (Collected words on the pharmacopeia). In *Xuxiu siku quanshu*, vol. 992. Shanghai: Shanghai guji chubanshe, [1624] 2002.

Ning Yuan 寧源. *Shijian bencao* 食鑒本草 (The dietary mirror). Beijing: Zhongguo shudian, [c. 1590] 1987.

Niu Wen'ao 紐文鰲. *Bencao minglan* 本草明覽 (A clear overview of the pharmacopeia). In *Zhongguo bencao quanshu*, vol. 169. Beijing: Huaxia chubanshe, [1854] 1999.

Norton, Marcy. "Tasting Empire: Chocolate and European Internalization of Mesoamerican Aesthetics." *American Historical Review* 111, no. 3 (June 2006): 660–91.

Parasecoli, Fabio. "Food and Popular Culture." In *Food in Time and Place*, ed. Paul Freedman, Joyce Chaplin, and Ken Albala, 322–39. Berkeley: University of California Press, 2014.

Peng Huairen 彭怀仁, ed. *Zhongyi fangji da cidian* 中医方剂大辞典 (Dictionary of Chinese medicine formulas). 11 vols. Beijing: Renmin weisheng, 1993.

Pilcher, Jeffery M. "Introduction." In *Oxford Handbook of Food History*, ed. Jeffery M. Pilcher, xvii–xxviii. Oxford: Oxford University Press, 2012.

Porter, Edgar. *The People's Doctor: George Hatem and China's Revolution.* Honolulu: University of Hawai'i Press, 1997.

Ptak, Roderich. "Ming Maritime Trade to Southeast Asia, 1368–1567: Visions of a System." In *China, the Portuguese, and the Nanyang: Oceans and Routes, Regions and Trade (c.1000–1600)*, by Roderich Ptak. Aldershot, UK: Ashgate Variorum, [1998] 2004.

Qian Shifu 錢實甫, ed. *Qingdai zhiguan nianbiao* 清代職官年表 (Chronological tables of Qing period officials). 4 vols. Beijing: Zhonghua shuju, 1980.

Qian Yunzhi 錢允治. *Shiwu bencao* 食物本草 (Pharmacopeia of edible items). In *Zhongguo bencao quanshu*, vol. 67. Beijing: Huaxia chubanshe, [1620] 1999.

Qin Wuyu 秦武域. *Wenjian banxiang lu* 聞見瓣香錄 (Records of knowledge and incense). In *Congshu jicheng xubian*, vol. 88. Shanghai: Shanghai shudian, [1793] 1994.

*Qu Dajun 屈大均. *Guangdong xinyu* 廣東新語 (News from Guangdong). Hong Kong: Zhonghua shuju, [1680] 1974. [Earliest record for chiles in Guangdong.]

Quanguo zhong caoyao huibian bianxie zu 全国中草药汇编编写组, ed. *Quanguo zhong caoyao huibian* 全国中草药汇编 (Collection of Chinese herb medicines from the whole country). 2 vols. Beijing: Renmin weisheng, 1988.

Quirino, Carlos, "The Mexican Connection: The Cultural Cargo of the Manila-Acapulco Galleons," paper presented at the Mexican-Philippine Historical Relations Seminar in New York City, June 21, 1997. http://filipinokastila.tripod.com/FilMex.html.

Reid, Daniel. *Chinese Herbal Medicine*. Boston: Shambhala, 1992.

Ridley, Henry N. *The Dispersal of Plants Throughout the World*. Ashford, UK: L. Reeve, 1930.

Rozin, Paul, and Deborah Schiller. "The Nature and Acquistion of a Preference for Chili Pepper in Humans." *Motivation and Emotion* 4, no. 1 (1980): 77–101.

Schafer, Edward. "T'ang." In *Food in Chinese Culture: Anthropological and Historical Perspectives*, ed. K. C. Chang, 85–140. New Haven, Conn.: Yale University Press, 1977.

Scheid, Volker, Dan Bensky, Andrew Ellis, and Randall Barolet, comps. and trans. *Chinese Herbal Medicine: Formulas and Strategies*. 2nd ed. Seattle: Eastland Press, 2015.

Schurz, William L. *The Manila Galleon*. New York: Dutton, 1939.

Shen Liansheng, ed. *Colored Atlas of the Compendium of Materia Medica*. Beijing: Huaxia, 1998.

Shen Lilong 沈李龍. *Shiwu bencao huizuan* 食物本草會纂 (Collected compilation of the pharmacopeia of edible items). 1691.

Shen Youpeng 沈又彭. *Nüke jiyao* 女科輯要 (Essentials of gynecology). [1850], 1862.

Shiwu bencao 食物本草 (Pharmacopeia of edible items). Palace edition. In *Zhongguo bencao quanshu*, vol. 27. Beijing: Huaxia chubanshe, [c. 1550] 2000.

Shiwu bencao 食物本草 (Pharmacopeia of edible items). 1621.

Shuijing yueguang 水晶月光 [pseud.] *Shuijing Yueguang: Chuanwei biji* 水晶月光: 川味笔记 (Shuijing Yueguang's notes on Sichuan flavors). Hangzhou: Zhejiang kexue jishu, 2014.

Simoons, Frederick. *Food in China: A Cultural and Historical Inquiry*. Boca Raton, Fla.: CRC Press, 1991.

Snow, Edgar. *Red Star Over China*. New York: Modern Library, 1938.

Song Yingxing 宋應星. Yeyi 野議 (Unofficial opinions). Shanghai: Shanghai renmin chubanshe, [1636] 1976.

Song Zuying 宋祖英 (singer), Lu Song 鲁颂 (composer), and Xie Dingren 谢丁仁 (lyricist). "Lajiao ge 辣椒歌" (Chile pepper song). In *Zhongguo Hunan minge* 中国湖南民歌 (Hunan folk songs), track 2. Guangzhou: Guangdong Zhujiang yinxiang chubanshe, 1990.

Song Zuying 宋祖英 (singer), Xu Peidong 徐沛东 (composer), and She Zhidi 佘致迪 (lyricist). "La Meizi 辣妹子" (Spicy girls). In *Jingdian jingxuan* 经典精选 (Collection of classics), track 1. Guangzhou: Guangzhou xinshidai chuban, 1995.

Spence, Jonathan. "Ch'ing." In *Food in Chinese Culture: Anthropological and Historical Perspectives*, ed. K. C. Chang, 261–94. New Haven, Conn.: Yale University Press, 1977.

Stockard, Janice E. *Daughters of the Canton Delta: Marriage Patterns and Economic Strategies in South China, 1860–1930*. Stanford: Stanford University Press, 1989.

Sun Xingyan 孫星衍, ed. *Shennong bencao jing* 神農本草經 (Shennong's classic pharmacopeia (revised)]. Shenyang: Liaoning kexue jishu, [1799] 1997.

Sun Yikui 孫一奎. *Yi zhi xu yu* 醫旨緒餘 (Extraneous medical purports). In *Yingyin Wenyuange siku quanshu*, vol. 766. Taibei: Shengwu, [1596] 1983.

Swislocki, Mark. *Culinary Nostalgia: Regional Food Culture and the Urban Experience in Shanghai*. Stanford: Stanford University Press, 2009.

Tagliacozzo, Eric. "A Sino-Southeast Asian Circuit: Ethnohistories of the Marine Goods Trade." In *Chinese Circulations: Capital, Commodities, and Networks in Southeast Asia*, ed. Eric Tagliacozzo and Wen-Chin Chang, 432–54. Durham, N.C.: Duke University Press, 2011.

*Taihai caifeng tukao 臺海菜風圖考 (Treatise on Taiwan's flora and fauna). In *Taiwan shiliao huibian*, vol. 8. Beijing: Quanguo tushuguan wenxian, [1746] 2004. [Earliest record for chiles in Taiwan.]

Taiyiyuan 太醫院 (Imperial Medical Office). *Yaoxing tongkao* 藥性通考 (General overview of the properties of medicines). Beijing: Xueyuan chubanshe, [1849] 2006.

Tang Xianzu 湯顯祖. *Mudan ting* 牡丹停 (*The Peony Pavilion*). Beijing: Renmin wenxue, [1598] 1978.

Teng Youde 滕有德. "Sichuan lajiao 四川辣椒 (Sichuan chiles)." *Lajiao zazhi*, no. 1 (2004): 6–9.

Tewksbury, Joshua, and Gary Nabhan. "Directed Deterrence by Capsaicin in Chillies." *Nature*, no. 412 (2001): 403–4.

Tewksbury, Joshua, et al. "Evolutionary Ecology of Pungency in Wild Chilies." *Proceedings of the National Academy of Sciences* 105, no. 33 (2008): 11808–11.

**Tian Wen 田雯. *Qian shu* 黔書 (Account of Qian [Guizhou]). In *Yue ya tang congshu*, vol. 25. Taibei: Yi wen yin shu guan, [1690] 1965. [Earliest record for chiles in Guizhou.]

Tong Yuejian 童岳荐, attrib. *Tiao ding ji* 調鼎集 (The harmonious cauldron). Beijing: Zhongguo fangzhi, [c.1790] 2006.

Tu Cuizhong 屠粹忠. *Sancai zaoyi* 三才藻異 (Embellishments on the Sancai encyclopedia). 1689.

Tu Daohe 屠道和. *Bencao huizuan* 本草彙纂 (Compilation of the pharmacopeia). In *Zhongguo bencao quanshu*, vol. 139. Beijing: Huaxia chubanshe, [1851] 1999.

Turner, Jack. *Spice: The History of a Temptation*. New York: Vintage, 2004.

Unschuld, Paul. *Medicine in China: A History of Ideas*. Berkeley: University of California Press, 1985.

"Vitamin A." In *Health Encyclopedia*. University of Rochester Medical Center. Accessed September 9, 2019. https://www.urmc.rochester.edu/encyclopedia/content.aspx?contenttypeid=19&contentid=VitaminA.

Wakeman, Frederic Jr. *The Great Enterprise: The Manchu Reconstruction of Imperial Order in Seventeenth-Century China*. 2 vols. Berkeley: University of California Press, 1985.

Waley-Cohen, Joanna. "The Quest for Perfect Balance: Taste and Gastronomy in Imperial China." In *Food: A History of Taste*, ed. Paul Freedman, 99–133. Berkeley: University of California Press, 2007.

Walsh, Danielle. "When to Use Dried Chilies vs. Fresh vs. Powder vs. Flakes." *Bon Appétit*, March 3, 2014. http://www.bonappetit.com/test-kitchen/cooking-tips/article/how-to-use-chiles.

Wang Ang 汪昂. *Zengbu bencao beiyao* 增補本草備要 (Supplement to the *Bencao beiyao*). Shanghai: Guang yi shuju, [1690] c. 1920.

——. *Zengding bencao beiyao* 增訂本草備要 (Revised and enlarged *Bencao beiyao*). In *Xuxiu siku quanshu*, vol. 993. Shanghai: Shanghai guji chubanshe, [1694] 2002.

Wang Fu 汪紱. *Yilin zuanyao tanyuan* 醫林纂要探源 (Exhaustive essential compilation of the forest of medicine). N.p.: Jiangsu shuju, [1758] 1897.

Wang, Hongjie. "Hot Peppers, Sichuan Cuisine and the Revolutions in Modern China." *World History Connected* 12, no. 3 (October 2015). https://worldhistoryconnected.press.uillinois.edu/12.3/wang.html.

Wang Kentang 王肯堂. *Zheng zhi zhun sheng* 證治準繩. In *Yingyin Wenyuange siku quanshu*, vol. 767–71. Taibei: Shengwu, [1596] 1983.

*Wang Lu 王路. *Huashi zuobian* 花史左編 (Supplement to the history of flowers). In *Xuxiu siku quanshu*, vol. 1117. Shanghai: Shanghai guji chubanshe, [1618] 2002. [Earliest record for chiles in Anhui.]

Wang Maohua 王茂華, Wang Cengyu 王曾瑜, and Hong Seung Tae 洪承兒. "Lüelun lishi shang dongya sanguo lajiao de chuanbo, zhongzhi yu gongyong fajue 略論歷史上東亞三國辣椒的傳播: 種植與功用發掘" (Overview and exploration of the history of chiles in the three East Asian countries, including their spread, cultivation and use). *Zhongguoshi yanjiu* [S. Korea], no. 101 (April 2016): 287–330.

Wang Qixian 汪啟賢. *Shiwu xu zhi* 食物須知 (Essential knowledge of edible items). In *Zhongguo bencao quanshu*, vol. 100. Beijing: Huaxia chubanshe, [1696] 1999.

Wang Siming 王思明. "Meizhou yuanchan zuowu de yinzhong zaipei ji qi dui Zhongguo nongye shengchan jiegou de yingxiang 美洲原产作物的引种栽培及其对中国农业生产结构的影响 (The introduction and cultivation of American crops and their influence on the Chinese agricultural production structure)." *Zhongguo nongshi*, no. 2 (2004): 16–27.

Wang Shixiong 王士雄. *Suixiju yinshi pu* 隨息居飲食譜 (Food and drink recipes of Suixiju). Beijing: Zhongguo shangye, [1863] 1985.

Wang Xiangjin 王象晉. *Qun fang pu* 群芳譜 (The assembly of perfumes). In *Siku quanshu cunmu congshu bubian*, vol. 80. Jinan: Qi Lu shushe, [1621] 1997.

Wen Ermao 文二毛. "Mao Zedong de yinshi guan: bu chi lajiao bu geming 毛泽东的饮食观: 不吃辣椒不革命" (Overview of Mao Zedong's eating and drinking: without chiles there would be no revolution). *Renmin wang*, November 21, 2010 [published by *People's Daily*]. http://history.people.com.cn/GB/198593/13272886.html.

Wilbur, Marguerite Eyer. *The East India Company and the British Empire in the Far East.* New York: Smith, 1945.

Wilkinson, Endymion. *Chinese History: A New Manual.* Cambridge, Mass.: Harvard University Asia Center, 2013.

Williams, C. A. S. *Outlines of Chinese Symbolism & Art Motives.* New York: Dover, [1941] 1976.

Wilson, Thomas. "Sacrifice and the Imperial Cult of Confucius." *History of Religions* 41, no. 3 (2002): 251–87.

Wu Daoyuan 吳道源. *Li zheng hui can* 痢證匯參 (An assemblage of evidence about dysentery). In *Xuxiu siku quanshu*, vol. 1004. Shanghai: Shanghai guji chubanshe, [1773] 2002.

Wu Qian 吳謙 et al., eds. *Yi zong jin jian* 醫宗金鑑 (The golden mirror of medicine). In *Yingyin Wenyuange siku quanshu*, vol. 780–82. Taibei: Shengwu, [1743] 1983.

Wu Qijun 吳其濬. *Zhiwu mingshi tukao* 植物名實圖考 (Illustrated treatise on the names and natures of plants). N.p. 1848.

Wu Tang 吳瑭. *Wenxintang wenbing tiaobian* 問心堂溫病條辨 (A small debate on warm illnesses from the Wenxing pavilion). In *Xuxiu siku quanshu*, vol. 1004. Shanghai: Shanghai guji chubanshe, [1813] 2002.

Wu Wenbing 吳文炳. *Yaoxing quanbei shiwu bencao* 藥性全備食物本草 (The complete preparations of medicines for the pharmacopeia of edible things). In *Zhongguo bencao quanshu*, vol. 77. Beijing: Huaxia chubanshe, [1593] 1999.

Wu Xingqin 吳省欽. *Baihua qiangao* 白華前稿 (Baihua's [Wu Xingqin] early drafts). N.p., 1783.

Wu Yigu 吳貽谷 and Song Liren 宋立人, eds. *Zhonghua bencao* 中华本草 (Chinese bencao). 10 vols. Shanghai: Shanghai kexue jishu chubanshe, 1998.

Wu, Yi-Li. "The Qing Period." In *Chinese Medicine and Healing: An Illustrated History*, ed. T. J. Hinrichs and Linda Barnes, 161–207. Cambridge, Mass.: Harvard University Press, 2013.

Wu Yiluo 吳儀洛. *Bencao congxin* 本草從新 (A refreshed pharmacopeia). In *Xuxiu siku quanshu*, vol. 994. Shanghai: Shanghai guji chubanshe, [1757] 2002.

Wu Youxing 吳有性. *Wenyi lun* 瘟疫論 (Discussion of epidemics). In *Yingyin Wenyuange siku quanshu*, vol. 779. Taibei: Shengwu, [1642] 1983.

Wu Zhengyi and Peter H. Raven, eds. *Flora of China*, vol.17: *Verbenaceae Through Solanaceae*. St. Louis: Missouri Botanical Garden, 1994.

Wu Zhengyi, Peter H. Raven, and Hong Deyuan, eds. *Flora of China*, vol. 11: *Oxalidaceae Through Aceraceae*. St. Louis: Missouri Botanical Garden, 2008.

Wu Zhiwang 武之望. *Chongding Jiyin gangmu* 重訂濟陰綱目 (To benefit yin: a comprehensive guide). N.p., [1620] 1728.

Xia Zengchuan 夏曾傳. *Suiyuan shidan buzheng* 隨園食單补証 (Additions to (Yuan Mei's) *Recipes from the Sui Garden*). Beijing: Zhongguo shangye, [c.1883] 1994.

Xiao San 蕭三, ed. *Geming minge ji* 革命民歌集 (Collection of revolutionary people's songs). Beijing: Zhongguo qingnian chubanshe, 1959.

Xu Dachun 徐大椿. *Lantai guifan* 蘭臺軌範 (Standards from the Orchid Platform). In *Yingyin Wenyuange siku quanshu*, vol. 785. Taibei: Shengwu, [1764] 1983.

——. *Shennong bencao jing baizhong lu* 神農本草經百種錄 (Myriad records of *Shennong's classic pharmacopeia*). In *Yingyin Wenyuange siku quanshu*, vol. 785. Taibei: Shengwu, [1736] 1983.

Xu Ke 徐珂. *Qing bai lei chao* 清稗類鈔 (Categorized collection of minor Qing matters). 13 vols. Beijing: Zhonghua shuju, [1916] 1984–1986.

Xu Wenbi 徐文弼. *Xinbian shoushi chuanzhen* 新編壽世傳真 (New compilation of the transmitted truths on longevity). In *Xuxiu siku quanshu*, vol. 1030. Shanghai: Shanghai guji chubanshe, [1771] 2002.

Yan Jie 嚴潔. *Depei bencao* 得配本草 (A harmonious pharmacopeia). Shanghai: Shanghai kexue jishu, [1761] 1965.

Yang Chongkui 楊崇魁. *Bencao zhenquan* 本草真詮 (True annotations to the pharmacopeia). In *Zhongguo bencao quanshu*, vol. 63. Beijing: Huaxia chubanshe, [1602] 1999.

Yang Jun 楊濬. *Shanghan wenyi tiaobian* 傷寒瘟疫條辯 (A brief debate on typhoid pestilence). In *Xuxiu siku quanshu*, vol. 1004. Shanghai: Shanghai guji chubanshe, [1785] 2002.

Yang Xuming 杨旭明. "Hunan lajiao wenhua de neihan jiqi zhenghe kaifa celüe 湖南辣椒文化的内涵及其整合开发策略" (The culture of chiles in Hunan as well as the development of their integration). *Hengyang shifan xueyuan xuebao* 34, no. 5 (2013): 171–73.

Yao Huoshu and Christina Lionnent. "Hunan's 'Spicy' Women." *Women of China* (English Monthly), no. 9 (2004): 26–29.

Yao Kecheng 姚可成, attrib. *Shiwu bencao* 食物本草 (Pharmacopeia of edible items). Beijing: Renmin weisheng chubanshe, [1642] 1994.

Yao Lü 姚旅. *Lu shu* 露書 (Book of dew). In *Xuxiu siku quanshu*, vol. 1132. Shanghai: Shanghai guji chubanshe, [1611] 2002.

Yi Su-gwang 李睟光. *Jibong yuseol* 芝峰類說 (Topical discourses of Jibong). Annotated by Nam Man-seong 南晚星. 2 vols. Seoul: Euryu munhwasa, [1614] 1994.

Yü, Ying-shih. "Han." In *Food in Chinese Culture: Anthropological and Historical Perspectives*, ed. K. C. Chang, 53–83. New Haven, Conn.: Yale University Press, 1977.

Yuan Mei 袁枚. *Suiyuan shidan* 隨園食單 (Recipes from the Sui garden). In *Xuxiu siku quanshu*, vol. 1115. Shanghai: Shanghai guji chubanshe, [1790] 2002.

"*Zanthoxylum simulans.*" *The Plant List.* Accessed March 6, 2017. http://www.theplantlist.org/tpl1.1/record/kew-2469033.

Zelin, Madeleine. *The Merchants of Zigong: Industrial Entrepreneurship in Early Modern China.* New York: Columbia University Press, 2005.

Zeng Yi 曾懿. *Zhong kui lu* 中饋錄 (A cook's records). Beijing: Zhongguo shangye, [1907] 1984.

Zhang Huizhi 張撝之 et al., eds. *Zhongguo lidai renming dacidian* 中国历代人名大辞典 (Dictionary of Chinese historical names). 2 vols. Shanghai: Shanghai guji, 1999.

Zhang Jiebin 張介賓. *Jingyue quanshu* 景岳全書 (Complete records of Jingyue [Zhang Jiebin]). In *Yingyin Wenyuange siku quanshu*, vol. 777–78. Taibei: Shengwu, [1624] 1983.

——. *Lei jing* 類經. In *Yingyin Wenyuange siku quanshu*, vol. 776. Taibei: Shengwu, [c. 1640] 1983.

——. *Shiwu bencao* 食物本草 (Pharmacopeia of edible items). In *Zhongguo bencao quanshu*, vol. 67. Beijing: Huaxia chubanshe, [1624] 1999.

Zhang Lu 張璐. *Ben jing feng yuan* 本經逢原. In *Xuxiu siku quanshu*, vol. 994. Shanghai: Shanghai guji chubanshe, [1695] 2002.

Zhang Maochen 張懋辰. *Bencao bian* 本草便 (Abridged pharmacopoeia). In *Zhongguo bencao quanshu*, vol. 57. Beijing: Huaxia chubanshe, [c. 1550] 1999.

Zhang Mu 章穆. *Tiao ji yinshi bian* 調疾飲食辯 (A discussion of suitable drinks and food for illnesses). Beijing: Zhongyi guji, [1823] 1999.

Zhang Qigan 張其淦. *Mingdai qian yimin shi yong* 明代千遺民詩詠 ([Biographies] of 1,000 poets from the Ming dynasty). In *Qingdai zhuanji congkan*, ed. Zhou Junfu, vol. 66–67. Taibei: Mingwen shuju, [1929] 1986.

Zhang Renxi 張仁錫. *Yaoxing mengqiu* 藥性蒙求 (Enlightening account of the properties of medicines). In *Zhongguo bencao quanshu*, vol. 139. Beijing: Huaxia chubanshe, [1856] 1999.

Zhang Tingyu 張廷玉, et al, eds. *Ming shi* 明史 (History of the Ming dynasty). In Hanji quanwen ziliao ku. http://hanchi.ihp.sinica.edu.tw/ihp/hanji.htm.

Zhang Yushu 張玉書, Watanabe Atsushi 渡部温, and Yan Yiping 嚴一萍, eds. *Jiaozheng Kangxi zidian* 校正康熙字典 (Corrected Kangxi character dictionary). Taibei: Yiwen yishu guan, 1965.

Zhang Zhicong 張志聰. *Bencao chongyuan* 本草崇原 (Lofty original pharmacopeia). Beijing: Zhongyi yao chubanshe, [c. 1674] 1992.

Zhang Zhijie 張之傑. "*Taihai caifeng tukao dian, zhu* 臺海菜風圖考點註" (Annotations to *Taihai caifeng tukao*). In *Zhonghua keji shixuehui congkan*, vol. 1. Xinbei City: Zhonghua keji shixue hui, 2011.

Zhao Qiguang 趙其光. *Bencao qiuyuan* 本草求原 (Seeking origins for the pharmacopeia). In *Lingnan bencao guji sanzhong*. Beijing: Zhongguo yiyao keji, [1848] 1999.

Zhao Xuemin 趙學敏. *Bencao gangmu shiyi* 本草綱目拾遺 (Correction of omissions in the *Bencao gangmu*). In *Xuxiu siku quanshu*, vol. 994–95. Shanghai: Shanghai guji chubanshe, [1803] 2002.

Zhencun mifang 珍存秘方 (Treasury to preserve secret formulas). N.p., c. 1900.

Zheng Dianyi 鄭奠一. *Wenyi mingbian* 瘟疫明辨 (On clearly distinguishing pestilences). In *Xuxiu siku quanshu*, vol. 1003. Shanghai: Shanghai guji chubanshe, [1752] 2002.

Zheng Quanwang 鄭全望. *Zhangnüe zhinan* 瘴瘧指南 (Guide for malaria). In *Xuxiu siku quanshu*, vol. 1003. Shanghai: Shanghai guji chubanshe, [1609] 2002.

Zheng Xuan 鄭玄. "*Yili* jiao 儀禮校" (Commentary on the *Yili*). In *Shisan jing* 十三經 (The thirteen classics), 1815 ed. In Hanji quanwen ziliao ku 漢籍全文資料庫. http://hanchi.ihp.sinica.edu.tw/ihp/hanji.htm.

Zheng Zhu 郑褚 and Zang Xiaoman 藏小满. "Chuancai shi zenyang bian la de? 川菜是怎样变辣的?" (How did Sichuan cuisine become spicy?). *Guoxue wenhua*, no. 4 (2009): 56–68.

Zhi Weicheng 支偉成. *Qingdai puxue dashi liezhuan* 清代樸學大師列傳 (Biographies of masters of textual studies of the Qing dynasty). In *Qingdai zhuanji congkan*, ed. Zhou Junfu, vol. 12. Taibei: Mingwen shuju, [1924] 1986.

Zhongguo nongye baikequanshu 中国农业百科全书 (Encyclopedia of Chinese agriculture). Beijing: Nongye chubanshe, 1995.

"Zhongguo shei zui bu pa la 中国谁最不怕辣?" (Who is the most unafraid of spice in China?). *Zhongguo lajiao*, no. 4 (2002): 23.

Zhongguo shehuikexueyuan yuyan yanjiusuo 中国社会科学院语言研究所, ed. *Xiandai Hanyu cidian* 现代汉语词典 (Modern Chinese dictionary). Beijing: Shangwu yinshuguan, 2012.

Zhongyi changyong caoyao, Zhongyao, fangji shouce 中醫常用草藥, 中藥, 方劑手冊 (Handbook of commonly used plant-based medicine, traditional medicine, and formulas for Chinese medicine). Hong Kong: Yiyao weisheng, 1972.

Zhongyi shijia: zhongyao xue 中医世家: 中药学 (Houses of Chinese medicine: studies of Chinese drugs). Accessed May 13, 2015. http://www.zysj.com.cn/lilunshuji/zhongyaoxue/index.html.

Zhou Yangjun 周揚俊. *Wenre shu yi quanshu* 溫熱暑疫全書 (Complete book on hot summer pestilences). In *Xuxiu siku quanshu*, vol. 1004. Shanghai: Shanghai guji chubanshe, [1679] 2002.

Zhu Benzhong 朱本中. *Yinshi xuzhi* 飲食須知 (Points for attention about food and drink). In *Zhongguo bencao quanshu*, vol. 63. Beijing: Huaxia chubanshe, [1676] 1999.

Zhu Yizun 朱彝尊. *Shi xian hong mi* 食宪鸿秘 (Guide to the mysteries of cuisine). Beijing: Zhongguo shangye, [1680] 1985.

Zou Shu 鄒澍, ed. *Benjing shuzheng* 本經疏證 (Commentaries on the pharmacopeia classic). In *Xuxiu siku quanshu*, vol. 993. Shanghai: Shanghai guji chubanshe, [1849] 2002.

INDEX

Page numbers in italics refer to epigraphs and boxes; those in boldface refer to figures and maps.

138, 192; for expelling damp, 34, 86–87, 102–3, 161–62, 167–68, 172, 181, 191; for snakebites, 97, *98*; side effects, 80, 98–103; for toothaches, 97, 99; for vitamins, 32, 62, 64, 73, 76, 92, 102, 163, 172, 192; for warming, 88–89, *90*, 97, 102, 124, 146

Chile Pepper Feng. *See* Wang Xifeng

Chinese medicine. *See* traditional Chinese medicine

class: and gazetteers, 15–16, 48–49, 62; impact on adoption of chiles, 30–31, 33, 74, 92, 106–8, 110, 112–14, 119, 125, 128–29, 163, 168, 189, 194; and raw chiles, 71–72. *See also* elites; farmers

climate, 8–10, 45, 59, 64, 158, 166–68, 180–82; and *qi,* 85, 91, 95. *See also* geography; regional adaptations

Columbus, Christopher, 9–10, 13, 206n8

Confucianism, 21, 86, 115–17, 127, 150, 173

corn. *See* maize

cuisine styles: eastern (Jiangnan), 114, 125–26, 159–60, 193–94; Hunan, 35, 48, 71–73, 161, 166, *167,* 170–74; northern (Beijing), 114, 158–60; Shaanxi, 73, 107, 140–41, 158, 162–64, 187; Sichuan, 35, 156–57, 164, 179–83, *184, 185, 186,* **187**; southern (Cantonese), 159–60; western (spicy), 161–62, 164

dan. See subtle flavoring

Daoism, 22, 117, 131, 141–42

decorations. *See* aesthetics; chile pepper, as decoration

Dennis, Joseph, 16, 207n31, 207n32, 225n5

difangzhi. See gazetteers

douban jiang. See chile pepper, paste

Dream of the Red Chamber, 6, 114, 145, 147–50, 174–76, 189, 193. *See also* Cao Xueqin; Wang Xifeng

Dunlop, Fuchsia, 162, 166–67, *184, 185,* 218n85, 231n32, 235n27, 235n33, 235n34, 236n43, 236n46, 237n47, 238n74, 238n76

duo lajiao. See chile pepper, salted

economics. *See* chile pepper, economical

Edwards, Louise, 149–50, 232n39

eggplant, 8, 72–73, 113, 127

elites, 22, 33, 113–14, 134; and desire for precedent, 53, 118–27, 138, 194, 197–202; and patronage of crops, 2, 7, 27, 125; and perpetuation of privilege, 15–16, 49, 106–8, 125; and reticence toward chiles, 2, 30, 54, 71–72, 76, 106–7, 109–13, 115–16, 118–19, 124–25, 134–35, 137–38, 173, 189, 193–94, 197–202; and shift toward adoption of chiles, 54–55, 74, 114, 123, 126–28, 190, 194–95

environment. *See* climate; geography; regional adaptations

60–61; in Hunan cuisine, 73, 166, *167*, 168, 172, 174; and minorities, 62, 64; as preservative, 73, 166–67, 180–81, 183; scarcity of, 64, 74, 192; in Sichuan cuisine, 73, 180–81, 183–84, 186

sauce, chile. *See* chile pepper, paste

Shaanxi, 24, 26, 29, 34, 48, 52, 56–57, 73, 107, 140, **141**, 151, 158, 162–64, **187**

Shandong, 40–42, 48–49, 52, 126–27, 133–34, 141, **142**, 158

Shengjing, 23–26, 40–42, 48, 52, 189

She Zhidi, 176–78, *189*

Shiwu bencao, 7, 28, 31–32, 34, 43, 77–78, 83, 85, 88, 91–92, 107, 112, 118–19, 133–34, 199–200

Sichuan, 1, 28, 33, 37, 50, 52, 60, 63–64, **67**, 69–70, 73, 121–22, 128, 137–38, 156–57, 161–62, 164; chile as identity marker for, 140, 179–86, **187**, 188; and health, 103, 180–81; recipe, *184*, *186*. *See also* cuisine styles, Sichuan; regional adaptations, Sichuan; salt, in Sichuan cuisine

Sichuan pepper, **35**, 36, 46, 73, 132, 166; chile as substitute for, 31, 39–42, 48–51, 75, 191; decline in use of, 2, 31, 35, 37, 49–51, 75; as flavoring, 22, 35, 180–81, 183–84; in *ma-la* flavor, 36, 50, 182, *184*, 185–86; in medicine, 35, 86; names, 22, 35, 37–42, 120–21, 213n16; as pungent

flavoring, 31, 35–37, 39–41, 166, 181; in recipe, *50*, *184*, *186*

Simoons, Frederick, 158, 205n1, 218n87, 222n54

Snow, Edgar, 151–52

songs, 102, *129*, 152–53, 171–74, 176–77, *189*. *See also Peony Pavilion*

Song Zuying, 6, 176–79, *189*, 190, 236n44

Spain, Spanish, 9–13, 21, 132, 206n8

spice trade, 9–10, 12, 14; chiles not part of, 10–11, 13, 21, 31

spicy (*la*), 1–2, 34, 140, 161, 164, 168–69, 180, 182; chiles as, 29, 31–32, 39, 42–43, 46, 48–50, 52, 75, 85–86, 102, 110, 124, 132–33, 144, 146, 148–51, 163, 174–75, 185, 191–96; etymology of, 2, 31, 52–54, 85, 191; fear of nonspicy, 162, 177, 179, 233n11, 234n12; in *ma-la* flavor, 36, 50, 182, *184*, 185–86. *See also* chile pepper, Chinese names for; chile pepper, as flavoring; pungent

spicy girls. *See la meizi*

starchy foods, 30, 92, 114

substitution. *See* chile pepper, as a substitute for other flavors

subtle flavoring, 113–16, 125–26, 137, 159–61, 191. *See also* cuisine styles, eastern (Jiangnan); Jiangnan

Taiwan, 18, 22–23, 48, 52, 58–59, 64, 75, 156, 159, 170, 192

Tang Xianzu. *See Peony Pavilion*
Tian Wen, 48, 60–61, 74
tobacco, 7–8, 18, 21, 27, 109, 125
tomato, 8–9, 29, 37
Tong Yuejian, 43–45, *50*, 54, 194, 197
traditional Chinese medicine,
    4–5, 15, 32, 77–80, 98–105,
    118–26, 146, 194–95; and *bencao*,
    41, 80–84; and Five Phases,
    33–34, 53, 81, 85–87, 91–92, 95,
    99–100, 103–4; observed effects
    of chiles, 91–98; and *qi*, 90–91;
    regional adaptations, 167–68,
    180–81; and *yin* and *yang*, 81, 85,
    87–91, 98–99, 103, 150. *See also*
    chile pepper, as medicine; five
    flavors; pharmacopoeia; *shiwu
    bencao*

Unschuld, Paul, 78, 95, 221n34

vegetable gardens. *See* chile
    pepper, in kitchen gardens
vinegar, 43–44, 48–50, 73, 159, 166,
    183, 186, 191
vitamins. *See* chile pepper, as
    medicine, for vitamins

Wang Fu, 39, 86, 89, 97, 201
Wang Lu, *106*, 107, 110–13, 229n2,
    239n1
Wang Maohua, Wang Cengyu,
    and Hong Seung Tae, 52, 65,
    133, 203n4, 210n55

Wang Xiangjin, 40, 112, 133
Wang Xifeng, 148–51, 174–76, 178,
    193. *See also Dream of the Red
    Chamber*; Cao Xueqin
Wu, Yi–Li, 79–80, 104
Wu Qijun, **66**, 70–72, 87, 157
Wuxing. See traditional Chinese
    medicine, Five Phases
Wu Xingqin, 29, 45, 54, 74, 96–97,
    137–38, 159

Xu Ke, 158–59, 161, 225n9
Xu Wenbi, 77, 78, 94, 97, 99–100,
    201, 224n79, 226n12

Yang Xuming, *156*, 166, 234n12,
    237n55
yin and *yang. See* traditional
    Chinese medicine, and *yin*
    and *yang*
Yi Su-gwang, 24, 112
Yunnan, *5*, 17–18, 25–26, 50, 52, 60,
    70, 120–23, **143**, **154**, 161, 164,
    184, 199

Zhao Xuemin, 83–84, 87, *90*,
    94–97, 99, 123–26, 194–95
Zhejiang, 21–22, 42, 45, 48, 52, 71,
    110–11, 131, 134, 137, 159
Zheng Zhu and Zang Xiaoman,
    50, 188, 234n12, 238n67
Zhili, 40–42, 52, 71, 158
Zuo Zongtang, 128, 169–70,
    236n43

ARTS AND TRADITIONS OF THE TABLE:
PERSPECTIVES ON CULINARY HISTORY

Albert Sonnenfeld, Series Editor